Comments about *The Basketball Coach's Bible*
What coaches say…

"I definitely would recommend this to the thousands of coaches out there who have no guidelines and are coaching AAU, biddy basketball, church leagues, and for anyone else who wants to teach youngsters the finer points of the game."
Dale Brown, LSU Men's Coach

"An outstanding learning tool for all ages. A must read for all coaches."
Stephanie Gaitley, St. Joseph's Univ. Coach

"Your discussions of a planned agenda for every practice has inspired me for two years now and, in a great part, is responsible for my success during this time. Keep up the good work."
Tom Luker, 7th grade Coach

"I can say, without question, that this is an excellent tool for teaching the fundamentals."
Jim Calhoun, UConn , Men's Coach

"Very well thought out and organized; a great addition to anyone's basketball library."
John McArdle, Chestnut Hill Acad. Coach

This book is not only for the young coach, but it is also appropriate for coaches, experienced or not, at all levels."
Charlene Curtis, former Temple U. Coach

"Without question it is a very good book about fundamental basketball."
Tom Shirley, Phila. Textiles, AD & Coach

"Informative. I would recommend it to others, especially new coaches."
Tony Springman, Head Coach Girls

"It is one of the best teachers and guides for beginning coaches of young teams that I've seen ."
Jack Mckinney, Former NBA Coach

People who know basketball, coaches who care about players–not the ones on an ego trip–say this is the best book on fundamentals they have seen.
Robert Kuiserling, Odessa, MO, Youth Coach

"**The Coach's Bible** is a real winner! It offers a thorough insight into the basic foundations of basketball. A truly outstanding book. If you love basketball, you will love **The Coach's Bibl**e."
Jim Tucker, Englewood High School Coach

"[A] splendid job. I wish there was a similar book when I began coaching."
"Speedy" Morris, La Salle University Coach

"Any parent who wants his child to improve should buy this book."
Wayne Montgomery, Tournament Organizer

"The ideas in this book will be as helpful for you as they were for our team."
Bernie Ivens, former West Phila. HS Coach

"Great for any level of coaching. Being a fundamental fanatic, this is the best guide I have seen."
John Cornet, High School Coach, Tenafly, NJ

"[Y]our book was a huge help. I highly recommend this book to all coaches, young or experienced."
Scott Whaley, Head Jr. High Coach

Thank you for your efforts in putting this book together. It has proved invaluable… throughout our 7-12 program."
Steve Hartman, Beatrice, Nebraska, Coach

"My girls really benefited from this great program of individual and group skill development."
Jennifer Lynch, Youth Coach, Edmond, OK

"A labor of love."
Fran Dunphy, Univ. of Penna. Men's Coach

What sportswriters and reviewers say...

"These two...guides [with **The Basketball Player's Bible**] offer a remarkably detailed, painstaking organized approach to teaching and mastering basketball skills. ...Goldstein breaks down basketball's many teachable skills (shooting, passing, dribbling, cutting, rebounding, etc.) into their component parts and supplies incrementally more difficult lessons for each task. The lessons themselves ...are practical, well presented, and part of a unified whole. Directions are clear, and diagrams accompanying each lesson ... are always decipherable. ... The need for 'fundamentals' is a rallying cry at every level of competition: these books deliver the goods."
Booklist

"[This book] is great! "Where was this when I needed it?"... some 30 plus years ago..."
Richard Broderick, Sportswriter, Marco Island Eagle (FL)

"{A} minutely detailed analysis of all of the fundamentals."
"{I}deal for coaches working with beginner players."
Scholastic Coach

"Congratulations!!! Very impressive. Your book gives beginning coaches a good guide."
Wayne Patterson, Basketball Hall of Fame

"[A] wonderfully-informative book that lives up to its billing as "A Comprehensive and Systematic Guide to Coaching".
Bob Weiner, Lompoc(CA) Record

"One of the most comprehensive basketball books available."
Ontario Basketball Association

"I don't often endorse books or products but..."
"The book is sensational!"
"I highly recommend the book to coaches at any level, from 4th and 5th grade through high school and college."
R.D. Keep, Sports Editor, Oskaloosa(IA) Herald

"If you are looking for a guide to help you coach better, this is the one you're looking for."
Cleo Chaffin, The Healdton(OK) Herald

"[H]olds the potential for wide appeal for a variety of users involved with kids."
Midwest Book Review, The Children's Bookwatch

"Like basketball? To help you understand what is going on, get a copy .... It covers every aspect of the game."
Book Browsing, West Orange Times

"It is one of the most thorough books on basketball I have read."
Henry Dunk Beter, National Director of Biddy Basketball

"No aspect of the game is missed as Goldstein walks us through the game step-by-step, from warming up before the contest to warming down afterward to prevent injury."
Dennis Harrison, Sportswriter Chestnut Hill Local

WHY THIS BOOK IS UNIQUE

•This book presents a coherent, comprehensive and systematic scheme of lessons that work.

•These lessons not only work, but also yield the maximum improvement for each player.

•This book addresses and answers the most basic questions about teaching and learning basketball.

•This is a *do* book. Lessons comprise most of the book. Each one deals with action, not theory.

•This book is about the basics and only the basics. Player and coach start from the beginning. Emphasis is on the individual fundamentals, which are then woven into the team skills. Anyone can easily alter and combine these basic lessons to meet his or her needs.

•This book exposes many inappropriate sports mottoes and ideas.

•In this book I redefine the fundamentals and then break them down into teachable skills. Each lesson teaches part of a skill, an entire skill, or several skills combined.

•Each lesson gives vital information: skills needed, skill analysis of each lesson, directions and setup for players, time needed, use of managers and assistants, troubleshooting teaching and learning, weekly practice, number of players, physical effort needed, extensions of lessons and more.

•This book supplies the *know how* to successfully teach *all* players of all abilities. Learning takes place conspicuously during each practice session. Because of the simplicity and effectiveness of the lessons, players often use them to help each other.

Golden Aura's Nitty-Gritty Basketball Series
by Sidney Goldstein

See the description in the back of this book.

The Basketball Coach's Bible

The Basketball Player's Bible

The Basketball Shooting Guide

The Basketball Scoring Guide

The Basketball Dribbling Guide

The Basketball Defense Guide

The Basketball Pass Cut Catch Guide

Basketball Fundamentals

Planning Basketball Practice

Videos for the Guides soon available

HOW TO CONTACT THE AUTHOR

The author seeks your comments about this book. Sidney Goldstein is available for consultation and clinics with coaches and players. Contact him at:

Golden Aura Publishing
PO Box 41012
Philadelphia, PA 19127
215 438-4459

The Basketball Coach's Bible

Third Printing

A Comprehensive and Systematic Guide to Coaching

Sidney Goldstein

GOLDEN AURA PUBLISHING

The Nitty-Gritty Basketball Series

The Basketball Coach's Bible
by Sidney Goldstein

Published by:

GOLDEN AURA PUBLISHING

Post Office Box 41012

Philadelphia, PA 19127 U.S.A.

Goldstein, Sidney, 1945

  The Basketball Coach's Bible: A Comprehensive and Systematic Guide to Coaching / Sidney Goldstein.--1st ed.--Philadelphia : Golden Aura Pub., c1994

first printing Dec. 1994

second printing Jan. 1995, third printing Dec. 95

 370 p. : ill. ; 28cm. -- (The Nitty-Gritty Basketball Series)

Includes index.

1. Basketball--Coaching I. Title II. Series: Goldstein, Sidney. Nitty-Gritty Basketball Series.

GV885.3.G65 1994   796.323   93-80272

ISBN 1-884357-07-5

Softcover $24.95

Cover design and illustration by Lightbourne Images

copyright ©1994

Acknowledgments

The fact that you are reading this book at this moment is a testimony to the care of many who helped me both spiritually and factually. I am especially appreciative to the many coaches who read the manuscript and gave me feedback. I want to thank Tom Shirley, Athletic Director and women's coach at Philadelphia College of Textiles and Sciences, John McArdle of Chestnut Hill Academy, Bill Gallagher of William Penn Charter School, Stephanie and Frank Gaitley of St. Joseph's University, Charlene Curtis of Temple University, and Jon Wilson, a regional director of the Biddy League. A host of other coaches reviewed the book and supported my efforts. These include Dale Brown of LSU, Jack McKinney, now of AmPro Sportswear; Jim Calhoun of the University of Connecticut; Bob Huggins of the University of Cincinnati; Wayne Montgomery and Dunk Beter of the Biddy League; Fran Dunphy of the University of Pennsylvania; Ted Weiss of Abington High School, and Speedy Morris of La Salle University. I want to thank other coaches not mentioned above who supported my efforts.

My special thanks go to my neighbor Sally Brash who gave me critical assistance of every kind during the years that I worked on the book. Her son, Ed Brash, gave me a publisher's professional advice that I needed.

I also want to thank the many other Philadelphia Area Computer Society (PACS) members who answered many computer related questions for me. Folks at MacConnection and Deneba Software gave me invaluable explanations on how to use my computer hardware and software. This book layout was done is Pagemaker; the illustrations and diagrams are from Canvas; the tables are from Word.

Lynn Fleischman edited this mass of basketball knowledge as well as answered many other questions. Elaine Petrov proofread this material. I am lucky to have found these folks and it was a pleasure to work with them.

Other more literary, than basketball, people who gave me needed advice and guidance are Bob Whitman of the University of Connecticut Law School, Dr. James Kirschke of Villanova, and Wendy Schmaltz of Ober Associates.

These are some of the many people who assisted me. I want to heartily thank them and the many others who have inspired and helped me.

I dedicate this book to the lovers of basketball–the coaches, volunteers, and parents who spend zillions of hours each year teaching basketball to youngsters.

Sidney Goldstein

Brief Table of Contents

Contents

Part 2   Practice Planning and Teaching   59

Part 3   The Lessons   73

1

2

Section 6-Moves — 147

Section 7-Pressure Shooting — 165

14

15

16

17

18

19

List of Appendices   **319**

Foreword by Dale Brown

If you've ever wondered, "How can I get my players to shoot better?" or "Will I ever learn how to teach a player to dribble well?" this is the book for you. Nowhere else will you find a book that takes the basic skills of basketball as its end point, not its beginning.

This book really IS about basketball fundamentals. I say this because, although many books purport to focus on fundamentals, aside from repeating the adage about how important the fundamentals are, these books quickly move on to more "glamorous" aspects of the game–such as preset offensive plays–without once taking a step back to explore and demonstrate the skills players need to have mastered before they can execute the plays. This book stays with the fundamentals, explaining them in ways coaches, players, parents at all levels of the game can understand and benefit from. Which is not to say that the fundamentals are simple to understand and acquire.

Why should you bother to read a book about the fundamentals of basketball? Acquiring the fundamental skills of basketball is similar to the process of developing any healthy habit, say eating healthy. We might think such acquisition is "natural," that is, that we are born with the knowledge we need to choose a healthy diet. But most of us need to be taught (and many of us need to unlearn unhealthy habits!). We need knowledge about good nutrition that is broken down into step-by-step changes we can manage, we need the opportunity to practice making healthy food choices, and we need a coach who will guide and encourage us (sometimes we are our own coach). In basketball, we coaches sometimes fall into the habit of thinking that the fundamental skills are "natural" and players either have them or don't. We can use this as an excuse not to focus on the fundamentals–or we can recognize that we can develop these skills at every level and therefore we should teach them at every level.

The problem is, even if we recognize the need to focus on fundamental skills, what kind of teaching resources do we have available to us? In his introduction, Goldstein has detailed the difficulty he had finding information about basic skills. As he says, most books began where he wanted to end. Perhaps part of the problem is a loss of focus on the process of teaching itself.

The premise of this book is the same one that informs good teaching of any sort: to learn something we need knowledge of the topic, instruction in breaking down the topic into manageable parts, and time to master the components and integrate them. With these tools, EVERY learner will progress—though not at the same rate or to the same degree.

So then, this book is different from other books about playing basketball:

First, it assumes we can teach basketball. That is, all players, of either sex and at whatever age, level of play or expertise, will get better if they understand and practice the fundamental skills of the game. Although the book obviously acknowledges the existence of natural talent and the advantages of predetermined physical characteristics, it does not assume that just because you are a good basketball player (that is, you score points, can dunk the ball, have moves, etc.) that your fundamental skills are sound and not in need of any improvement. I certainly have had experience with stellar players who were nonetheless lacking in certain fundamental skills, which at critical times could, as they say, come back to haunt them and the team. Nor does the book assume that just because you do not appear to be a good player that you cannot become good (or at least much better) once you have mastered these fundamental skills. In other words, it assumes that fundamental basketball skills and techniques can and should be taught–though they rarely are–to everyone who plays the game.

Second, the book does not assume any particular level of understanding or expertise. Instead it identifies the fundamental skills needed to play the game effectively, breaks these skills into component that are teachable and learnable. It walks you through the parts, puts them back together, then shows you how to build upon them in increasingly complex ways.

Third, the book assumes that if you focus on teaching and learning, and not on winning, you will win games anyway. If you are a player focused on learning these skills, you will play better ball and contribute more to the team effort. If you are a coach focused on teaching these skills, you will produce better players and better teamwork. If you are a player, coach, or parent working your way through this developmental process, you will better understand how the parts relate to the whole, and, in the end, basketball will simply be more fun.

One other noteworthy characteristic of this book: Goldstein deals not only in skills fundamentals, but in attitudinal fundamentals. In an era of big time basketball as glitz biz, Goldstein's book returns us to the notion of playing and coaching basketball for the love of it. He clearly respects not only the game, but also the thousands of people–coaches, players, parents, officials– putting in hour after underpaid hour, sometimes forced to make do with inadequate equipment and confined to cramped, dingy gyms. And they put up with all of this for no tangible reward beyond an occasional "thanks, coach" or a pat on the back. This book is a return to our roots.

Dale Brown, LSU, January 1995

INTRODUCTION

Why I Wrote This Book

My uncle Inky's (Inky Lautman) photograph appears a half dozen times in the Basketball Hall of Fame in Springfield, Massachusetts. In the beginnings of professional basketball in the thirties, he was a high scorer for the Philadelphia SPHAA's. Even though his talent was not transmitted genetically, his interest in the game was. As a kid my only ambition was to play basketball for Overbrook High School in Philadelphia, where Wilt Chamberlain and Walt Hazzard, among other notables, once played. In 9th grade I inscribed **Overbrook High School** in big black letters on the back of several T-shirts. On others I wrote **Hazzard** or **Jones** (for Wally Jones) with a number below. In 10th grade, family problems led me to quit the cadet basketball team. In 11th grade, a chronic foot problem, still a mystery, prevented even a tryout. During my senior year, a sprained ankle just before tryouts doomed my chances. At less than 50% mobility, I played with great pain, only to be cut. I was dazed. My childhood dreams came to an abrupt end. Years of practice, often 3-5 hours a day, culminated without earning a big **O** or even a fair shake at a tryout. The next day I decided to tell the coach, Paul Ward, about my injured ankle. I asked if I could try out in a week when the ankle was better; I regularly played with the guys on the team, and I felt I was as good as any of them. He gave me the chance. Thirty years later I still have my orange and black warm-up jersey that came with big black letters already printed on it—**OVERBROOK HS VARSITY BASKETBALL.**

In college my thoughts of basketball lessened. Theoretical engineering, my course of study, required over 20 hours of class each week. I always needed a part time job as well. I played on some independent teams and made the all-star team at the Ogontz campus of Penn State. After college I played on many independent teams, often head to head against current college players or professionals-to-be.

Several years after I graduated with a degree in Biophysics, a colleague at Columbia School, a private school in Philadelphia, asked for help with the men's basketball team. After a few practices and games, he saw that I knew what I was doing and let me run the team. After a few more games we won the championship. My next coaching experience was at a public high school with the girls' junior varsity team. The lack of skill and dedication of these girls astonished me. Guys would break their necks to play, whereas a girl would quit rather than trim her nails. Even though these attitudes only mirrored societal gender expectations, I was not prepared to deal with the problem; I had a team to coach. That was problem enough. They practiced shots from midcourt even though they couldn't hit the rim from the foul line. (Over the years, I found that many other players of both genders practiced, if you can call it that, similarly.) At the beginning of the season on what turned out to be one of my best teams, the players could not consistently hit the rim (let alone make the shot) from the foul line. To run several lessons involving foul shots, I moved the players to half the distance. In one of my first scrimmage games we had 8 players on the court because several failed to report out. I yelled a lot to correct matters. The layup, the dribble, and every other skill seemed advanced ones that most players completely lacked. Even the cardinal rule of basketball that requires players to dribble the ball, rather than just run down court with it, was foreign to some.

I didn't have a clue. I wondered, "Where do I start teaching? What and how do I teach?" I thought that you couldn't teach layups and dribbling as well as many other skills. Other coaches only reinforced this idea: kids need to possess some natural talent. My game demeanor was as clueless as my practices. I thought if I yelled loudly enough that players would get the idea. The yelling during my first season helped; it helped the other team. We lost 7 of 7 close games. My other mistakes are too numerous and embarrassing to mention.

Coaching skilled players is kid's stuff compared to teaching unskilled novices. My learning started abruptly that first day at practice. During the next 7 years of coaching, I read everything I could get my hands on about basketball. Most books started where I wanted to end up. They assumed players knew the basics or they thought an explanation of the basics, without any methods to accomplish them, was all that was needed. As a gag, a revered men's coach gave me a 20-year-old book about women's basketball. The women on the cover were wearing old-fashioned uniforms with skirts and shoulder straps (tunics I am told). This coach and the other gym teachers watching this presentation didn't expect me to read it, but I did. Even though not detailed nor explanatory, it did give me an idea where the beginning was. I remember best the 6 or 7 types of passes described, most of which we never bother to teach.

I attended many basketball (as well as volleyball and one ice hockey) clinics. Often the top basketball coaches that were invited offered more general information than definite detailed advice. One women's volleyball coach, who at the time seemed old, short, and unathletic, did impress me at one clinic. She had known nothing about volleyball when she started but quickly learned how to teach the basics. Year after year she beat all the teams in the area. She thought her teams won because her teaching methods were better. The other coaches disliked her, especially the men. She offered free clinics so the other teams could do as well. Few, if any, took her up on it. Her attitude was so refreshing. Once I even attended an ice hockey clinic hoping to pick up some related tips. The Czech national team practiced three-person fast breaks off ice with a basketball, believe it or not.

I watched the basketball practices of many college, high school, and other teams as well as talked to many coaches. Each night I often spent hours planning practice. I began to realize that teaching the skills was a puzzle that I could unscramble. To find more effective ways required study, planning, and innovation. I realized that with limited practice time, a coach can only teach the most basic skills. Coaches need to identify and then teach the more dependent individual skills first. Lessons need to focus on one thing at a time, not impart many skills at once. This was both the key to teaching and the biggest impediment to learning. Some things took years to figure out. Others, like learning that yelling at players during games did no good, took only one season. (Players echo your nervous state, so be calm. I remember losing only one other close game, when the score was tied in the last minute, during the next six years.)

While I worked on my puzzles, the program developed at our high school, West Philadelphia HS. With the varsity coach, Bernie Ivens, we transformed a women's program that had no respect, no uniforms, and no facility (at first I used the school hallways for part of each practice) or equipment. In five years the result was a public league and city championship as well as a victory over the best of New York's five boroughs in a tournament.

Over many years of coaching, planning, and studying, I found ways to teach each and every skill even to the most unskilled player. This scheme of learning did not come from any book. I tried things in practice. I modified them till they worked. Even players who could not simultaneously chew bubble gum and walk learned the skills. I believe you too can benefit from my work.

Who Can Use This Information

The book for coaches is the perfect tool for anybody who wants to coach and teach basketball:

- A little league or recreation league coach

- A high school or junior high school coach
- A college coach, a professional coach
- A women's or a men's coach
- A parent who wants to teach his or her child

All words in this book are unisex; all lessons are as well. Sixth graders spend more time learning the fundamentals than professionals; however, both the kind and the number of fundamentals are the same for everybody. There are not 10 skills for beginners and 50 for the pros or visa-versa. (Some pros might be happy to possess the foul shooting or dribbling skills of a good 9th grader.)

In addition this is an ideal text to use at clinics for teaching either players or coaches as well as in courses at universities. Internationally, where basketball know-how and expertise lag far behind the USA, this book has even greater application because of its fundamental nature.

How This Book Will Help You

This book will help you in many ways. It supplies field-tested, successful lessons ready for use. It not only teaches the fundamentals to players, but also to you. It shows you how to both plan practice and run practice to give and get the most out of your players. It does more than just save you much time; it gives you methods and ideas that work.

A Word About Teaching

Teaching involves more than just eloquent explanations and eye-catching demonstrations to spellbound our audience. It is an attitude that says a player's or student's ability to learn is only limited by the teacher's ability to teach even though we know players, as well as we ourselves, do have limits. If we go into practice without this idea the chance for learning and teaching is greatly decreased because we can simply say the players are not good enough, talented enough, or smart enough to learn. So, we don't need to spend that extra time planning and thinking of new ways to teach.

Teaching encourages the opposite: the desire to understand both the needs of your players and the basics of basketball and then the commitment to spend the time needed for success. The result of these teaching efforts gives a player a method or a way to learn, something that yields significant improvement with practice.

The Coach's Manual–What It Is and How to Use It

Part 1 gives you an overview and discussion of the fundamentals, as I have defined them, of basketball. Carefully scrutinize both the flow chart and outline. The next part, Part 2, involves planning practice and teaching at practice. One chapter discusses planning a practice and provides a guide, called the **Practice Planning Guide**, to help plan daily practices. The other discusses the principles of practice teaching, which I incorporated into each lesson. Part 3, the largest part of the book, presents the lessons. One chapter describes the many features of each lesson. The other chapter, Chapter 9, presents over 170 lessons and extensions in a learnable order arranged by fundamental skill. Start with the first one in each skill section–there are 19 of these–and then progress in order as the players learn. Coordinate teaching the many skills using the **Practice Planning Guide** and the information supplied in each lesson.

The appendices, labeled **A** through **G**, include much useful information. The first gives pregame and game coaching tips and things to do at the beginning of the season. Another gives **The Table of Lessons,** which lists every lesson and extension by number along with seven other useful pieces of information. **The Table of Individual Skills** lists the lessons by skill in the order that you would teach one player. The after practice **Warm Down** presents a stretching routine for players. Another appendix explains how to keep **game statistics** and analyze them. Included also are blank forms to be copied for use in each game. **Sample practices** for three different age levels and three different season times are given. Included also are blank forms for **daily** and **weekly planning of your practice**. A form for keeping **inside shot statistics** is also supplied. The **Index** allows you to find information by topic.

The Basketball Coach's Bible

PART 1 | THE FUNDAMENTALS

Chapter One
1

A Philosophy of Fundamentals

Every coach agrees that the fundamentals of basketball are important. How does this translate to what we, coaches, do every day in practice? Are we just giving them lip service or do we really believe in fundamentals? Let's examine some facts:

1. The pros' foul shot percentage has always been between 63% and 78%. Why is it so low? The pros are the best players, and they surely have time to practice. What's the problem? The answer–shooting technique.

Shooting 100 foul shots does not improve your shooting technique. Shooting technique is a fundamental that both 7th graders and the pros need to practice regularly. If coaches emphasized technique, foul shooting percentages would go up 10-15%.

2. After reading many books, attending many clinics and watching many high school and college practices, I find little time spent on fundamentals. Even when they are addressed, the methods and explanations usually lack detail, completeness, and effectiveness.

3. I also perceive a widely held attitude by coaches, men's coaches in particular, that fundamentals are for little kids, little girls. These folks should calculate their team's foul shooting percentage. They should also count the number of good dribblers on their team. These numbers won't add up to nearly the number of players on the team.

4. In clinic after clinic and book after book, I find tons of info about offensive plays. I'm sure there are many entire books devoted to this topic. What's the problem? Your team's offense needs to react to the other team's defense. This involves not only adjusting to each opponent but also adjusting to each play of the game. You

can't teach these adjustments by just practicing predesigned plays! Teaching the fundamentals of both individual and team offense is the only way to do it. Emphasis needs to be shifted away from plays to the fundamentals.

5. Many coaches at the high school (including myself initially) and lower levels of play think that zone defense is easier to teach than person-to-person defense. However, players in a zone must know how to cover players one-on-one in every situation, as well as how to shift properly in the zone. Thus, zones are more difficult if you look at the fundamentals involved.

If the fundamentals of basketball are like the fundamentals of physics, house building, or any thing else, then they are the building blocks for learning and doing. Skipping them at any level of play, from 7th graders to the pros, leads to problems: if you were a house builder the building would fall down. In basketball skipping these steps leads to a vacuum of information on the fundamentals and second rate training methods. Can you imagine a builder not bothering to make a strong solid foundation because the building style is so sophisticated? Yet coaches routinely ignore laying a strong foundation in favor of developing fancy "architecture."

The fundamentals are more than the building blocks. You can combine the individual and team basics to perform any skill or move or play. Slightly altering the lessons in this book can produce more configurations than you ever imagined. An example: after I spent months teaching one-on-one defense, my 10th grade players learned a 2-1-2 shifting zone in 5 minutes–actually during a double timeout in a game. Anybody can do this if he or she understands the power and significance of the fundamentals.

Another misconception about fundamentals is that they are easy to learn. This is hardly the case. They are very difficult to learn, practice, apply, and even recognize. Seventh graders will not be able to perform adequately half the things in this book. Most pros can do better, but not by as much as you think.

Many folks may have another misconception about how skillfulness relates to a player's basketball ability. They think that basketball prowess goes hand-in-hand with skill; not entirely so. This may be a surprising statement from a person who is writing about the need to emphasize fundamentals. Here is one example: how would Magic Johnson, Wilt Chamberlain, or Michael Jordan do if he were a foot shorter? Would we even know their names today if this were true? This book teaches fundamentals, not how to make great players. If you want to turn out great players, then you need to also work on genetics, speed, and strength.

This is a book of fundamentals. It is a step back to the basics and a step forward to improved training methods. It is a place to start and to return again and again. I have tried to explain the fundamentals without skipping steps for coaches at all levels. All lessons in this book can and should be modified and combined to suit your own purposes. No matter what you do, the fundamentals do not change. You will reap great rewards by recognizing, practicing, and applying them to your situation.

(Notes)

The Basketball Coach's Bible

Chapter Two

The Court

2

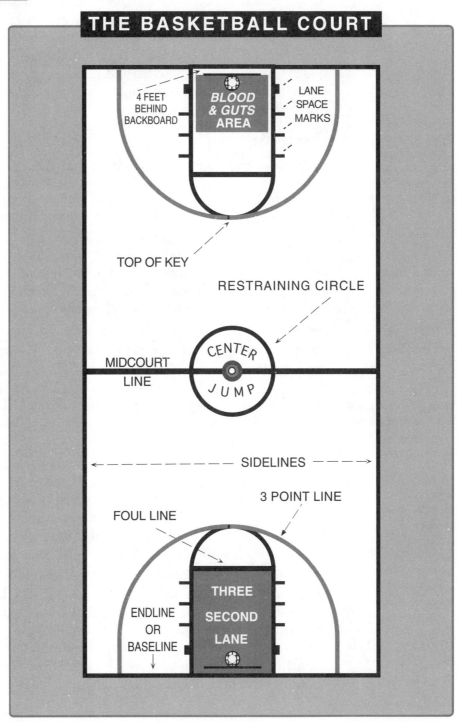

THE BASKETBALL COURT

4 FEET BEHIND BACKBOARD

BLOOD & GUTS AREA

LANE SPACE MARKS

TOP OF KEY

RESTRAINING CIRCLE

CENTER JUMP

MIDCOURT LINE

SIDELINES

3 POINT LINE

FOUL LINE

ENDLINE OR BASELINE

THREE SECOND LANE

The Court

If the court were real estate worth $1000, the area around the basket would be worth $999.99. I call this the **blood and guts area**. Games are won and lost here. However, simply stating that this is the most important area on the court is inadequate. You need to practice and teach every lesson with this focus.

Most coaches are not aware that the court extends four feet behind the backboard. Great rebounders devastate opponents moving to the ball from this area. You need to teach offensive rebounders to use this area to their advantage. Defensive players must learn how to box out players rebounding from this direction. See lesson section 11 on rebounding and lessons 12.4-6 on defense.

The Lines

All lines on the court are two inches thick. The endlines (or baselines) and sidelines border the court. The center restraining circle is twelve feet in diameter. The three second lane is bounded by the foul line on one end and the baseline on the other. The midcourt line divides the court in half. This information is hardly surprising to most people. If you step on a line you are **out** if it is an out-of-bounds line or the midcourt line. You are **in,** if it is any other line. In either case, out or in, the lines can work against you. Players must watch where they step.

The three point line, if your court has any, is a semicircle about 20 feet (more for the pros) from the basket. Since the basket is 4-6 feet from the endline, the three point line straightens out about 5 feet from the endline.

The top of the key is a point that intersects the three point line straight away from the basket. I don't think there are any rules concerning the top of the key now. In the distant past there may have been. The semicircle at the court end of the lane also has no function now. It was part of another restraining circle when jump balls were held near the tie up position. Now teams alternate possessions after a tie up in most leagues.

The foul line or free throw line is 19 feet from the baseline and 13 feet from the front rim of the basket. The basket itself is 18 inches in diameter and is 6 inches from the backboard. Note that these measurements are standard for courts in the U.S.A. at this time. Note also that measurements will vary slightly depending whether you measure from the inside or outside of the line. See the diagram on the next page.

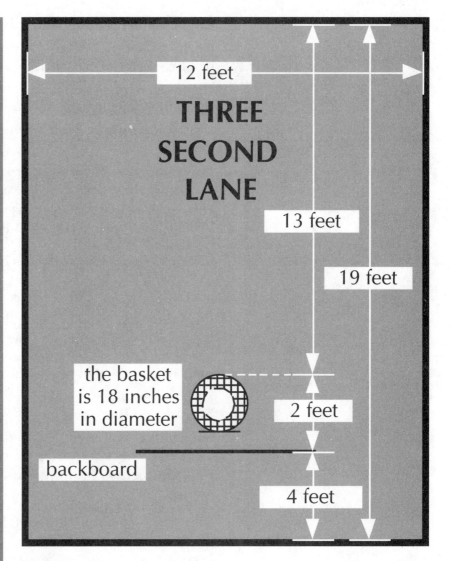

Areas

The three second lane contains the **_blood and guts_ area**. Offensive and defensive players line up alternately on the lane for foul shots. The defense takes the position on the lane closest to the basket inside the innermost space mark. On offense, players can stay in the lane for a maximum of three seconds unless the ball is either shot or loose. Defensive players prevent the offense from having easy access to the lane. See lessons 12.4-6. To enter the lane unopposed, offensive players must fake and then make quick charges into this area for the ball. See lessons 10.5-7.

Other Terms

Backcourt–away from your own basket. Backcourt players are guards. In men's basketball, a backcourt violation occurs when a player crosses midcourt with the ball and then goes back.

Boards or **off the boards**– a rebound

Corner–the area directly to either side of the basket near the baseline. You can not use the backboard for corner shots.

Discontinuing–a dribbling violation; dribbling for a second time after stopping.

Double dribble–a dribbling violation; dribbling with 2 hands.

Forecourt and **backcourt** are not on the court. These are not specific locations. The forecourt is where the forwards play on offense. It is fore or closer to the basket than where the guards play. In a full court press when the guards take the ball out from the baseline, the forecourt could be near midcourt. In a regular offense the forecourt is around the basket and baseline. Farther away from the basket or back are the guards in the backcourt.

Foul line extended–walk on the foul line toward the left or right sideline. This area or line you walk on outside the foul line is the foul line extended area. With a paint brush you could extend the foul line to the sidelines. These extensions on the left and right sides are considered the foul line extended.

Free throw line–foul line

Give and go– Passing, then cutting to the basket (or other area) expecting to receive a return pass.

Head-to-head or **belly-to-belly**–play tight one-on-one defense.

Help out–moving into position to cover and covering another player's offensive assignment.

Inside–closer to the basket, usually in the lane. The defense usually takes an inside position. The offense always wants to pass inside.

In–in bounds; inside.

Man-to-man–archaic term for person-to-person defensive coverage.

On-off ball–On ball refers to defensive coverage on the ball. Off ball is the coverage on the other 4 players without the ball. On ball coverage is usually tight, whereas off ball coverage is usually much looser.

One-on-one–person-to-person defensive coverage.

Outside–farther from the basket. Teams do not want to take too many outside shots. Shorter players usually play outside.

Out–out-of-bounds; outside.

Over and back–a men's game violation; when you cross half court with the ball and then go back.

Paint–the three second lane. On most college and professional courts it is painted one color, often a color of the home team.

Palming–a dribbling violation when the palm of the dribbling hand is turned upward (and then downward) to better control the ball.

Ready position– a player's body position when on the court. The body should be in a half down position, feet shoulder width apart. Body weight is on the balls of the feet. Bending is from the knees, not the back. The fingers are spread apart, clawed. The ready positions for rebounding, defense, and offense are similar.

Screen or pick–when a stationary offensive player is used as, or sets up as, a block or impediment on the defensive player assigned to another offensive player. It is a violation if the screen moves to cause contact with the defense.

Shooting range or **range**–the maximum distance from which you can shoot well. Players often shoot from beyond their range.

Slough off–the defense moves away from the offense.

Strong- weak-side–The ball side of the court is called the strong side. The defense needs to guard closely here. The weak side is the off ball side of the court. The defense can slough off individual coverage and move toward the lane to help out.

The Lane–the 3 second lane.

Three second lane–the lane: the paint.

Tied up–when the offense is not able to pass or move the ball because the defense either gets their hands on the ball (jump ball) or prevents ball movement for 5 seconds (a violation).

Transition or **transition game–** moving from offense to defense or vice-versa. Players need to make quick transitions, especially from offense to defense.

Traveling–see "walking" below.

Violation–against the rules. The other team is awarded the ball out-of-bounds.

Walking–traveling; sliding the pivot foot while holding the ball or taking more than one-and-a-half steps while holding the ball. The half step is actually another step. Another way to say this is that it is a violation to take 2 full steps with the ball. When catching, a player takes the half step first. When passing or dribbling, the half step is the second step.

(Notes)

Chapter Three

3

Flow Chart of the Fundamentals

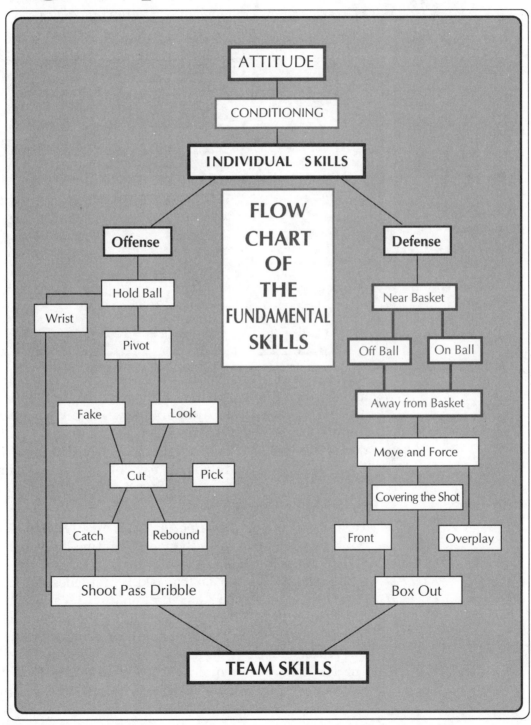

ATTITUDE

CONDITIONING

INDIVIDUAL SKILLS

FLOW CHART OF THE FUNDAMENTAL SKILLS

Offense

Hold Ball

Wrist

Pivot

Fake

Look

Cut — Pick

Catch

Rebound

Shoot Pass Dribble

Defense

Near Basket

Off Ball

On Ball

Away from Basket

Move and Force

Covering the Shot

Front

Overplay

Box Out

TEAM SKILLS

The Flow Chart

This flow chart introduces the fundamentals taught in the lessons. You can more easily recognize relationships between the skills in this form. The more basic ones, taught first, are at the top; more dependent and complex skills are further down. It is one way to look at the fundamentals. Lesson sections devoted to a particular skill are in parenthesis ( ) after the name. Words from the chart like pivot, look, and fake are used interchangeably with the _ing_ ending-pivoting, looking, and faking.

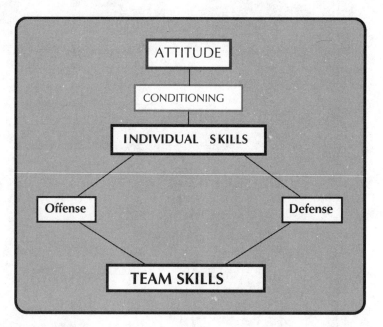

Attitude is at the top because it determines both the teaching and learning that transpires. What you do reflects your attitude, not what you say or even how you say it. **Conditioning** allows players to remain fresh enough to apply skills during the last quarter of a tight game. **Conditioning** also improves a player's athletic ability. This is at least as important as, if not more than, skill. Speed, strength, and quickness ensure successful execution.

Teach **individual offensive** (1-11,13) and **defensive** skills (12,13) before team skills (bottom). Planting individual seeds early permits immediate growth that continues during the entire season. Working on team skills postpones individual growth and wastes time and effort on things players are unprepared to do. There are more than double the number of individual **offensive** fundamentals as **defensive** ones. For this reason offense takes much longer to teach than defense. These skills are more intertwined and need to be taught separately before combined; defensive skills mostly require effort.

Offense

The offensive ball handling skills–shooting, passing, dribbling, catching–begin with **Holding the ball** (1). It is so simple–it takes only 5 minutes to teach–why bother mentioning it? Holding the ball properly not only positions the hands to catch the ball (the ready position), but also to shoot, pass, and dribble. Problem diagnosis in these areas start here. Another key, usually the missing key, to ball handling is **wrist** (3) movement. It is similar for shooting, passing, and dribbling even though the arms are in different positions.

After acquiring the ball, players need to **pivot** (2) in order to shoot, pass, or dribble. Lacking pivoting expertise measurably detracts from all other skills. Two other commonly overlooked

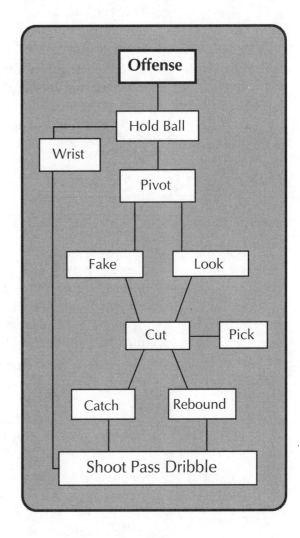

fundamentals are **fake** (parts of 6,8-10,12) and **look** or **communication** (parts of 10,12-19). **Faking** is the finishing touch that enables players to successfully execute any **move**. Players fake with the ball, without the ball, and even on defense. ***Looking*** is something that coaches figure will just come naturally. Not so. It needs to be taught. All players must know where the ball is at all times as well as where the other players are. This includes dribblers, (especially) and passers, knowing who is behind them as well as in front. (Eyes behind the head are helpful.) ***Looking*** both to pass or before cutting involves much communication; it is not random. I've seen championships lost because players were not ***looking*** in the right place. Another key to offense, especially team offense, is ***cutting*** (10). Working against a press or attempting to pass or catch the ball inside involves a combination of ***looking***, ***faking***, and ***cutting***. ***Picking*** or ***screening*** (13) involves ***cutting*** both to set the pick and to use it. Players, especially novices, ***cutting*** to the ball must stop running *after* ***catching*** (10) the ball; stopping *before* ***catching*** permits the defense an easy interception. For novices, a ***catch*** without walking after a cut to the ball is a difficult task.

Rebounding is another form of ***catching*** the ball with ***cutting*** and ***looking*** combined. Combine all of these offensive skills with shooting (5-8), passing (9), and dribbling (4), and you are ready to teach the team skills (14-19).

Defense

Even though defense (lessons 12-13) is most important to me, less practice time needs to be spent on it for many reasons. There is not only less to learn, but also many offensive lessons develop skills used in defense (not because defense is played in the lesson). All conditioning lessons help as well because defense is 90% effort. All dribbling lessons help defense because dribbling position is similar to defensive position. You may have noticed that good dribblers are usually good on defense. For the reasons mentioned above, a team's defensive play usually varies less than its offense.

Defense is most important ***near the basket*** because this area is the easiest place to score. I estimate that teams shoot over 80% within 3 feet of the basket compared to less than 50% overall. Defending the ***blood and guts area*** is the key to team defense. Games are won or lost there.

One-on-one coverage of the player with the ball is not as important as you think, though it is important. Only one player is ***on*** the ball while four are ***off***, away from the ball. Any offensive player can beat one defender. However, it is difficult for one player to beat five players if the other four help out. ***Off ball*** defenders prevent the offense from taking advantage of the defense. They also close down access to the ***blood and guts area***.

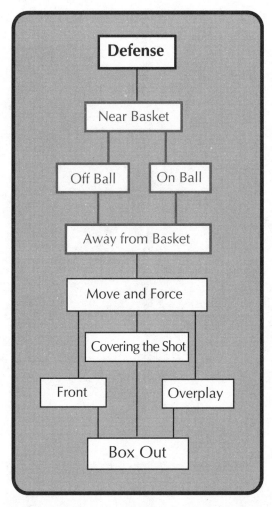

The main defensive skill is ***move and force*** (12), which includes ***fronting*** (12), ***overplaying*** (12), and ***covering the shot*** or defending the shot (12). ***Move*** means to stay with (or one step ahead of) the offense with or without the ball. ***Force*** a player with the ball either to the opposite hand or to the sidelines while dribbling down court, or to the center of the court near the basket. ***Fronting*** (face-guarding) involves playing the offense face-to-face (belly-to-belly is a more apt description). Covering both the ball and players during out-of-bounds plays, as well as in ***boxing out,*** are situations where fronting is used. ***Overplaying*** is used to cover players without the ball. The objective is to prevent passes, cuts near the basket, and offensive rebounding. ***Covering*** the shot means to set up properly on players with the ball when they are in scoring position. Most often the defense should force players in the center of the court to their opposite hand; force players on the sides to the center toward help, since there usually is no help on the baseline. Players ***box out*** after shots whether they are ***fronting***, ***overplaying***, or ***covering the shot.***

The Basketball Coach's Bible

Chapter Four 4

Outline of the Fundamentals

This outline complements the flow chart. It presents relationships between the skills in more detail. The main headings are Practice or Pregame Skills, Individual Skills, and Team Skills. The next chapter discusses these topics even though the outline could stand on its own. Read through it.

The first section on practice and pregame skills are those that do not fit into the other categories. Most of this outline involves individual skills, Section II. I divide it into four parts–non-ball skills, ball skills, going-for-the-ball skills, and defensive skills. The last section on team skills presents half and full court setups as well as ways players should react in each situation.

THE TEACHABLE SKILLS

I. Practice or Pregame Skills

A. Attitude

1. Teaching
2. Winning
3. Recruiting

B. Conditioning

1. Cardiovascular
2. Body–Legs, Trunk, Arms

C. Warm-Up and Warm Down

D. Hustle

E. Game Procedures

1. Reporting In and Out
2. Bench Behavior

II. Individual Skills

A. Offensive Non-Ball Skills

1. Looking & Communication

a. Locate Ball at All Times
　　　b. Where to Cut
　　　c. Where to Pass
　　　d. Out-of-Bounds Plays
　　　e. Deception–Before Passing, Cutting, Stealing
　　　f. Dribbling
　　　g. Team Looking on Defense
　2. Pivoting
　3. Faking
　　　a. With Body, Head, Eyes, Ball
　　　b. Before Passing, Dribbling, Cutting, Shooting
　4. Occupying the Defense
　5. Picking or Screening

B. Individual Ball Skills

　1. Holding the Ball
　2. Wrist Skills
　　　a. Dribbling
　　　b. Shooting
　　　c. Passing
　3. Moves
　　　a. Around the Basket
　　　b. To the Basket
　　　c. Before Shooting

C. Going-for-the-ball Skills

　1. Catching
　2. Cutting
　3. Loose Ball
　4. Rebounding

D. Individual Defensive Skills

　1. Body Position
　2. On Ball-Covering the Ball
　　　a. Near Basket
　　　b. 12 Feet Away
　　　　(1) Near Side Lines
　　　　(2) Near or In Lanes
　　　c. Near Midcourt

(Notes)

The Basketball Coach's Bible

Chapter Five
5

Discussion of the Fundamentals

Practice or Pregame Skills

Attitude

This book reflects my attitude and ideas because it describes what I did. I explain the things that work well. Many more things did not work well; that is another book. In the Do Not section of the **Principles of Practice Teaching** chapter I describe some of these field-tested mistakes.

Whenever I was uncertain of what to do or how to handle players, I kept three things in mind:

> **1.** Teach each individual as though everything depends on it. (It does.) Do what is best for each individual; this is what is best for the team.
>
> **2.** Minimize differences among players.
>
> **3.** Be specific when talking to players; don't waste their time; no BSing.

In the end, your players will reflect your attitude.

Every jock and good ole boy (or girl) adage that I have ever heard reflects an attitude antithetical to teaching. I must comment on one in particular. I am not unaffected by these ideas and speak from experience.

"Winning is the only thing" declares this famous, widely quoted (or misquoted) sports proverb. This idea encourages coaches to judge both their team's and their own individual success based on winning and losing. "We won, so we must have played well. I also did a great job coaching and planning." Or "We lost. We need more practice. I must work harder." None of this is necessarily correct. Coaches need a more concrete basis for evaluation. Thinking this way there is none.

Winning also becomes a moral issue. Winners are good in every sense–good in basketball, good as people, morally righteous. Losers are folks that are no good in every way and, further, do not deserve any consideration. Try to get a job in competition with the home town star. Often the poorer players on a team are invisible or are considered lesser people. The coach thinks, "Why spend time with a player who will not help me win?" Good players yield good or worthwhile people.

We will spend the time to make sure they get to class and pass the algebra test.

Winning also corrupts. If winning is the only thing, what is to prevent illegal and unethical actions to achieve this end? I've too often seen recruiting violations, pacts between coaches and referees, corruption among timers and official scorers, and, in general, too many non-game related things done to take advantage of others.

How many times were you angry at players in practice or a game for making a mistake? Winning demands players do things right whether or not they know how. **Teaching** says that the only limit to a player's ability to learn is the teacher's ability to teach. Face it, players' mistakes stem from your inabilities. **Teaching** encourages coaches to study basketball and to examine themselves; it is giving of yourself, whereas winning only demands, takes, and uses.

Winning paradoxically always makes you a big loser because nobody wins all the time. Only one team wins the championship. All the others lose. On the other hand, when you **teach** you win all the time. **Every practice and every game are wins if your players learn.** This book shows you how to be a winner in a real sense. It will also inadvertently help you score more points than the other team.

My most satisfying day as a coach was neither the day we won the city championship nor when we won games against favored opponents. I was absent on my most satisfying day as a coach. My captain ran a practice that we had planned and discussed the previous day since I knew I would be absent. Another coach in the gym said *the players practiced as if I were there.* This may not sound like much to you, but it means everything to me; my practices are tough.

Conditioning

In the recipe for successful coaching, *conditioning* is one of the most important ingredients. I notice that players often tire in the second half, particularly near the end of the game. The conditioned team gets all those loose balls; the tired team is much slower. The conditioned team has an easier time on offense and continues to play tight defense; tired teams do not think well, execute directions well, play tight defense, or even shoot well. There is no match between tired and conditioned teams. I have seen better skilled and more talented tired teams lose to lesser conditioned teams innumerable times at the high school and college level.

So, one objective that is pervasive throughout every practice is conditioning. Explain this to your players just as I have done above. How do you condition your players in a time efficient and effective way? The answer is surprisingly simple–a continuous movement or motion lesson. Lessons 1.2 and 1.3 are examples.

A continuous movement lesson means just that. Players do not stop moving or running at any time during the lesson. The skills involved in these lessons are often the same ones that you want to teach. Initially they involve the basic ball handling skills. Add practice shooting and team skills to these lessons as well. As the season progresses you can find a way to make any lesson continuous motion.

At the beginning of the season, we move for 15 minutes and then gradually work up to 30 minutes. Adjust this to the condition of your players. We want long-term cardiovascular conditioning, not anaerobic or sprinting activities; many other lessons involve sprinting. A great mistake is to force out of shape players to go faster; just keep them moving. A thoroughbred will run at a very fast pace whereas a heavy player will barely move. It takes time to get in shape; injury takes little time. Players greatly strengthen their legs as well in these drills.

Here are three instructive examples of how to and not to get in shape.

1. A friend always had trouble getting in shape. He ran hard. He was always out of breath. His feet would be bloody after running around the track. His legs would be sore. It always worked this way, and it was nearly impossible for him to improve his condition. He always just gave up or had to quit because of pain and injury.

2. George, a friend's brother, wanted to get in shape. I went out jogging with him. I walked, he jogged. Since this was his first time jogging, I told him not to jog faster than I was walking. We had an enjoyable conversation while exercising for about 10 minutes. He said it was difficult to go that slowly. I told him it was the only way to start without injury. Less than a year later I ran into George's brother who told me that George was running 9 miles a day.

3. When I get in shape, I go slowly. I go from 0 minutes to 1 hour of jogging per day without injury, stiffness, or even getting much out of breath. If I am out of shape, I just walk for an hour or so a day. In one case I remember being totally out of shape before going on a trip to

England. During the first three weeks there, I walked all day around London, Edinburgh, and the Lake District. At Oxford I met some friends who wanted to go for a jog around the area. I warned them of my poor condition, that I would need to go slowly and even then I could not last long. We jogged for over 45 minutes. I had no difficulty breathing and no soreness afterward. I had walked myself into shape.

There is a phrase too often used in sports about conditioning that I must comment on. Every one has heard it or used it– "NO PAIN, NO GAIN." Pain is often a warning sign to your body that you are overdoing it. Overdoing it causes stiffness and injury. It is a step backward because it puts you out-of-business. Sensible conditioning gets you where you want to go without injury. There is no choice - *easy does it* all the way. Adding to this well-known credo places it in its rightful context–*No Pain, No Gain, No Brain.*

All sports mottoes have one thing in common. They substitute emotion in place of planning. It is easier to spit out trite mottoes urging your players to victory than to study basketball. It is easier to blame players for their poor play than to spend more time planning your practice. A new motto to replace some old ones is *Plan Hard, Improve Much*. We need to spread around some sensible ones. Please send them to me. See the address on the order form at the back of this book.

Warm-Up and Warm Down

You do not need a special warm-up. Any moderately paced movement loosens muscles; even shooting around before practice will do. The continuous motion lesson is also a good warm-up. Stretching tight muscles before they are loose can cause injury. On the other hand, after practice leg muscles are loose and will tighten up. Stretching after practice prevents this. It is also a good time for players to cool off before going outside. A player leads the lesson while you talk to your players; plant ideas, give homework and reminders. Appendix B presents a warm down.

Hustle

Hustle is another skill that many think you **just can't teach**. Nothing is further from the truth; it is easy to teach. It takes no talent to learn. Some of the many lessons that teach hustle include *Go Fetch-It (10.1), Catch-Up (7.2), Fronting (12.4), Overplaying (12.5),* all transition lessons, etc. Hustle lessons are part of the everyday practice. Every player I have coached learned to hustle.

Game Procedures

Experience taught me that novice players need practice reporting into and out of games. Once it took several minutes during a scrimmage to corral a group of replaced players who continued to play. Rehearse reporting in and out.

Avoid substitution problems in a game by informing the substituted players ahead of time. Advise him/her to watch the player being replaced. Before reporting in *the player tells you* the offensive and defensive positions.

Practice bench behavior, especially with younger players. Some simple rules are:

> **1.** Players always remain on the bench always when not in the game. No going for water or anywhere else without permission.
>
> **2.** Fans root, players control themselves despite what some pros and college players do.
>
> **3.** During time outs, bench players give up their seats to those in the game. Then they form a semicircle around you so they can easily hear the directions and you can more readily talk, if there is a noisy crowd.

Setup for Time-Outs
P = players in game
X = other players
C = coach

Offensive Non-Ball Skills

Looking and Communication

These are both teachable, distinct fundamentals taught in tandem with others. Usually coaches do not teach these skills because they do not perceive them as skills.

Whether on offense or defense, each player must always know where the ball is; this involves *looking*. Many defensive lessons, involving strong- and weak-side play and overplaying, emphasize watching *(looking* at) both the ball and the offense. In addition, defensive players must watch (*look*) for cutting, especially near the basket. Rebounding also involves *looking* at shot arcs to predict where the ball will go.

On offense *looking* means more than watching the ball; it is directed, not random. Players evaluate situations to find openings. Always look to pass inside. Look long in out-of-bounds plays under the opponent's basket even before picking up the ball; look short under your own basket. Passers and dribblers especially must be aware of everything both in front and behind them. Communicating to another player a cut or pass to a particular spot are other *looking* skills incorporated into many lessons. Some of these are 9.51, 9.52, 10.61.

Pivoting

The first move after a player touches a ball is a pivot. Picking up a loose ball, rebounding, catching a pass, driving, shooting, or dribbling all involve pivoting. A lack of ability to pivot affects a player's ability to perform all the above tasks. One can never practice enough pivoting. Eventually players practice it in tandem with all other skills. See section 2.

Faking

The difference in the effectiveness of much of what we do depends on *faking*. Players *fake* before passing, shooting, dribbling, or cutting. On defense as well, players *fake* to steal passes or a dribbled ball. Players fake with the ball, head, eyes, and/or body.

One big difference between skilled and unskilled players is the ability to fake. This discrepancy only happens because faking is usually not taught, even though it is not an advanced skill. Lesson 10.5 teaches faking separately, whereas lessons 6.0-6.6 (plus others) teach faking in tandem with other skills. Inexperienced players can readily learn and use fakes.

Offense Off the Ball

A player without the ball on offense (4 of 5 players) either wants to hide or be seen intentionally by the defense. Both of these involve *faking*. See 10.5.

•To be seen is easier. The player's objective is to occupy the eyes and attention of the defense. This prevents the defense from helping out on the ball. To accomplish this distraction players overtly act as if they want the ball or are going to cut to the basket. Stay in view; fake cuts away from the ball.

•The offense *hides* before a cut to the ball so that the defense cannot react quickly to the play. A player accomplishes this move several ways:

    1. Stay out of the normal view of the defense. Move to the side or behind the defense.

    2. Act like you are sleeping, not paying attention to the game.

The offense should do both. The defense either does not see or ignores the offense.

Screening or Picking

Screening is important when the defense is strong. This is rarely the case with young players. Therefore, screening is one of the last skills taught (section 13). Players often use picks in two situations:

1. When the defense is person-to-person
2. During out-of-bounds plays.

Individual Ball Skills

Holding the Ball

One of the most overlooked skills is *holding the ball*. It is a prerequisite to learning all the ball handling skills, such as shooting, passing and catching, and dribbling. For this reason it is the first lesson. Novice and other players exhibiting problems with any ball handling skill need only a few minutes of instruction. I heard somewhere and others have confirmed the fact that one former great NBA shooter, Pete Maravitch, slept holding the ball.

This first lesson will immediately help the many players labelled *butterfingers*, who have difficulty catching the ball. Difficulty catching the ball often leads these players to be afraid of it. They turn away from hard passes or attempt to catch passes with their eyes shut. As a result they often injure fingers in the attempt to catch the ball, and they rarely catch the ball. This is all for naught.

Examine how a butterfingered player holds the ball: by using much of the palms and lower parts of the fingers. To control the ball, players need to hold it with the **fingertips**, not palms. Only the fingertips touch the ball. (The term *touch,* as in shooting *touch,* alludes to this.) Try catching a ball the butterfingered way with your palms. Have your players try this as well. It is difficult, if not impossible.

The first step of the correct way to catch the ball involves making the hands into claws. Hold the ball in these claws with contact only at the fingertips. The first lesson, 1.0, details this.

Wrist Skills

Shooting (5,7,8), passing (9), and dribbling (4) are wrist skills, because the fluid motion of the wrist along with the hand is the major limiting factor to improvement. Before practicing any ball skills, 1-2 minutes of wrist work pays off in great dividends. Besides making the motion more fluid, it also strengthens the wrist. Improvement can occur without even touching the ball. See Lesson 3.0 for details.

The wrist skills are the most difficult ones to learn, in part because they involve the entire body, not just the wrists.

Players need much coordination to perform them well. In addition, coaches rarely teach these skills. Often coaches use naturally talented players in lieu of teaching this skill and then readily claim, "*You just can't teach it.*" Every shooting lesson that I have read or watched was academic in nature (even the Wizard of Westwood, John Wooden, did it that way in a video); a beautiful explanation at best. Nowhere do coaches give players a way or technique to practice. Nowhere do coaches break the skills down into learnable parts. The obvious fact that even some pros (Hall of Famers too) do not have the technique of well-instructed 9th graders attests to the horrendous state of teaching. This applies to passing and dribbling as well.

Start teaching the wrist skills immediately so players can practice them correctly on their own.

Moves

A *move* is what I call a more advanced scoring skill, although coaches, as well as I, often use this term more broadly to mean any series of movements. The purpose of all moves is to score. Moves are often considered *slick* since they fake out the defense. Players often invent them during games, making it difficult to present them all. The section on *moves* (6) gives players a varied sample.

Going-for-the-Ball Skills

Catching (10), cutting (10), going for loose balls (10+), and rebounding (11) are the *going for the ball skills*. All of these skills involve looking to start, hustle in the middle, and pivoting to end. In between, players use many other skills such as positioning, communicating, and grabbing the ball. Moving quickly helps also.

The most difficult part of catching involves cutting to the ball or to the open space. Practicing catching lessons without cutting is for naught. With the defense close, the player that catches the ball is the one who moves to the ball one step ahead of the opponent. Teams with *going-for-the-ball-skills* beat presses.

Rebounding is another *going-for-the-ball* skill not often taught. The keys to rebounding involve predicting where the ball will go and then moving to the best position. Section 11 divides rebounding into teachable parts.

Individual Defensive Skills

Defense (section 12) is easier to teach than offense because it is mostly physical; it takes little talent to learn. There are fewer defensive skills than offensive ones to master. Each skill is less complicated as well, so players learn much faster than offense. A team's shooting often varies from game to game, but the defense can be more constant, something you can rely on.

Often coaches forgo teaching person-to-person defense because the coach thinks, incorrectly, that a zone defense is easier to learn. Even in a zone players need to cover the player with the ball one-on-one. Under the boards the defense again must play low post players one-on-one. Each situation in a zone ends up with the defense playing the offense one-on-one. Zone players, in addition, need to know how the zone shifts. For these reasons zones are more difficult to teach and learn, not easier than one-on-one defense.

Most of the opponents' zones that my teams faced were only places for players to stand on the court. Any particular defensive player seemed to have no idea how to cover the player with the ball. Coaches need to teach players how to play one-on-one rather than where to stand on the court.

Some problems may arise using person-to-person defense. With inexperienced players you are more vulnerable under the boards since the players are not *all milling around there* as in most zones. Novice players also muddle the coverage by losing the player they are guarding or by picking up the wrong player. However, in the long run your players will do better than you would ever expect. They learn how to play defense, not take up space.

I break down individual defensive skills into four basic categories:

1. Body position
2. On ball–covering the ball
3. Off ball–preventing catches & cuts
4. Preventing rebounds

Body position is **the defensive position**. This position facilitates quick, fast movements in any direction. The body is low with feet shoulder-width apart. Lesson 12.0 gives the details.

Covering the ball means to cover the offensive player with the ball in any position on the court. **The keys to learning this skill are the Three Yard and Forcing lessons (12.1-12.2)** These teach a player to stay in the best defensive position one step ahead of the offense. Covering the shooter is another skill often not taught. Most players just attempt to block the shot, flailing their arms around the shooter. Often referees call a foul whether or not there is contact. See Lesson 12.7.

In a person-to-person defense only one player covers the ball. Four work to prevent the offense from catching it where they want. Overplaying (12.5) and fronting (12.4) teach this important skill.

Treat any offensive player going into the **blood and guts area** or already there very specially. In particular, prevent offensive rebounders coming from behind the basket. Lesson 12.6 combines fronting, overplaying, and boxing out in this area.

Team Skills

Individual skills make up most of the teachable skills. There are few team skills compared to the individual ones, or at least fewer than most people think. Team skills most importantly coordinate the movements of all players. They furnish players a court position from which they execute individual skills. However, players need to know *how to do it* well before they need to know *where to do it*.. That is why team skills, in my opinion, take a back seat to the individual ones. Even though I present a minimum of team skills, there is still enough here for a professional team.

The team skills include the center jump (14), the foul line setup and transition game (15), half court offensive (16) and defensive (17) setups, out-of-bounds plays (18), and full and half court pressure setups (19). Often I went into preseason games before teaching many team skills. I never taught zone defense in practice. However, I once did during a game. It took only one time out for the players to learn how to play an excellent shifting 2-1-2 zone defense. These were inexperienced 10th graders. They even surprised me.

Games start with a center jump, so teach it first. I have even taught it at the start of a preseason scrimmage. Teaching detailed center jump plays is a poor use of time especially since it is only used a few times a game. A simple defensive jump setup prevents you from "getting burned." Trickier plays can evolve with developing communication during the season.

The foul line setup is a great way to teach boxing out as well as the transition game skills. The transition game involves going from offense to defense or vice-versa quickly. It is one team skill that players need before the first scrimmage. You may find that shooting from the foul line may be difficult for novices. So, move novices closer to the basket. Shooting from too far destroys shooting technique. As shooting technique develops allow players to move back closer to the foul line.

The keys to team offense are:

1. Cutting to the open space

2. Communication between the passer and cutter.

Practice these as individual skills, not as part of practice plays. They take much time to learn. Keep offenses simple like *Plays 1,2,3* in Lesson 16.1. Guidelines for any practice play are:

1. The ending is a short shot or layup

2. All players go for the rebound

3. There is a transition made to the defense.

The most complex combination of the individual and team skills involves pressure offense against a pressure defense. Teach it as soon as your players are ready, not before.

(Notes)

PART 2 | PRACTICE PLANNING AND TEACHING

Chapter Six

6

Practice Planning

Planning is the key to teaching and learning. Plan for the season as well as for daily practices. The lessons and the guide below assist in making everyday plans. Seasonal planning depends on an evaluation of your players' ability; this evaluation determines both the number of lessons taught and how much time is spent on each. I caution you not to skip lessons. Consider spending less time on lessons your players execute well or combining several lessons. Skipping key fundamentals makes learning improbable, if not impossible. Skipping steps also has an effect opposite to the one you want, because learning is slowed down rather than speeded up.

Daily Planning

Use the **Practice Planning Guide** to plan your daily practice. It allows for great variation. There is a definite rationale for the **lesson order**; it is not random. Choose lessons from the **lesson section** as you would courses from a Chinese restaurant menu to teach the appropriate **lesson skill** topic. Keep in mind that I wrote the lessons in descending order of importance for the most part; sections 1 to 3 are more fundamental than sections 5 to 7. Within each skill section, the lessons also increase in difficulty. The **Time Needed** is a range that you must coordinate with the time ranges (for introduction and daily practice) given in the **Coach's Corner** section of each lesson. Young or inexperienced players need more time to complete any lesson; experienced players need less time. The introductory times for any lesson are nearly double the daily practice times. So initially, since all lessons are introductory, you will have a difficult time precisely following the guide.

Practice Planning Guide

Order Number	Lesson Skill	Lesson Section	Time Needed (minutes)
1	individual warm-ups	any 1-13	5-15
2	continuous movement (continuous motion)	1.2+,1.3, 9.32, 9.4+	15-30
3	individual skills - new lessons	1-13	15-30
4	shooting technique	3, 5-8	10-30
5	defense	12, 11.3	10-15
6	individual skills, transition, team	1-13, 14-19	10-15
7	lay ups	5.4-5.5, 5.8	5-10
8	warm down	see Appendix B	5-10
9	individual practice	any 1-13	0-20
TOTALS			75-175
APPROXIMATE AVERAGE			~2 HOURS

THE PRACTICE PLANNING GUIDE

Order Number

1. Individual Warm-Ups

The time spent on *individual warm ups* is extremely valuable. Ideally, players work on the skills they need most. Give individual instruction. Devise individual practice plans. If players work hard, extend the warm up; it will reduce the time needed for other lessons. Hopefully, players will continue to practice the same way on their own.

During warm-ups watch and work with players; this is not time for a coffee break. Watch for players shooting from great distances, practicing incorrectly, or wasting time. Given individual instruction, players readily recognize the great value of this time.

2. Continuous Movement

The *continuous motion lesson* conditions your players cardiovascularly while they practice many basic skills. You will need several days of introductory lessons, before running a continuous motion lesson. Initially, players perform simple ball handling skills while constantly moving for 15 minutes. Players need just move, not sprint. Gradually extend the length to 30 minutes. The complexity of the skills practiced can also increase.

Practice the continuous motion lesson first, because it is a good warm up. Do it before any sprinting. It also enables players to focus better at practice, just as jogging does for adults. After this warm up, players are ready to slow down and listen for a while. This is an opportune time, while the players are fresh, to teach something new.

3. Individual Skill, New Lesson

Initially, all lessons are new. So, several weeks might elapse before you introduce only one new lesson each day. Meanwhile use this time to teach individual skills not included in other parts of practice. These include pivoting, dribbling, and the going-for-the-ball skills–catching, passing, and cutting.

Pivoting and dribbling have priority over the going-for-the-ball skills. Pivoting is the last part of any going-for-the-ball skill, so players need pivoting expertise to complete any of these. Dribbling is a skill that players enjoy practicing on their own. So, teach dribbling as soon as possible. It is also part of many other lessons, especially the shooting lessons. After the first several weeks the team may need to spend little time on separate dribbling lessons.

4. Shooting Technique

After a difficult new lesson do an easy one. Shooting technique is easy to practice, not easy to perform well. Teaching it requires close supervision. Shooting technique, like dribbling, is happily practiced by players in warm-ups and outside practice. So, it is advantageous to teach it as soon as possible.

5. Defense

Defensive lessons require a maximum physical effort. This is a physically difficult lesson after an easy one. Players use little skill and thought so these lessons are easy to learn. Hustle (heart) is an integral part of all defensive lessons.

6. Individual Skill or Transition or Team

For the first several days, or weeks, teach individual skills in this slot. When players are ready, start teaching the team skills. You can also introduce team skills, especially transition lessons, in the new lesson slot as well.

7. Layups

Do layups as a team to end practice. Encourage the players to loudly count each shot made in a row. After making the required number from the left, right, and center positions, end the practice. This tactic wraps up practice on an up note.

8. Warm Down

Before players leave we have a warm down which involves stretching, cooling off, and talking. (See warm down in appendix.)

9. Individual Practice

Any individual practice after this needs to focus on a lesson, no playing or just shooting around since players do this enough on their own.

The Total Practice

Plan to spend 2 hours for a practice planned like the guide. The minimums and maximums for each section when added up indicate that practice can vary from about 1 hour (75 minutes) to 3 hours (175 minutes). Adjust the time spent on each lesson based on the needs of your players. A stop watch is helpful. If you spend additional time on the current lesson then partially cut one or several of the following lessons. With young players at the beginning of the season things will probably vary greatly. It takes a while before you can follow a complete practice plan. It is okay if you only complete half of the practice. Your kids need the time on the basics. You need time to learn what your players need.

There are several things you can do to help cut practice time:

- Encourage players to practice the lessons on their own.

- Give practice lessons as homework. For example, tell a player to do 100 pivots or take 50 one-foot shots.

- Use the warm-ups to full advantage to reduce the time needed for regular practice lessons.

- Cut the time for a lesson done frequently.

- Introduce less new material. Never rush if you are behind schedule.

- It is okay to go into preseason games with out teaching the center jump or press, etc.

- Plan to teach on game day while waiting for referees or the other team. Often there is 30 minutes of usable time.

- Plan teaching sessions before and even during a preseason scrimmage.

The schedule is always tight if you teach the fundamentals. Planning again is the key. The results are obvious.

Seasonal Planning

Looking at the great number of skills and lessons (over 170) can be overwhelming unless you do some seasonal planning. In particular, you need to plan weeks or even months ahead to teach each team skill. You don't have to stick to this schedule. Your plans will surely change, but this gives you reachable goals and a sensible framework to teach the individual skills. Planning the individual skills is easier; just go in order from the easiest one to the most difficult one. Alternate days and the amount of time spent on each lesson, so at the end of the week or month players have a complete dose.

The first team skill taught is a defensive center jump setup. Players learn this lesson in 15 minutes and do not require repeated practice. Because it is not a critical lesson, you can practice it any time before the first game. Teach the foul line setup next. Use this setup to teach boxing out and the transition game as well. Get to this as soon as possible.

Young players have very different needs than older high school players. The foul line transition and helping out on defense lessons are the only critical team skills for younger players. Be patient and wait to teach plays until players can cut and communicate well. The only additional critical skill for older players is offense against the press, because you will certainly be pressed if you have a lead near the end of a game.

Planning Scrimmages

Scrimmages, like games, act as tests for the players (and coach). Players want to be prepared for a test; they practice harder and listen more closely. Plan a scrimmage for the first week of practice and then immediately announce this to your players.

Schedule teams of similar ability. Great wins or losses may affect the learning process in a negative way. Eventually players understand that you care more about how they play than winning or losing. It may be a good idea not to keep a running score. Decide with the other coach how to run the scrimmage. Do you want to hire referees or referee yourself? Do you want a game or a scrimmage with 10-15 minute teaching timeouts? Do you plan to predominately use the best players or do all players play equal times? I favor self-refereed games with 10-15 minute teaching time outs for younger players initially. Self-refereeing also gives you the opportunity to spend a few extra seconds explaining calls to players and even showing them a better way to accomplish something. Game referees' seldom have time to give explanations, and they certainly will not instruct. Buy and read the rule book for your league, so you understand better the calls and rules.

Chapter Seven 7 | Principles of Practice Teaching

The principles of practice teaching have much to do with attitude. These methods of dealing with players derive from my deep seated beliefs, as I previously have explained.

1. Focus on individual skills. Team skills are just applications and combinations of these.

2. Write down your practice plan in a book for future reference as well as on a 3x5 card for practice. (Copy pages from the appendix.)

3. Use a stopwatch to time lessons. Don't force lessons into the allotted time. If you need more time for one lesson, cut from another. An assistant can help you time.

4. Involve all players every minute in practice. There is no sideline where unoccupied players go. Nobody sits.

5. Each player needs a ball. Any type of ball will do. Bob Cousy's signature can be missing. It can be lopsided. Use volleyballs or beach balls, if necessary. It is easy to acquire used balls from any school. They usually have closets full of old, used, lopsided balls taking up storage space, gathering dust. No excuses.

6. Do not let players dribble when lessons do not involve dribbling. Do not allow dribbling between lessons either. This activity not only wastes time, but also allows players to continue poor dribbling and looking habits. You need to supervise and control dribbling in warm-ups, practice, and warm downs especially with novice players.

7. Use what I call **shadows** when teaching team skills or skills involving many players. Shadows follow the same directions as the player you teach, only from a few feet behind. You may need to use two or more shadows sometimes. Often the shadows alternate position with the first player in line. This keeps all players actively involved and learning. The lessons instruct you when to use shadows.

8. Use all players in practice scrimmages, even if this means having 16 players on the court. The smallness of younger players readily allows this. With older, larger players you may want to limit the player number to 12 or 14.

9. Each player needs to learn the individual skills for each position. Tall players practice dribbling just like short ones. Short players learn boxing out.

10. Plant ideas in players ahead of time. It directs thinking and effort. The ideas can involve strategies in tomorrow's game, or skills that you will practice next week. Inform players when you will teach particular skills.

11. Give lessons for homework. There are many things players can practice without a court or even without a ball. (See the COURT and BALL sections of The Table of Lessons in the appendix.) If there is a ball and a court available at home, so much the better.

12. Make sure players practice correctly when you are watching. Hopefully players will continue to practice correctly on their own. Players should find practicing the way taught easy. However, there are millions of ways to do things incorrectly. Watch for these. Practicing perfectly makes perfect; practicing incorrectly facilitates bad habits that are difficult to change.

13. Do not play favorites. Good players are not better people or more important people. Bad players are not bad people. They are unique, worthwhile individuals. Treat all players as great people.

14. Keeping track of layups or short shots missed encourages players to do better. If needed, tell players how many shots they missed privately. The last resort is to make an announcement to the team. Never use this information to berate players. You can require a player to shoot 2 or 3 full court layups or shots after practice for each one missed. Keep these statistics in a book, so that you can readily peruse an entire week or month.

15. Make simple practice rules for the players.

16. Run each lesson at the appropriate effort level.

17. Be aware of the many Do Nots for coaches. See the Field Tested Mistakes section in this chapter.

18. Use managers. They are more than tremendous help; they are a necessity. Train them just like players.

19. Comment readily to a player when you see improvement. This will occur often when you use these methods.

Rules for the Players

1. Be at practice on time, dressed, ready to play.

2. Do not dribble or even hold a basketball while I (the coach) am talking or teaching a lesson. (Use *balls down* as the instruction before teaching to remind players to place all balls on the floor. Otherwise, balls slip out of players' hands causing distractions.)

3. Players may not leave the gym or a lesson without permission.

4. No 30 foot shots, or shots outside the foul line, at any time in the gym. The younger the players the closer the distance they need to practice.

5. Inform the coach of illness immediately by phone or by note.

Effort Levels of Lessons

For a lesson to be effective, you must be clear as to what physical effort is required by players. Should players shoot as if it were the game on-the-line, or should they take time squaring up and moving their arms into position? Should the defense play at 100% effort or should they offer token resistance? Each lesson in this book is run at one of the three effort levels below.

Level 1, The Technique Level–This level exaggerates the proper way to shoot, pass, dribble, etc. Perform technique level lessons slowly. Perform them this way in practice only, not in games. Practicing at this level reaps tremendous benefits. Improvement occurs in the ball skills without even using a ball. Minute for minute of practice, this is the best spent time for players. Coach for coach, these lessons are the least recognized and practiced.

Level 2, The Practice Level - Lessons at this level are the most common. Players normally practice most skills this way.

Level 3, Game Level - Game level lessons are the most advanced level of lessons. Exert game type pressure on the player. Transition and other hustle lessons that demand a maximum physical effort are game level lessons. Any offensive lesson with aggressive defense as well as all full speed defensive lessons are also game level lessons.

Using Assistants and Managers

Assistants are more than a tremendous help; they are a necessity.

•At games they set up the gym and keep score and time, as well as statistics.

•At practice they assist in a great variety of ways:

1. They act as offensive or defensive players (usually dummy) in lessons.

2. The assistant can spot such individual actions as walking violations. Assign one individually to assist a player.

3. They keep practice statistics such as number of missed layups.

4. They keep time using a stop watch for each lesson. Often I ask one manager to time the lessons. If one lesson takes longer than the scheduled time I need to cut back on another. The manager can inform you to stop when 5 or 10 minutes have elapsed. This keeps you approximately on schedule. Note that some lessons can readily be cut, others can't. This is one reason to use time ranges when you plan practice, instead of specific times.

5. They can keep players far apart minimizing chances of collisions and also direct traffic in lessons where players are close.

Each lesson gives other specific uses for managers.

Treat managers like players in every respect. They listen to the lessons; they do not practice shooting or dribbling on the side. They are there, ready to go, each day when you need them. They get letters, jackets, trophies, etc., just like any player. My warmest feelings toward any students are to my many basketball managers. Thanks again.

If you are a teacher, recruit your best students as managers. Older students are better managers. Use 5 or 6 managers if you can get them. Use males or females, regardless of the gender of your team. The critical selection criterion is interest. Teach one manager how to keep score or time or statistics. Then, have this manager train others. Always check on this training. As with the players, teach each manager every job. Have many keep official score at a game or scrimmage. As with players, keep them all working. Nobody just sits.

Methods That Do Not Work—Do Nots

This list could be longer than any other list in the book. There are many ways to do things poorly and ineffectively (I have tried them), fewer ways to do things well. Here are some Do Nots.

1. DO NOT play games in practice. The next section details why this is a big mistake.

2. DO NOT allow players to practice incorrectly. Make sure that they both practice needed skills and adhere to the lessons.

3. DO NOT spend much time teaching zone defenses until person-to-person is learned.

4. DO NOT practice foul shooting by taking 10 or 20 in a row. See the foul shooting technique lessons (5.6,5.7)

5. DO NOT practice shooting from more than four feet with novices, one foot is better. Use the specifically designed practice shooting lessons if you want players to practice at greater distances.

6. DO NOT have your players run without using basketball skills as they are running. No kamikaze drills (unless players dribble).

7. DO NOT get players overly excited or UP for a game. Usually they are UP. You need to do the reverse—calm players down.

8. DO NOT act nervous in games. This makes players nervous.

9. DO NOT come to practice unprepared. PLAN

10. DO NOT force players with small hands to shoot with one hand. This two-handed method is much more difficult than shooting one-handed. Players readily shoot with one hand when they are able. However, make sure they practice shooting technique with one hand. Practicing technique one handed will improve the two handed shot as well as ready players for a one handed shot.

11. DO NOT overuse praise. Players want your attention, consideration, and help. Praise is often used in lieu of these more important things.

12. Most importantly, *never think that the game is more important than any **one** of your players*.

These are just some of the Do Nots I have learned from personal experience. I'd like to hear some of yours.

Playing Games in Practice

More needs to be said about playing games in practice. It is a poor way for novices to learn or practice newly introduced individual skills. The reasons are many:

1. There is little repetition of any particular skill in a game compared to a particular lesson. Learning follows (correct) repetition. Each player may only take 5 shots in a 30 minute game, whereas each player can take 30 shots in two minutes of shooting practice. The same holds for the other skills as well.

2. Repetition in a game is not timely. Shooting for example, does not take place at regular short spaced intervals. Learning needs uninterrupted repetitions.

3. At any instant in a game, a coach will find it difficult to coach 10 players simultaneously, because each one moves uniquely. It is easy to allow players to continue to make errors.

4. In a game players use skills combined in groups. Players learn best when you teach each skill separately and then further break each skill into its components. Combine the skills after each is learned, not before.

Playing Street Ball-Half Court Basketball Outside of Practice

When I grew up playing half court, two-on-two and three-on-three, was very common, much more common than full court games. The basketball experience obtained by playing half court is useful, especially for developing individual moves, but not nearly as helpful as proper practice. Consider the number of playground players and the amount of time they spend on the court. If street ball were that worthwhile there would be many more stars coming off the playgrounds right into the college and pro ranks. This rarely, if ever, occurs. The fact that foreign players often play with great skill, despite their lack of street ball experience compared with Americans, only confirms this belief. Here are some reasons why playing too much street ball is a Do Not for players:

1. Conditioning usually does not take place because of the lack of continuous movement.

2. An important part of the game, the transition game, is not part of half court play.

3. Team play is not encouraged, since a player is always close enough to the basket to score.

4. Playing more rested in a half court game and then playing after sprinting down the court a few times are quite different.

5. Injuries are much more likely to happen in half court games, because there are so many quick direction changes.

6. Three second rules usually never apply in these games. So half court offenses do not work in real games.

There is no need to tell your players that half court is no good. Instead, encourage them to play full court outside practice, even if it is only two-on-two or one-on-one. Encourage players as well to use the three second rule in any type of game; tell them that other players may abide by this rule if someone calls this obvious violation. Most importantly, encourage players to practice the way you teach them.

(Notes)

PART 3 | THE LESSONS

Chapter Eight
8

Lesson Features

Table

The table that begins each section is part of the larger Table of Lessons found in Appendix G. At a glance this table gives a section overview that will aid in planning. Each section table supplies the name of each lesson as well as these additional features: lessons needed before, the number of players needed, the effort level, the estimated times to both introduce and practice the lesson on a daily basis, whether you need a ball and/or a court. The Coach's Corner section of each lesson supplies much, not all, of the same information. Note that you find the introduction and daily times for the extensions only in the table, not in the lessons.

Lesson Numbering

Each section teaches one and sometimes several intertwined skills. All lessons in a section have the same starting integer number like 1.0, 1.1, and 1.2 increasing by tenths. Zero level lessons like 1.0 and 2.0 present the first and most fundamental part of each skill. Often you need only 5-10 minutes to complete it. Some lessons like 6.0, Moves, and 8.0, Practice Shooting, do not contain a drill, but explain the lessons that follow. Read this explanation before doing anything else in those sections. Extensions of a lesson are numbered by hundredths; for example, 1.11 and 1.12 are extensions of 1.1. An extension usually takes a lesson one step further. Often, it uses the identical setup for players. Sometimes extensions provide the next small step in learning. In some cases, I divide a lesson into parts, instead of using extensions, because the skills involved are closely related. In this case, the lesson name includes the number of parts like Blocking Boxing Out 1-2.

Name

A name related to each lesson serves as a descriptive mnemonic device (I almost forgot that–oops!). When skills are executed simultaneously, their names are directly coupled like Pivot Pass or One Dribble Layup, where a player dribbles (only once) in for a layup. Lessons with skills performed separately are named like Pivot With Defense or Layup With Dribble, where the dribbling is done after the layup.

Brief

In one sentence (usually) the **brief** immediately familiarizes you with the lesson by stating the action and movement involved.

Fundamental Notes

What fundamentals do you practice in the lesson? How do they relate to each other? When do you use them in a game? What is the significance of the lesson? The Fundamental Notes section discusses these questions and more.

Setup

This specifies the physical placement of the players on the court. Diagrams point out specific court locations difficult to describe.

Directions for Players

These are the step-by-step directions for your players. It is for you, but it is directed to your players. This permits the dialogue to be more readable. Instead of telling you what to tell the players I directly instruct the players. A bullet (•) precedes information directed to the coach.

Troubleshooting Teaching and Learning

What problems will you have teaching? What common problems will players have? Here are some that I have encountered. Unfortunately, you will compile a list of your own. Send them to me.

•TEACHING - These are details that you need to emphasize.

•LEARNING - These are common difficulties exhibited by players. Expect them.

Use of Assistants

These are some of the many ways to use your assistants.

Weekly Practice

Weekly practice suggests the number of times to practice a lesson each week. Practice most lessons *daily* until players are ready for the next one. (Daily does not mean every day for the entire season.) Practice others only 1-3 times each week or season or as needed.

Extensions

Extensions of lessons are numbered using hundredths like 1.11 and 9.31. (1.11 is an extension of 1.1 and 9.31 is an extension of 9.3) Usually extensions add another step, combine another skill, or change one variable in a lesson. The write-ups vary greatly from one sentence in length to nearly complete lesson features. Each section *table* lists information about all extensions in the section.

Some lessons have 2-6 parts with no extensions whereas other lessons have only one part with 2-6 extensions. Why are things this way? The reason for this is paradoxical–some parts may appear so similar, that if discussed together, you might not see the difference, so I separate them into extensions. Other parts may not seem similar, but need to be taught together or one after the other; these become parts.

Coach's Corner

The **Coach's Corner** lists 5 morsels of information about each lesson that assists you in planning practice. The section table contains this information as well.

Lessons Needed Before

This feature lists each lesson needed before this current one. This helps you plan. Usually, you need to complete the previous lesson. Sometimes the current one requires many other skills. Players will not execute this lesson well without your teaching these other skills. A plus sign (+) indicates that a team skill lesson or another one requires too many lessons to list. *All 11* or *all-11,12* indicates entire sections are needed before teaching this lesson.

Number of Players

This gives the number of players working together in a lesson. A plus sign (+) next to a number, like 2+, indicates a passive person, a manager or coach, is required with the 2 other players. This person usually just stands in one place.

Effort Level

This details the physical effort involved. Level 1 lessons involve technique and are often called technique level lessons. Do them slowly; they often do not resemble the skill performed in a game, because two to five technique lessons often comprise a skill like shooting or catching.

Neither offense nor defense expends much effort.

Level 2 lessons are at the practice level and are called practice level lessons. Any skill practiced at a moderate pace, like shooting or pivoting, is at level 2. This level is a catchall for lessons between levels 1 and 3. Offense and defense make a moderate effort.

Level 3 lessons are at the game level (called game level lessons). Players sprint and perform at maximum effort. Exert pressure on players. Offense and defense go full speed against each other. Games are easy compared to these lessons.

The effort level of each lesson is important for planning practice. In practice it is smart to alternate game and technique level lessons so players run hard and then have a breather. Running two game level or technique level lessons in a row is usually a Do Not.

Introduction Time

This is a time **range** needed to introduce the lesson. Inexperienced players often need the maximum (or more) amount of time. Experienced players may take even less than the minimum. These times are a guideline. Experience with your players will enable you to make more exact estimates.

Daily Time

The more you practice a lesson, the less time you need to derive similar results. It often takes half as much time to practice a lesson, as it does to teach it the first time. Use these numbers as guides when practice planning.

FEATURES OF THE DIAGRAMS

Lines and Arrows

Solid lines usually indicate movement of players, whereas dashed lines usually indicate movement of the ball. One exception to this is when dashed lines are used to show pivoting direction. The types of arrows used are solid for movement and hollow for passes. A different type of arrow head is used for fakes. See the diagrams.

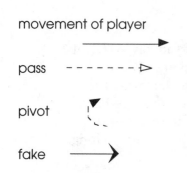

movement of player

pass

pivot

fake

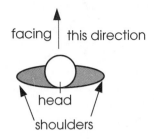

Body Position of Player

The body of a player is shown from an overhead view two ways. The line or the ellipse represents the shoulders. The circle shows the head. The player is always facing away from the shoulders toward the head.

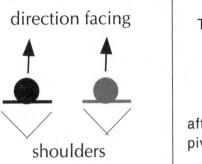

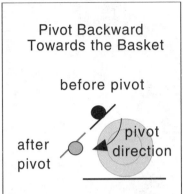

Shading for Different Positions

When a player is shown in two positions in the same diagram, the first or initial position is black or a darker shade, whereas the second is lighter in color. Often, the offense or defense are shown in light and dark shades. A narrow shaded line is also used to show the path or position changes of a player.

Numbers in Multistep Movements

Many drills involve multiple steps. Each step, as well, may have several timed movements that need to be executed in order. So, in the diagrams for each step, the numbers indicate the order of the movements. One (1) means first, two (2) second and so on. If two players move at the same time the numbers will be the same, so there may be several ones or twos in the diagram.

In the diagram below, from lesson 16.1, there are three ones in the diagram. This indicates that these players move at the same time. There are two twos; one indicates a cut, while the other indicates a pass.

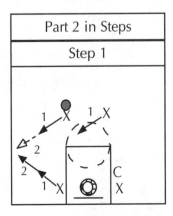

The Basketball Coach's Bible

Chapter Nine

9

The Lessons

A. Sections 1-13
   The Individual Skills

B. Sections 14-19
   The Team Skills

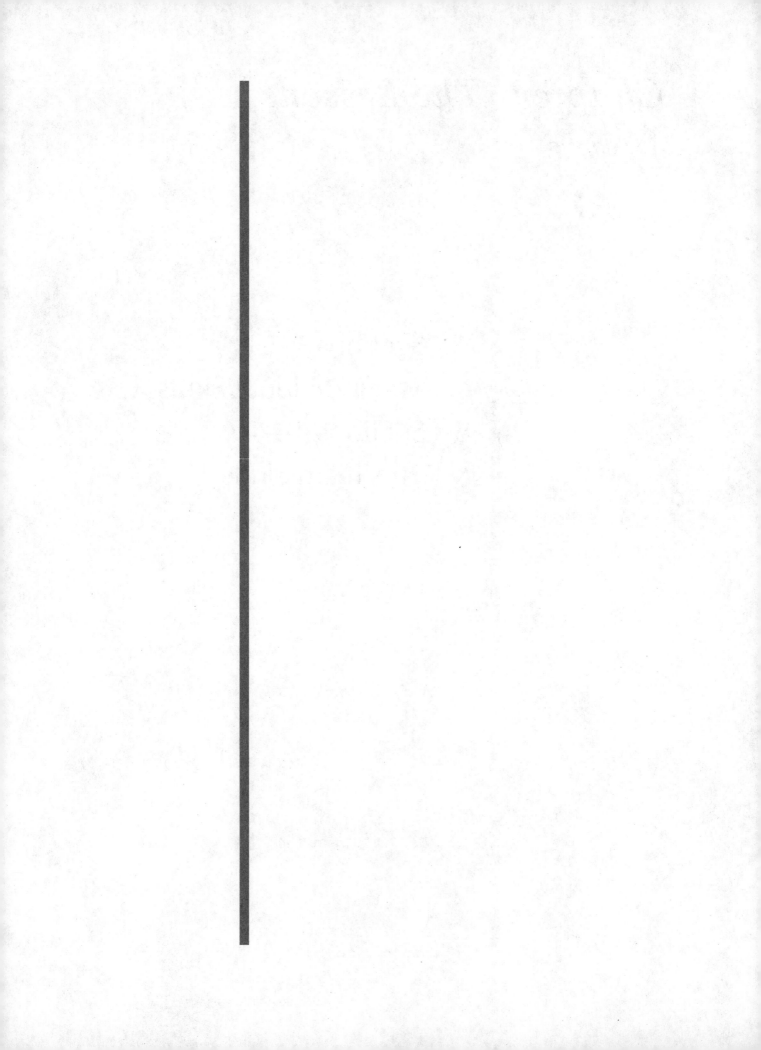

Section 1
Ball Handling

L E S S O N #	NAME	P L A Y E R S	C O U R T	B A L L	E F F O R T	LESSONS BEFORE	L E S S O N #	INTRO TIME	DAILY TIME
1.0	**Holding the Ball**	1	-	x	1	none	**1.0**	5-10	1-2
1.1	Take Away	2	-	x	1	1.0	1.1	5-10	1-5
1.11	Hold High	2	-	x	1	1.1	1.11	-	1-5
1.12	Hold Low	2	-	x	1	1.1	1.12	-	1-5
1.2	Grab Full Court	2	x	x	2	1.1, 5.4	1.2	10-20	10-20
1.21	Short Pass Full Court	2	x	x	2	1.2	1.21	-	10-20
1.22	Tricky Pass Full Court	2	x	x	2	1.2	1.22	-	10-20
1.3	Line Lesson	T	x	x	2-3	1.1, 1.2	1.3	15-55	5-15
1.4	Move Ball	2	-	x	3	1.1	1.4	5-10	2-5

1.0 Holding the Ball

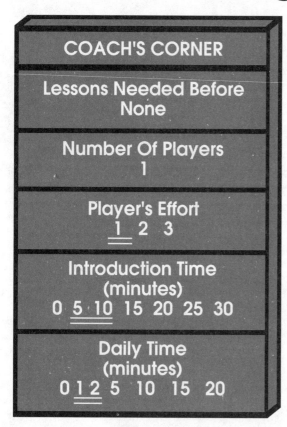

BRIEF:

The ball is held in an exaggerated position in contact with the fingertips.

Fundamental Notes

This lesson is the beginning of teaching and learning basketball. Both players and coaches at all levels need to recognize that shooting, passing, dribbling, and especially catching, depend on how the ball is handled or held–handle the ball with the fingertips. This lesson increases the sensitivity of the fingertips. Sensitivity is another name for *touch*, a word used in connection with shooting. However, *touch* is needed just as much for passing, catching, and dribbling.

Setup

Players line up side by side each with a ball.

Directions for Players

1. Shape each hand into a claw and growl (like a *small* lion).

•The fingers will naturally spread far apart when the player growls.

2. Hold the ball so that only the fingertips touch the ball. Now, overdo it by holding the ball with your fingertips only. Long fingernails make this difficult. Trim them.

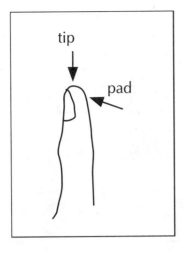

tip

pad

3. Hold the ball tightly, while I explain the importance of this lesson.

4. The fingertips control the ball when you shoot, dribble, pass, and catch. This lesson overdoes the way to hold the ball. Practicing this way improves your ability to shoot, pass, catch, and dribble, without even practicing these skills. You can do this at any time during practice, or at home. In the past you may have heard of a player who slept with a ball. Sounds funny, but some of the greats did it. It sensitized their fingertips which enabled them to control the ball better. They awakened better players or at least better ball handlers!

Troubleshooting

1. Novice players claw their hands and growl (really). Make sure the growl is fierce enough, so that players spread their fingers far apart.

2. Players tend to underdo, not overdo, it. The palm must stay far from the ball.

Use of Assistants None

Weekly Practice

Do this lesson at least once, regardless of the players' level. Novices may need to repeat this lesson many times. Players can hold the ball this way while you explain another lesson. After one week ask players if this helps. It should be obvious. If you catch players practicing this lesson throughout the season, it is a sign of success.

Extensions None

Holding the Ball

OVERDOING IT
Palms far away from the ball.
Fingertips touching.

MORE NORMAL-UNDERDOING IT
Palms closer to the ball.
More finger pads touching

IMPROPER-UNDERDOING IT
Palms too close to the ball.
Only finger pads and fingers touch

1.1 Take Away

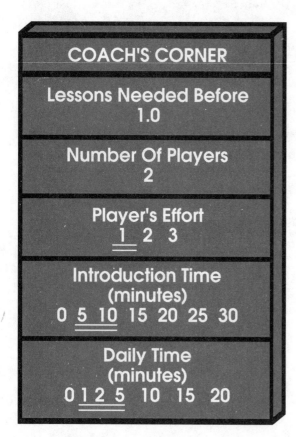

COACH'S CORNER

Lessons Needed Before
1.0

Number Of Players
2

Player's Effort
<u>1</u> 2 3

Introduction Time
(minutes)
0 <u>5 10</u> 15 20 25 30

Daily Time
(minutes)
0 <u>1 2 5</u> 10 15 20

Brief:
One player holds the ball while the other grabs and then pulls it away.

Fundamental Notes

Grabbing is a precursor to both catching and rebounding. Do this lesson slowly at the technique level. Note that pivoting is not involved in this lesson. Complete lessons 2.0 and 2.1 before adding the pivot.

Setup

Each group is 3 yards away from every other group.

Directions for Players

1. One player tightly holds the ball at waist height with the fingertips.

2. The other player grabs the ball with the fingertips, and then rips it 2-6 feet away.

3. Switch roles and repeat. Continue for the allotted time.

Troubleshooting

1. Emphasize that the ball needs to be both held and grabbed using the fingertips. Overdo it. Palms do not touch the ball.

Take Away Setup

hold out ball

grab and pull away

Hold High

Hold Low

2. Grab the ball away with much effort. This is similar to grabbing a rebound or stealing the ball. Players may pivot.

3. Players tend to underdo all technique level lessons. Watch closely and (over)emphasize overdoing it.

Use of Assistants

Watch the palms of the players; the palms stay far from the ball.

Weekly Practice

Do this everyday, until it becomes part of the continuous motion lesson.

Extensions

Introduce these extensions the second day with novice players. More experienced players can do them the first day.

1.11 Hold High

Hold the ball high overhead in 1.1. The other player must reach high for it. Without a partner, a player can duplicate this move by tossing the ball a foot overhead and then grabbing it.

1.12 Hold Low

One player places the ball on the floor. The other player stretches low for the ball, grabs it, and pulls the ball away. A player can readily do this lesson without a partner.

1.2 Grab Full Court

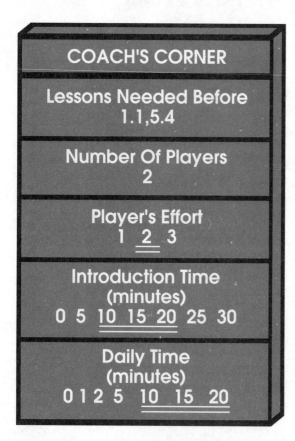
Brief:

Players run a full court circuit while executing the grabbing lesson.

Fundamental Notes

This lesson is a continuous motion or conditioning lesson. While practicing the ball handling skills, players move continuously for the allotted amount of time. They move around a circuit between the two baskets without dribbling. The grabbing lessons are executed while moving. It may look funny, but it is of great value. Besides practicing ball handling skills and becoming more conditioned, players shoot a layup at each basket. Players also need to communicate to avoid both collisions and passing other groups close to the basket. Note also that more coordination is needed to grab the ball while running than when stationary. Run at a comfortable pace. Encourage out of shape players to go slower. Players tend to go too fast at first.

Setup

Players line up equidistant around the circuit on the full court in groups of two. Each group has a ball.

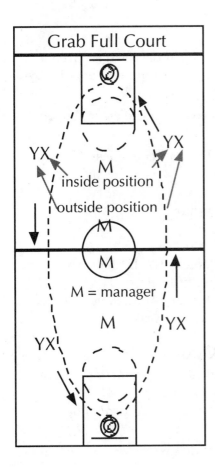

Grab Full Court

M = manager

Directions for Players

1. This is a continuous movement lesson and it means just that, no stopping. We move for 15 minutes today and will add to this each day. You do not need to run at top speed; pace yourself so that you can finish. As you run grab the ball back and forth as you did in the previous lesson.

2. Run down the right side of the court. Shoot a layup at the basket, then run down the other side of the court to the other basket. Alternate shooting the layup.

3. At no time does the ball bounce on the ground.

4. Every few minutes I will signal you to change direction. Stop, turn around and go in the opposite direction.

5. Switch inside and outside positions as well, after each basket. Inside, in this case, means away from the sideline, toward the center of the court. Outside means toward the sidelines. Switch so that you alternate the passing direction each time you come down the court.

•Demonstrate this step with players.

6. Each minute the grabbing position will change. We start out holding the ball at waist level. *Grab high* means to hold the ball over your head. *Grab low* means to gently roll the ball, not bounce it, on the ground ahead of the other player.

•See the extensions below to add more variety to this lesson.

Troubleshooting

1. The ball never bounces on the floor—while grabbing, before shooting, or on the rebound.

2. Remind players of many things:

•Keep your heads up so that you do not run into each other. Do not run past a group just before reaching the basket.

•Run down the sides of the court so that there are no collisions.

•Stop or slow down before taking the layup.

3. Players want to dribble, so emphasize that there is no dribbling.

4. Players also attempt to hand the ball off, rather than make their partner reach and then grab for the ball.

5. There will be mismatches in terms of conditioning. A well conditioned player will be matched with a player in poor shape. Suggest switching partners, if necessary. A manager can run with a player at the appropriate speed.

6. After each basket, make sure players switch inside-outside positions.

Short Passes from 1.21

hand off

lateral

hook

behind back

bounce

Use of Assistants

1. Pair a manager with a player if necessary. Often a manager is in better shape. Most of my managers were several years older than the players.

2. Station managers in the center of the court, between the baskets, to prevent collisions.

3. Managers closest to the basket keep track of layups missed.

Weekly Practice Everyday

Extensions

Many extensions can be added to 1.2. Dribbling will interfere with the ball handling skills, so don't add it. Listed below are some extensions. All involve the way the ball is transferred between players.

1.21 Short Pass Full Court

There are many types of short passes that can be practiced in the continuous motion lesson. All of these improve not only the particular pass, but also all ball handling skills.

1. The **hand off** is actually not a pass. One player gives it to the other.

2. The **lateral** is a short pass. It is thrown under handed.

3. The **overhead hook** pass is practiced with each hand.

•Players need to stay close for the hook and the following passes.

4. The **behind the back** pass needs to be practiced with each hand.

5. The **bounce** pass is the exception to the no bounce rule.

1.22 Tricky Pass Full Court

Do these near the end of the lesson. Players will have difficulty and some fun. If they lose the ball, demand that they speed up to recover it.

1. The **between the legs** pass is a lateral type pass. Do it with each hand.

2. The **bounce between the legs** pass is another easier one that can be done. Do it with each hand as well.

3. Invent a pass by combining two types of passes. For example, players can move the ball around their back, then throw a hook or lateral pass.

4. Another combination—move the ball between the legs; no bouncing; then use a bounce pass. Their are many combinations to try. Don't worry about walking initially (or ever), unless your players are experienced.

5. With more experienced players one partner or manager can harass the shooter.

1.3 Center Line Lesson

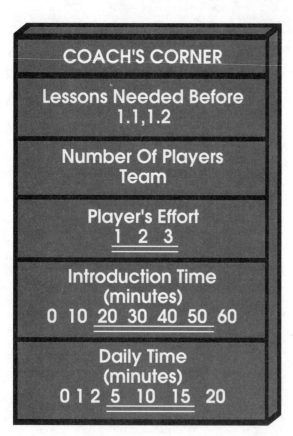

COACH'S CORNER

Lessons Needed Before
1.1, 1.2

Number Of Players
Team

Player's Effort
1 <u>2</u> 3

Introduction Time
(minutes)
0 10 <u>20 30 40 50</u> 60

Daily Time
(minutes)
0 1 2 <u>5 10 15</u> 20

Brief:

Rapid fire ball handling is practiced while the players move in a circuit around the center line or any other court line.

Fundamental Notes

This continuous motion lesson is more difficult to teach than the first one. With young players, under 9th grade, you may want to skip this entirely or teach it in parts. Three parts are presented. Part 1 explains the circuit. Part 2 explains the basic lesson. Part 3 adds things to make it interesting. The skills involved are all ball handling skills. Besides being fun, this is very time efficient, once it is learned. For this reason use this lesson as a game warm-up.

Setup

The players line up on one side of the midcourt line (any other line can be used) about one foot away. They walk down one side of the line to the sideline, step across it, and then walk back on the other side of the line. This makes a circuit. Spread the players out so that they are equidistant apart, not more than 5 feet from one another. Shorten the circuit at the ends if needed.

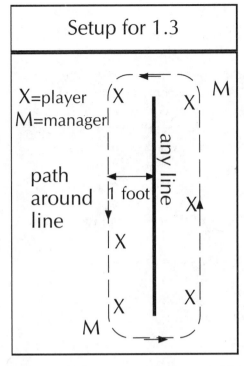

Setup for 1.3

X=player
M=manager

path
around
line

1 foot

any line

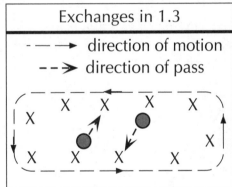

Exchanges in 1.3

- - -→ direction of motion
- - -⇢ direction of pass

Directions for Players

This lesson is difficult to teach. After you give a direction observe how the players react before you continue. Since there are many long breaks in your presentation, the directions are given for the coach, rather than the players.

Part 1 The Circuit

1. The players walk and then jog around the circuit. They need to stay equidistant at all times.

2. Reverse the direction several times.

3. When players stay equidistant go to **Part 2**. This takes 5-30 minutes depending on the level of your players. Youngsters have difficulty with this concept.

Part 2 The Basic Lesson

4. Give one player near the center of the line a ball. Tell them to hold the ball toward the other line, so that the other player can easily grab it away.

5. The first player on the other side of the line that passes the ball grabs it away. Continue grabbing the ball back and forth across the line.

6. Reverse the players' direction each minute.

Part 3 Three Enhancements

7. One, add several other balls to the center of the line. Two or three is normal. Five is a maximum. I often add as many as possible for the last minute of the lesson.

8. Two, change the ball handling skill practiced every 30 seconds. Here is a list: hand off; grab away high, low, and waist high; lateral pass; bounce pass; etc. Use any pass from 1.2 and the extensions.

9. Three, speed up the movement around the circuit. The proximity of the players limits this. Start slowly, even walking, the first day. Gradually speed up to a quick jog over weeks of practice.

Troubleshooting

1. It may take several days before players can do this well. Be ready.

2. Have 5 or 6 balls handy. End the lesson when things go awry because of the overloading of basketballs.

3. Note the difference between a hand off, a grab, and a lateral. In a hand off the ball is given to the other player. In a grab the other player must reach for the ball and take it away. A lateral is a short underhanded pass.

4. Emphasize that the technique part of this lesson involves overdoing the holding of the ball with the fingertips.

5. YOUNG players do not comprehend the word equidistant. For a teacher, this situation is reminiscent of a Piagetian conservation task where you can never convince a fourth grader that five pennies in line, close together, are as much as the same five pennies spread apart. Expect problems, not surprises.

Use of Assistants

1. Place an assistant at both ends of the line, so players know where to turn.

2. Another assistant hands you the balls as you need them.

Weekly Practice

This is used either as part of the continuous motion lesson or as a separate lesson.

Extensions

After the first month of practice use this as a regular part of game warm-ups, because this lesson allows players to practice a lot of ball handling in a short period of time.

1.4 Move Ball

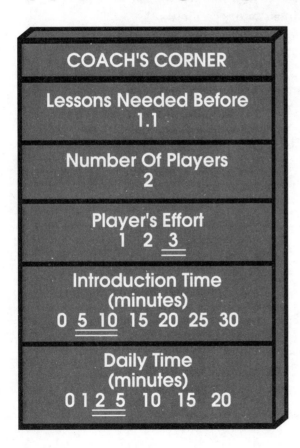

COACH'S CORNER

Lessons Needed Before
1.1

Number Of Players
2

Player's Effort
1 2 <u>3</u>

Introduction Time
(minutes)
0 <u>5</u> <u>10</u> 15 20 25 30

Daily Time
(minutes)
0 1 <u>2</u> <u>5</u> 10 15 20

Brief:

One player quickly moves a ball right in front of another who attempts to take it away.

Fundamental Notes

Closely covered offensive players must move the ball quickly to avoid getting tied up. This type of ball movement is used in other moves. The defense learns how to tie up the offense without fouling. Young players, in particular, often flail their arms and hands at the ball when going for it. Fouls are called, not only when there is actual contact, but also when it looks like contact. This lesson helps to prevent unnecessary fouls and players' fouling out.

Setup

Two players, 2 feet apart, face each other. One player has the ball. Each group is 3 yards apart.

Directions for Players

1. Do not move your feet once you are set.

2. The defense goes after the ball without fouling. Flailing the arms without contact is considered a foul. If you foul in this way or by contact you stay on defense. Loudly count to 10 and then stop.

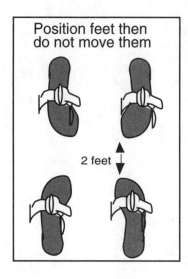

Position feet then do not move them

2 feet

Move the Ball

high to low

left to right

near to far

3. The offense moves the ball quickly, keeping it away from the defense. You can bend your knees, rotate your hips, and move the ball high to low, left to right and near to far from the body. Call out contact fouls.

4. The defense can move their feet more as the offense becomes more adept at moving the ball.

5. Switch roles and repeat this 2-4 times.

Troubleshooting

1. The objective is to move the ball, not the body. Keep both feet in place.

2. The offense calls contact fouls. Flailing fouls can be called by the coach, managers, or the players.

3. Offensive players tend to move their feet and body to protect the ball. Keep the ball out in front.

4. Young defensive players readily foul the offense. This is why the offense must loudly call fouls.

Use of Assistants

Each assistant watches one or two groups. They point out excessive body movement on offense, flagrant fouling, and flailing to the players.

Weekly Practice Every other day

Extensions

After 2-4 weeks players learn the skills. A natural extension is Pivot with Defense, Lesson 2.21.

Section 2
Pivoting

L E S S O N #	NAME	P L A Y E R S	C O U R T	B A L L	E F F O R T	LESSONS BEFORE	L E S S O N #	INTRO TIME	DAILY TIME
2.0	**Start Pivoting**	1	-	-	1	none	**2.0**	10-15	5-10
2.1	Pivoting with Ball	1	-	x	2	1.0, 2.0	2.1	15-20	2-20
2.2	Pivot with Defense	2	-	x	3	1.4, 2.1, 7.1	2.2	15-20	5-10
2.21	Pivot with D Pass	2+	x	x	3	2.2	2.21	10	5-10
2.22	Pivot 2 on D	3	x	x	3	2.21	2.22	10	5-10
2.23	Pivot 2 on D Pass	3+	x	x	3	2.22	2.23	10	5-10

2.0 Start Pivoting

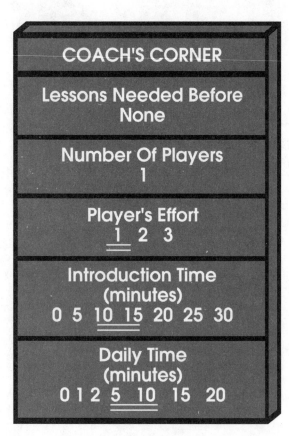

COACH'S CORNER

Lessons Needed Before
None

Number Of Players
1

Player's Effort
<u>1</u> 2 3

Introduction Time
(minutes)
0 5 <u>10 15</u> 20 25 30

Daily Time
(minutes)
0 1 2 <u>5 10</u> 15 20

Brief:

Players pivot forward and back-ward using each foot.

Fundamental Notes

Each time a player touches the ball, he or she must pivot. Shooting, passing, catching, and rebounding ability depends on a player's ability to pivot. All players need to be experts in pivoting before they can learn and perfect these other skills.

Setup

Players are 6 feet apart in one or two rows.

Directions for Players

1. The feet are shoulder-width apart.

2. Start with the left foot as the pivot foot. Put all of your weight on the ball of the left foot. Then, shift your weight to the right foot.

3. Do these actions together. Move the right foot forward, making a circle around the left foot, swiveling (pivoting) on the ball of the left foot. Act like you are stomping on bugs with the right foot.

•The players make 2-4 revolutions each time. Watch the ball of the foot of each player.

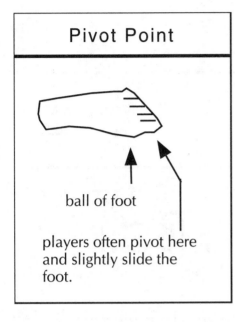

Pivot Point

ball of foot

players often pivot here and slightly slide the foot.

4. Now, stomp on bugs moving backward. Make 2-4 revolutions.

5. Now, switch pivot feet. Put all of your weight on the ball of the right foot. Switch your weight to the left foot.

•Repeat the directions to pivot forward and then backward.

Troubleshooting

1. The "stomping on bugs" idea works better than more technical descriptions for beginners.

2. Players pivot slowly, unless you want them dizzy. Initially, small steps are better than large steps.

3. Watch closely to make sure that: 1) players pivot on the ball of foot and 2) players do not slide the foot while pivoting.

4. Players tend to pivot on some part of the foot other than the ball, such as the toes. Note that a player can, by the rules, pivot on any part of the body without walking. This includes toes, behind, or even the head. These more unusual pivot points are sometimes employed when players scramble on the floor for the ball. However, using the ball of the foot is the most practical and easiest way to pivot.

5. Players also tend to slide the ball of the foot. This is a walking violation.

Use of Assistants

Assign assistants to watch players having difficulty.

Daily Time

Direct players as needed to repeat this lesson during warm ups or after warm downs or for homework. A homework assignment can be 100 pivots, twenty-five each way. Or, tell players to stomp on 100 bugs; 25 both forward and back on the left foot; repeat with the right foot. (Tell them also not to look for bugs.)

Weekly Practice

This lesson is primarily for novices. Doing this in practice everyday for two weeks is sufficient for anybody.

Extensions

As soon as possible advance to the next lesson that involves pivoting with the ball. More experienced players can start there.

2.1 Pivoting with Ball

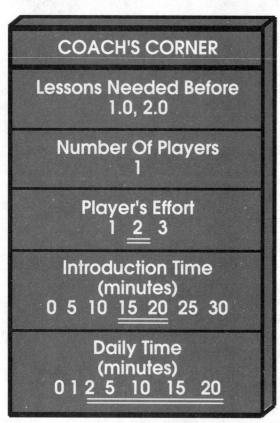

COACH'S CORNER

Lessons Needed Before
1.0, 2.0

Number Of Players
1

Player's Effort
1 _2_ 3

Introduction Time
(minutes)
0 5 10 15 20 25 30

Daily Time
(minutes)
0 1 2 5 10 15 20

Brief:

Players pivot while moving the ball high and low, left and right, and close and far from the body.

Fundamental Notes

Pivoting, as previously discussed, has applications in everything done with the basketball. This lesson combines pivoting with ball movement. Ball movement is used to keep the ball away from opponents as well as fake before shooting, passing, or dribbling. This skill is the key to all offensive moves.

Setup

Players line up 6 feet apart each with a ball.

Directions for Players

1. The skills in this lesson are applicable to everything done with the basketball. Hold the ball at waist height; feet shoulder-width apart. The left foot is the pivot foot.

2. Take one long step to the right and push the ball to the far right, low to the ground. The ball is to the right of your foot.

3. Pivot 180 degrees forward, halfway around, and push the ball high overhead.

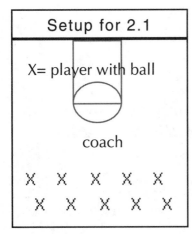

Setup for 2.1

X= player with ball

coach

X X X X X

X X X X X

• Repeat steps 2-3 until the players pivot around twice.

• Repeat pivoting backward with the same pivot foot.

• Switch the pivot foot and repeat pivoting forward and backward.

• Then repeat this entire lesson. Assign a player to lead the lesson as soon as possible.

Troubleshooting

1. Demonstrate that pushing the ball is a quick powerful movement.

2. After you demonstrate this lesson, assign a player to lead it. The leader faces the same direction as the team to avoid the mirror image confusion of facing the players. At first the players look at the leader's back. When everybody pivots around, the players will not see the leader. So, verbal cues are needed. Use "stretch low...okay, pivot high" or other cues.

3. Initially, concentrate on learning the routine. Gradually work to improve the movements.

Use of Assistants

Assist players having difficulty.

Weekly Practice Everyday

Extensions

Most lessons in this book involve pivoting. The applications are almost endless. Novices cannot practice this enough at the beginning of the season. Assign it for homework. Assist players with it in the warm-ups. All offensive moves start here. That is why this is such a pivotal lesson.

2.2 Pivot with D

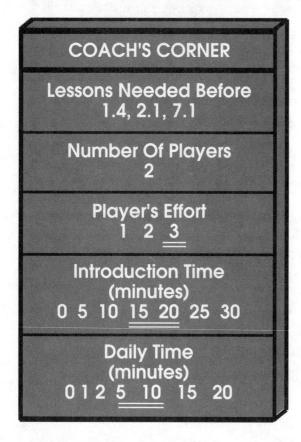

COACH'S CORNER

Lessons Needed Before
1.4, 2.1, 7.1

Number Of Players
2

Player's Effort
1 2 **3**

Introduction Time
(minutes)
0 5 10 **15 20** 25 30

Daily Time
(minutes)
0 1 2 **5 10** 15 20

Brief:

The offense pivots away from a defensive player attempting to steal the ball.

Fundamental Notes

This lesson makes players pivot in a game like situation. They move the ball away from the defense as well as look to pass under pressure. The defense learns to go after the ball without fouling.

Setup

Groups of two set up 3 yards apart. The defense lines up 2 feet from the offense. The offense has a ball.

Directions for Players

1. The offense starts with the left foot as the pivot foot, ball waist high.

2. The directions for the defense are simple—go after the ball without fouling. Move around the offense for the ball instead of reaching with the arms.

3. The offense pivots backward and forward holding the ball in the high-low, left-right, close-far positions practiced in Lesson 2.1.

4. The defense slowly counts to 5 then stops. The offense calls fouls.

5. Repeat with the offense pivoting on the right foot. Then, switch roles.

Troubleshooting

1. If the defense goes after the ball very aggressively, more so than even in a game, the offense gets better practice.

2. If the offense just pivoted away from the defense, the purpose of the lesson would be defeated. The offense must face up to the defense and then prevent a steal by moving the ball and the body.

3. Remind the defense that flailing their arms, even without contact, results in a foul call.

Use of Assistants

Assistants watch for walking or flailing.

Weekly Practice Everyday

Extensions

2.21 Pivot with Defense Pass

During this lesson, 2.21, ask the pivoter for a pass. This is a more realistic situation. Use only hand gestures to get the pivoter's attention, since the purpose is to make the pivoter look while protecting the ball. Make it more difficult for the passer by constantly walking around and by asking for a pass after variable amounts of time; one second one time, 5 seconds another. Always ask immediately, if the player is not looking. Assistants can do this as well.

2.22 Pivot 2 on D

Position another defensive player behind the pivoter. Demonstrate how to protect the ball, and simultaneously block out the defensive player behind with your body and elbow. The dribbler boxes out this player behind, as if the dribbler were going for a rebound. The offensive player must also push the ball hard, like in Lesson 2.1, low to the far left or right and then pivot 180 degrees. This defensive situation arises after a successful trap. Make sure the defense does not foul.

2.23 Pivot 2 on D Pass

Ask the dribbler for a pass in the previous Lesson, 2.21. This lesson is the goal for the pivoting skills.

Section 3
Wrist Movement

L E S S O N #	NAME	P L A Y E R S	C O U R T	B A L L	E F F O R T	LESSONS BEFORE	L E S S O N #	INTRO TIME	DAILY TIME
3.0	**Flick of the Wrist - Shoot,Pass,Dribble**	1	-	-	1	none	3.0	10-15	2

3.0 Flick of the Wrist- Shoot, Pass, Dribble

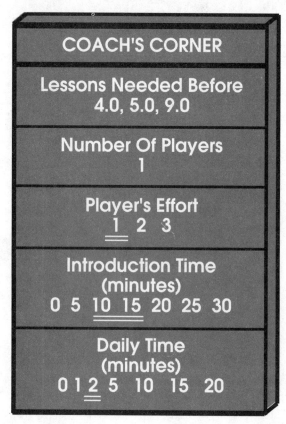

COACH'S CORNER

Lessons Needed Before
4.0, 5.0, 9.0

Number Of Players
1

Player's Effort
<u>1</u> 2 3

Introduction Time (minutes)
0 5 <u>10</u> <u>15</u> 20 25 30

Daily Time (minutes)
0 1 <u>2</u> 5 10 15 20

Brief:

Players move their wrists back and forth with the arms extended first down at the sides and then overhead.

Fundamental Notes

This lesson is the key to learning all the ball handling skills - shooting, passing, and dribbling. Practicing with the wrists significantly improves a player's shooting, passing, and dribbling without even touching a ball! Only a small amount of time is spent on this lesson, but the reward are great. All ball handling skills become doable for everyone - young, old, short, tall, male, female, clumsy, athletic. The consequences of skipping it, because you consider it too easy, are much greater. Count the good dribblers (or shooters or passers) on the court in any game from sixth grade level to a professional all-star game. It will not add up to ten, as it should. Some Hall of Famers do not even have the skills of many 12 year olds.

Professionals, and the rest of us as well, lack

Hand Movement for Dribbling

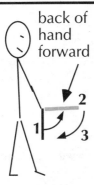

back of hand forward

1. flick upwards
2. bend wrist up as far as possible
3. allow hand to naturally move back

Hand Movement for Passing or Shooting

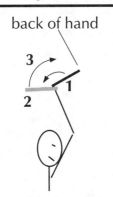

back of hand

1. flick backwards
2. bend wrist back as far as possible
3. allow hand to naturally move forward

many fundamental skills because coaches do not recognize them. This lesson teaches a vitally important, usually ignored skill. Make sure your players do this.

Setup

Players line up side by side, 4 feet apart.

Directions for Players

1. Let your arms loosely hang at your sides. To loosen your hands, shake them both back and forth and to the sides. The fingers also need to be loose.

•Continue for 10-30 seconds. Check each player's hands for looseness.

2. Let your hands hang loosely at your sides again. Turn your arm so that the back of your hand is facing forward; the palms face backward. Let your hands hang loosely. Using your arms, not the wrist or hand, flick your wrists forward only. Let them come back to the original position without using extra effort. The wrists and hands move like a waving wet noodle. The elbows are only slightly bent.

3. Continue to flick your wrists while I am talking. This simulates the motion of the wrist while dribbling. Do this for a minute on your own everyday. Your dribbling will improve.

•Continue for 1-2 minutes. Check each player's wrists for looseness.

4. To simulate shooting and passing, raise your arms directly overhead. Now, the back of the hands face backward; the palms face forward. The elbows are slightly bent forward, not to the sides. Rotate the elbows slightly inward to make the elbows point forward. You may need to slightly rotate the hand outward to keep the palm facing forward.

5. Loosen the wrists and hands. Flick your wrist and hand backward only. Let them come forward without additional effort.

Continue this for 1-2 minutes. Practice this on your own for one minute each day.

Troubleshooting

1. This lesson is a key to learning how to shoot, dribble, and pass.

2. Emphasize these directions:

    a. The hands and wrists need to be loose.

    b. The motion is forward and back, not sideways.

    c. The elbows point slightly forward or back, not to the side.

3. Flick in one direction only, toward the back of the hand.

4. Young players make every mistake possible. Elbows will be bent outward; wrists and hands will be tight; fingers will be together; the flick will be sideways or forward instead of back. You need to work individually with each player.

5. Young players also tire quickly. They have difficulty lasting for 1-2 minutes. This lesson builds up the arms and wrists as well.

Use of Assistants

Assistants look for sideways flicks, bent elbows and tight hands.

Weekly Practice Everyday

Extensions

Do this lesson every day of the season. Spend 10-20 seconds on it before each shooting, passing, or dribbling lesson. Players immediately see the benefits. Hopefully, you will see players working on their wrists in warm-ups without your urging.

Section 4
Dribbling

L E S S O N #	NAME	P L A Y E R S	C O U R T	B A L L	E F F O R T	LESSONS BEFORE	L E S S O N #	INTRO TIME	DAILY TIME
4.0	**Dribbling D Position**	1	-	x	1	3.0	**4.0**	5-10	1-2
4.1	Look at the Leader 1-2	1+	x	x	2	4.0	4.1	20-30	5-15
4.11	Look and Count	1+	-	x	2	4.1	4.11	"	"
4.12	Watch the Game	1+	-	x	2	4.1	4.12	-	-
4.13	Twist Around	1	-	x	2	4.1	4.13	-	5-15
4.2	Follow the Leader	1+	-	x	2	4.1, 4.13	4.2	15-20	5-15
4.21	Follow Step Ahead	1+	-	x	2	4.2	4.21	-	5-15
4.22	Follow Back & Sideways	1+	-	x	2	4.2	4.22	-	1-5
4.23	Twister	1	-	-	2	4.22	4.23	5-10	1-5
4.24	Twister with Ball	1	-	x	2	4.23	4.24	-	5-10
4.3	Protect Ball	2	-	x	2-3	4.2	4.3	10-25	5-10
4.31	Protect with 2 on D	3	-	x	3	4.3	4.31	-	5-10
4.32	Dribbler Vs Dribbler	2	-	x	2	4.3	4.32	-	10-20
4.4	Dribble with D Layup	1+	x	x	2-3	4.3, 5.41	4.4	15-25	10-20
4.5	Dribble Pass with D	3	-	x	3	4.4, 9.3, 9.6, 10.5	4.5	20-30	10-20
4.51	Dribbler Shoots Ball	3	x	x	3	4.5	4.51	-	10-20
4.52	With D on Cutter	4	x	x	3	4.5	4.52	-	10-20

4.0 Dribbling D Position

COACH'S CORNER

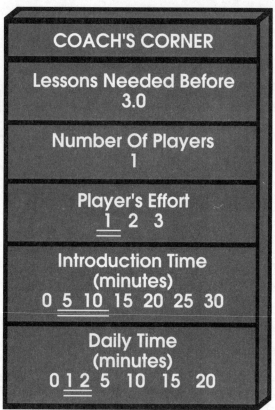

COACH'S CORNER

Lessons Needed Before
3.0

Number Of Players
1

Player's Effort
<u>1</u>　2　3

**Introduction Time
(minutes)**
0　<u>5　10</u>　15　20　25　30

**Daily Time
(minutes)**
0　<u>1 2</u>　5　10　15　20

Setup for 4.0

X=players　C=coach

3 feet apart

C

X---X　X　X　X　X　X　X　X

up　half down　full down

Brief:

Players move their body and wrists in the dribbling defensive position.

Fundamental Notes

It is no coincidence that most good dribblers are also good defensive players. The body positions for both defense and dribbling are similar. They can be practiced together. In both cases players need to be able to move in any direction as quickly as possible. The body is low to the ground with feet slightly greater than shoulder-width apart. The dribbling position is more demanding than the defensive one, since it entails twisting and swiveling of the head, shoulders, hips, and legs in different directions. Being able to perform these twisting movements while handling the ball and looking is the key to dribbling well. This is covered in Lesson 4.1.

Setup

The players line up 3 feet apart.

Directions for Players

1. The body position for dribbling and defense are very similar. We practice these skills together. Put your feet shoulder-width apart. Keep the trunk straight and bend at the knees. Overdo it by bending down all the way. This is the full down position. Move half way up. This is the half down position. Stay in it now.

•Move the players between the full and half down positions several times.

2. Let your arms hang straight down at the sides. The back of your hands face forward, the palms face backward.

3. Flick the wrists upward and let them come back without any additional effort like we did in a previous lesson.

•Do this for 30 seconds.

4. Move to the full down position. Continue flicking the wrists.

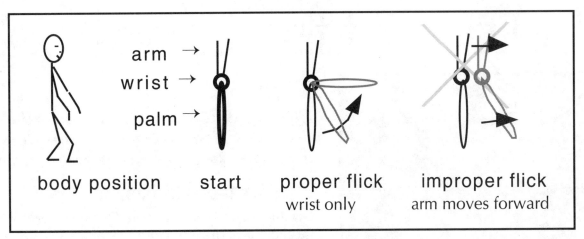

arm →
wrist →
palm →

body position start proper flick
wrist only improper flick
arm moves forward

The Ready Position

The Unready Position

The back is bent too much and the legs too little.

•After another 30 seconds move players to the up position. Move through the various positions - up, half down, and full down - for another minute while continuing to flick.

Troubleshooting

1. Emphasize that the wrists are loose and then flicked upward only; the elbows and trunk are straight.

2. Players tend to flick the wrists forward, not up. This distinction may seem slight but the lesson has value only if the wrists are flicked upward. The diagram shows the difference between a forward and an upward flick. In the upward flick, the hand rotates nearly 90 degrees more than the forward flick. Often a player moves the entire arm forward in a forward flick.

3. The half down position is also called the ready position. Players use this exclusively when on the court whether on offense or defense. Since players tend to bend the trunk of their body, rather than their legs, regularly do this lesson and all extensions in the full down position. Demonstrate in the up position, so you don't injure yourself.

Use of Assistants

Watch for flicking wrists and straight elbows.

Weekly Practice Everyday

Extensions

The natural extension of this lesson is Lesson 4.1 where dribbling with the ball and swiveling are covered. All of the lessons involving dribbling can be done without the ball, as well as with the ball, with great benefit to players.

4.1 Look at the Leader 1-2

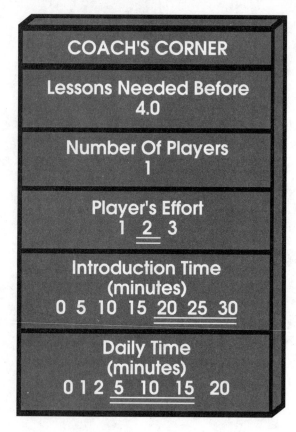

COACH'S CORNER

Lessons Needed Before
4.0

Number Of Players
1

Player's Effort
1 <u>2</u> 3

Introduction Time
(minutes)
0 5 10 15 <u>20 25 30</u>

Daily Time
(minutes)
0 1 2 <u>5 10 15</u> 20

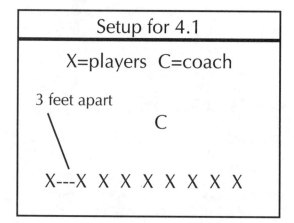

Setup for 4.1

X=players C=coach

3 feet apart

C

X---X X X X X X X X

Brief:

Players dribble with each hand as well as swivel the head, shoulders, and hips in every conceivable way.

Fundamental Notes

Dribblers do two things well. One involves the movement of the hand and the wrist. The hand is clawed; only the fingertips touch the ball: the wrist is loose; flicks of the wrist propel the ball, not arm movement. The other involves body position. The head readily glances in any direction. The shoulders, hips, arms, legs, and other body parts are positioned to sprint, as well as to ward off the defense. Give instructions visually, instead of orally, as much as possible, to insure that players keep their heads up. Use the full down position to emphasize:

1. the need to bend legs, not backs.

2. that it is easier to dribble if your hands are near the ground.

Part 1 teaches the dribbling positions without the use of the ball. This enables you to readily diagnose wrist and body position problems before the ball is used in Part 2.

Setup

Players line up side by side, 5 feet apart, each with a basketball.

Directions for Players

Part 1

1. Start in the full down position, feet shoulder width, arms extended straight downward, elbows only slightly bent, hands straight down.

•Old bones are not required to stay in the full down position (thank God), flick wrists, or even dribble the ball in Part 2.

2. Mirror my movements. Continue to flick upward from each position I show. Each position is about 6 inches from the foot.

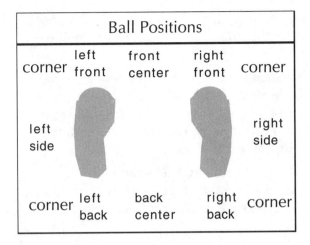

Ball Positions

corner	left front	front center	right front	corner
left side				right side
corner	left back	back center	right back	corner

Dribbling in the Full Down Position

Dribbling in the Half Down Position

•See the diagram located below the Coach's Corner feature in this lesson that shows nine (9) dribbling positions (if you add corner positions the total is 13). Players need to dribble in each position with each hand. This yields 18 positions. Name the position only after everyone is in it.

3. Since I am facing you, my right hand is your left, my left is your right.

•Use your left hand first. This is the right hand for players. Move your hand to this position. Hold the first few positions for 10-15 seconds so that you can verbally correct a player. After this hold them for 3-8 seconds. It is useful to name the positions, even though the instructions are nonverbal, so players can use this in other lessons. An ordered list is below. There is no need to direct players to use the right or left hand because they can readily see this. Here is the list: *right side, right front, front center, left front* (continue with the same hand), *left side, right back, left back, back center*. Repeat these movements with the left hand. Closely watch the wrists.

Part 2

4. Dribble the ball about six inches from your foot in each position. Do not turn around to dribble in back or awkward positions. Keep your head forward so you can follow the directions. Stay in the full down position.

•Follow the same directions as in Part 1. Hold each position long enough to correct each player.

•Repeat all of these dribbling positions using the other hand.

5. I am going to move more quickly now. Keep your heads up and follow.

•Move the ball to every position. Hold each position for a maximum of 3 seconds. Continue for 15-30 seconds.

6. Move to the half down position and follow me.

•Players have more difficulty dribbling in the half down position because they dribble higher.

Their elbows need to be extended, not bent. Their backs need to be straight vertically, not bent as well. Continue for another minute.

•To end this lesson do some tricky movements. Move the ball to the *center back* position and then through the legs to a *center front*. Repeat using the opposite hand. Then go from the *center front* to the *center back*. Repeat using the opposite hand. If anyone is still dribbling stop them. C'est fini.

•Change the feet positions after doing this lesson several times. Put the left or right foot forward at any time during the lesson. Make sure the players follow these movements as well as the ball movements.

Troubleshooting

1. Emphasize that the hands and palms do not touch the ball. The hand is shaped like a claw. Only the fingertips touch the ball. Flick the wrist to dribble; do not move the arms.

2. The ball is inches off the ground.

3. Both arms are in the same ready position for dribbling; they hang straight down at the sides with the elbows slightly bent. After more practice, move the nondribbling arm to a defensive or protective position with the elbow bent.

4. Players often dribble the ball in the wrong position with the wrong hand because their heads are down. Stay on top of this. Yell "Heads up, Bob," to a player looking down, "I'm dribbling at the right front position."

Use of Assistants

Managers watch elbows, fingertips, backs, and other parts of players.

Weekly Practice Everyday

Extensions

4.11 Look and Count

There are other ways to do Lesson 4.1. One other way is to give the prompts verbally, i.e. right hand, right front, center, left front, left back, left hand, etc. The advantage is that you do not need to move the ball or your hand. The big disadvantage of this method is that players need not keep their heads up to follow the directions. To remedy this drawback, instruct players to yell out the number of fingers you flash every few seconds. Another way to do this lesson (and relax) is to allow one of your players to lead the lesson. Whisper directions to the leader, if need be.

4.12 Watch the Game

A lone player or small group dribbles while watching a game or people warming up. The dribblers move the ball to every position as well as between the legs as they watch. It is a worthwhile use of time that usually is wasted. Novice players do this exercise from the full down position.

4.13 Twist Around

This lesson makes an OK dribbler a very good one. It forces a player to dribble in the unusual positions needed to evade the defense and protect the ball. The setup and directions are the same as for Lesson 4.1 except that the players line up with their sides or backs, instead of their fronts, facing you. In order to see you the players must rotate their heads, hips, and shoulders toward you. They do not swivel their feet around; the feet remain pointed away from you. Novices do this in the full down position first. This lesson can be done with verbal prompts and flashing fingers. A player can also be the leader.

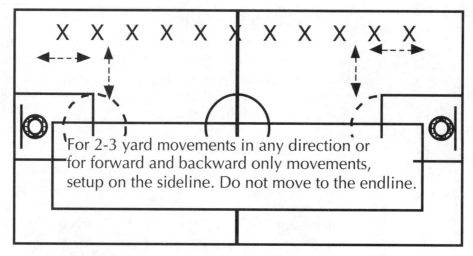

For 2-3 yard movements in any direction or for forward and backward only movements, setup on the sideline. Do not move to the endline.

4.2 Follow the Leader

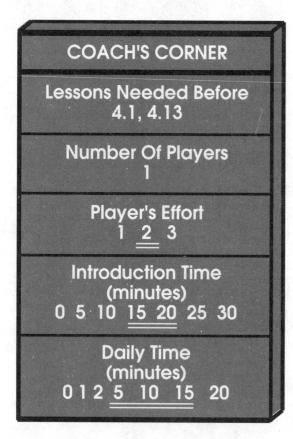

COACH'S CORNER
Lessons Needed Before 4.1, 4.13
Number Of Players 1
Player's Effort 1 <u>2</u> 3
Introduction Time (minutes) 0 5 10 <u>15</u> <u>20</u> 25 30
Daily Time (minutes) 0 1 2 <u>5</u> <u>10</u> <u>15</u> 20

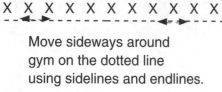

Move sideways around gym on the dotted line using sidelines and endlines.

Brief:
Players dribble as in Lesson 4.1 while moving.

Fundamental Notes

This lesson is a step closer to game type dribbling. It is identical to Lesson 4.1 with the addition of movement. Learn Lesson 4.1 well before doing this one.

Setup

There are several setups you can use. To see players better, keep them in one row.

•For sideways movement, players set up 4 yards apart on the sideline and move around the court on the out-of-bounds line. Players can move in a circuit without obstacles.

•For forward and backward movement, players must set up on one sideline, nobody on the endline. Otherwise players collide at corners on forward movement.

•If you want players to move only 2-3 yards in any direction then they can set up on the sideline.

Directions for Players

1. This lesson is like the previous lesson with the addition of movement. Move around the court on

the out-of-bounds line. Keep moving when you reach the baseline. Forward and backward motion is inward and outward toward or away from the center. I will point in the direction of motion.

2. Start in the half down position with the ball on the floor out of the way. When you take steps to the right, do not bring your feet close together. Do not slide your feet. If you take this step quickly, it resembles a jump. So, I call it a jump-step. Let's do it. Jump-step right.

•Instruct the players to jump-step left, forward and backward as well. Continue for several minutes.

3. Pick up the ball. Jump-step in the direction that I point. Dribble in the position that I show.

•Point in a different direction every 5-20 seconds. Point left and right initially. After more practice point forward and back. Decrease the time as players move in one direction as they become more expert.

•Hold your hand in the dribbling position for only a second. Change positions every 5-10 seconds initially. Decrease the time between changes as players become more expert. Deliberately put players in difficult positions as soon as possible. Some difficult positions include: moving right and dribbling on the left side with the right hand; moving left while dribbling on the right side with the left hand; dribbling in the back and back center positions anytime.

•Players must line up on the sideline, not the endline, before moving forward. Otherwise, endline and sideline players collide.

•Keep all prompts visual. This way players with heads down stand out like sore thumbs.

Troubleshooting

1. Space players far enough apart to avoid collisions.

2. Players must move slowly, at the same pace as well, to avoid collisions.

3. Players keep the nondribbling hand in the same position as the dribbling hand.

4. High dribbling is more difficult than low dribbling. If players keep the knees bent, and the elbows straight, the ball should be only inches off the ground.

5. Players initially move at different speeds, often bouncing balls off the feet of adjacent players. Expect scrambling for loose balls.

6. Players tend to bend the back, instead of the legs. This prevents quick movement.

7. Players that have difficulty dribbling are usually dribbling high. Work on hand and wrist movement as well as body stance.

Use of Assistants

Line up close to the players to keep players equidistant.

Weekly Practice Everyday

Extensions

4.21 Follow Step Ahead

This lesson is the same as 4.2 except that the players stand with one foot forward. Practice this extension with the left and then the right foot forward.

4.22 Follow Back & Sideways

This lesson is the same as 4.2 except that the players line up with either their backs or sides facing you. There are many possible positions–besides left side, right side, and back, in each position the left foot or the right foot can also be forward. Players often must swivel at the hips and shoulders to see you.

4.23 Twister

This lesson is best done individually, one player at a time. Players act like they have a ball. They move through a self imagined Globe Trotter like routine. They move in every direction, spinning around, putting the ball behind their backs and through their legs. If you watch each player closely, it is easy to diagnose dribbling problems. The flick of the wrist may not be strong enough. The hands may be too high off the ground. The hands may not be in the claw position for ball handling. The legs may be bent too little while the back may be bent too much. Correct problems before the player uses a ball. Players perform the twister routine with the ball, just like they do it without the ball. Even though this lesson seems strange (like many others), it is very beneficial.

4.24 Twister with Ball

This time, players use a ball. Flash fingers every few seconds to make sure players are looking up. They must call out the numbers as you flash. Players do this individually.

4.3 Protect the Ball

COACH'S CORNER

Lessons Needed Before	4.2
Number Of Players	3
Player's Effort	1 <u>2</u> 3
Introduction Time (minutes)	0 5 <u>10</u> <u>15</u> <u>20</u> <u>25</u> 30
Daily Time (minutes)	0 1 2 <u>5</u> <u>10</u> 15 20

Setup for 4.3

X= a group of 2 players

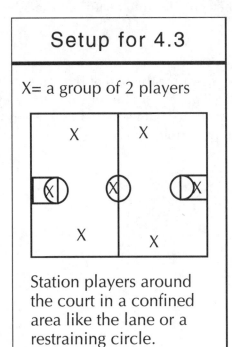

Station players around the court in a confined area like the lane or a restraining circle.

Brief:

The dribbler protects the ball from an aggressive defensive player.

Fundamental Notes

This lesson forces players to protect the ball while dribbling. An aggressive defense goes after the ball with more than normal abandon, staying in body contact with the dribbler. The dribblers are allowed to turn and swivel in a particular area, but cannot run away. The body, especially the arms, wards off the defense. Both the dribbler and defense overdo it. Technically, both constantly foul each other initially, but players need an opportunity to dribble with contact. This is the best way to learn. Require more legal play after several days. Insisting on it immediately undermines the purpose of the lesson. Because the defense works at maximum effort, this is a hustle lesson.

Setup

Groups of two set up as far apart as possible. One player has the ball.

Directions for Players

1. The defense goes aggressively after the ball for about 20 seconds; it is okay to make body contact; no flailing is allowed. Knocking over players is also not allowed. When the offense turns, do not stay behind, facing their back. Hustle after the ball.

2. The dribbler continuously dribbles in the area assigned. Running away, besides causing a collision, defeats the purpose of the lesson. Turn and swivel one way or the other. Listen for the signal to switch dribbling hands.

3. Protect the ball using the arm without the ball as well as your body. Push the defense away if necessary. This is a foul, but it is okay now.

4. I will give the signal to start and stop. Switch roles each time.

•Each player dribbles twice. Initially give the signal to change dribbling hands every 5-10 seconds. Initially, give the signal orally. When the players are accustomed to the lesson, give cues with your hand.

•Flash fingers for expert dribblers. They call out what they see.

Troubleshooting

1. The defense goes after the ball aggressively, causing body contact. A lazy defense makes this lesson of less worth. The defense continuously runs around, not through, the offense for the ball.

2. Allow players to foul each other for a week at most.

3. Initially, many players lose the ball. Make it clear that the offense runs after the lost ball. The offense also runs back.

4. If you see players with their heads down, yell "look up."

Use of Assistants

Station managers between groups to avoid collisions. They watch for two things: one, an aggressive defense; two, a heads up dribbler. Managers can flash fingers as well.

Weekly Practice Everyday

4.31 Protect with 2 on D

This lesson is the same as 4.3 with two players on defense (if you dare). The offense always keeps one defensive player on their back, boxed out, so they only need to deal with the other one in front.

4.32 Dribbler Vs Dribbler

Each dribbler aggressively goes after the ball of the other, while protecting their own dribble. They must stay in a small area to avoid collisions with other groups. Managers stand between groups. Give cues to switch the dribbling hand.

4.4 Dribble with D Layup

COACH'S CORNER

Lessons Needed Before
4.3, 5.41

Number Of Players
1+

Player's Effort
<u>1</u> 2 3

Introduction Time (minutes)
0 5 10 <u>15 20 25</u> 30

Daily Time (minutes)
0 1 2 5 <u>10 15 20</u>

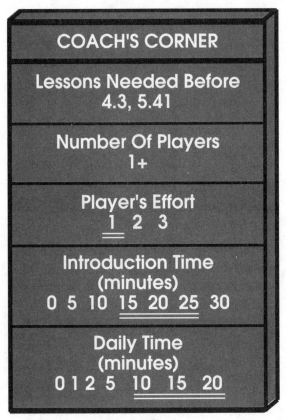

Setup for 4.4

→ Lines of players

M= managers

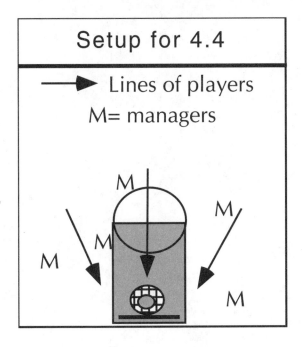

Brief:

Managers, as well as other players, go for the ball of a player dribbling back to the layup line.

Fundamental Notes

This lesson provides game-like dribbling practice during any layup lessons (e.g. 5.4+ extensions, 5.5+ extensions). In this layup lesson a player shoots, rebounds, and then dribbles to the other layup line. Managers and other players go for the ball while the player is dribbling. The dribbler must look in all directions, even behind, to protect the ball. After this, dribbling in a crowd in a game is easy by comparison. Players improve quickly.

Setup

This depends on which layup lesson you are doing. Use any 5.4 or 5.5 extension or 5.5. Station managers around the layup lines.

Directions for Players

•See 5.4 or 5.5 for the layup lesson directions.

1. Managers, go after every ball near you. Be tricky in your efforts to knock the balls far (very, very far) away from the players. Look especially for players contemplating their sneaker laces. Don't run after players.

2. Players, protect the ball at all times. If it gets knocked away, run after it. Run back as well.

3. Go after the ball of other players, especially players looking down.

Troubleshooting

1. Nobody chases players around the gym. A 1-3 second effort is enough.

2. Managers should knock the ball in a direction away from the layup lines.

3. Players hustle after batted balls and then back to the layup line.

4. Initially, many players will be chasing balls around the gym. After a few days they will be much wiser (if not much older).

Use of Assistants
Use as many assistants as possible. Ten is okay.

Weekly Practice Everyday

Extensions None

4.5 Dribble Pass with D

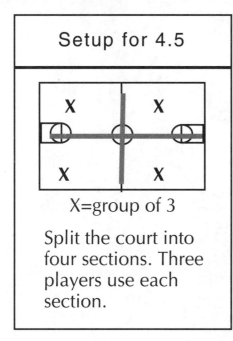

Setup for 4.5

X=group of 3

Split the court into four sections. Three players use each section.

Brief:

While dribbling downcourt covered by defense, the dribbler passes to a cutter at the basket.

Fundamental Notes

This advanced level lesson involves many skills. Related lessons are in parenthesis. The dribbler is covered closely (13.1,9.6) while dribbling downcourt looking to pass (4.4). At the correct moment, a pass (9.3) is thrown so that the cutter (11.1,10.5) and the ball meet at the basket (9.5).

Setup

Split the court in half (not really) at the midcourt line and then again basket to basket to form four sections. Three players set up in each area. Alternately use the left and right sides of each basket. Use side baskets, if they are available.

Directions for Players

1. The cutter starts in the corner. Cut within 5 seconds after the dribbler starts dribbling.

2. Starting at midcourt the dribbler moves toward the basket. Pass to the cutter, then follow the pass to the basket.

3. Time the pass so that it meets the cutter at the basket.

4. The defense covers the dribbler. Follow the pass to the basket. If the shot is missed, go for the rebound.

5. Quickly move to the sidelines, rotate positions, and go again after the other group finishes. Rotate from dribbler to defense to cutter. Each rotation moves a player closer to the basket.

6. Rotate to each position twice.

Troubleshooting

1. This lesson is not for novices. It is helpful to add one transition and one boxing out lesson to the long list of lessons needed.

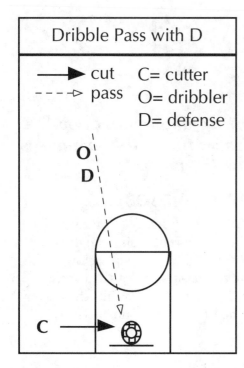

Dribble Pass with D

→ cut C= cutter
- - -▷ pass O= dribbler
D= defense

2. Players hustle during this lesson, as well as moving off and on the court. Each drill is executed in rapid fire succession.

Use of Assistants

Assistants spur players to reset to their new positions after the lesson is completed.

Weekly Practice As needed

Extensions

4.51 Dribbler Shoots It

This is the same as 4.5 except that the cutter cuts to the low post, catches the pass, and then gives the ball back to the dribbler for a layup. Passing off and then cutting to the basket, or toward the ball, is called give and go.

4.52 With D on Cutter

This is the same as 4.51 except that another defensive player covers the cutter. Rebounding and boxing out skills (11.0-11.3) are needed before doing this. Covering a cutter (12.5 or 16.21) is also needed.

Section 5
Shooting

L E S S O N #	NAME	P L A Y E R S	C O U R T	B A L L	E F F O R T	LESSONS BEFORE	L E S S O N #	INTRO TIME	DAILY TIME
5.0	**Shot Technique Wrists**	1	-	-	1	none	**5.0**	10-15	2
5.1	Flick Up	1	-	x	1	5.0	5.1	10-20	2-5
5.11	Opposite Hand Flick Up	1	-	x	1	5.1	5.11	-	2-5
5.12	Flick Up High	1	-	x	1	5.1	5.12	-	2-4
5.13	Shoot Up	1	-	x	2	5.12	5.13	-	1-2
5.2	One-Inch Shot	1	x	x	1	5.13	5.2	10-30	5-10
5.3	One-Foot Shot	1	x	x	2	5.2	5.3	10-20	5-15
5.31	Regular One-Foot Shot	1	x	x	2	5.3	5.31	-	5-10
5.32	One-Foot Shot +Dribble	1+	x	x	2	4.3	5.32	-	5-15
5.33	One-Foot Jump Shot	1+	x	x	2	5.31	5.33	-	5-10
5.4	The No-Step Layup	1	x	x	1	1.0	5.4	15-30	5-20
5.41	One Step Layup	1	x	x	1	5.4	5.41	-	5-20
5.42	Layup Lesson	T	x	x	2	5.41	5.42	10-20	10-15
5.43	Layup with Dribble	1	x	x	2	4.2, 5.42	5.43	15-20	5-15
5.44	Layup with Passing	T	x	x	2	5.42, 9.1	5.44	15-25	5-15
5.5	One Dribble Layup	1	x	x	2	4.2, 5.42	5.5	15-25	5-15
5.51	Two Dribble Layup	1	x	x	2	5.5	5.51	-	5-15
5.6	Foul Shot Technique	1	-	x	1	5.3	5.6	10-15	2-5
5.61	Technique Short Shot	1	-	x	1	5.6	5.61	10-15	5-15
5.62	Technique Longer Shots	1	-	x	1	5.61	5.62	-	5-15
5.7	Foul Shot Practice	1	x	x	3	5.6	5.7	5-15	5-15
5.8	Lateral Layup Lesson	T	x	x	2	2.1, 5.43, 9.5, 10.61	5.8	15-25	5-15
5.81	Bounce Pass Layup	T	x	x	2	5.8	5.81	-	5-15

5.0 Shot Technique-Wrists

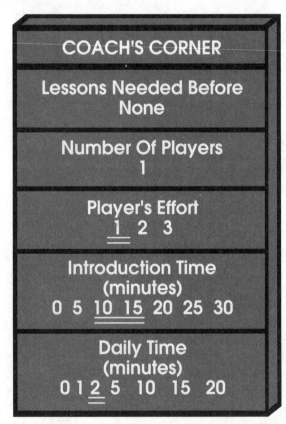

Brief:

In shooting position, players flick their wrists. (This is similar to 3.0.)

Fundamental Notes

The importance of wrist motion in learning and improving shooting, passing, and dribbling cannot be over emphasized. This lesson is applicable to players at ANY level from novice to professional. Practicing this lesson improves every type of shot.

Setup

Players set up 4 feet apart with a ball.

Directions for Players

1. Relax your hands. With arms at your sides, shake your hands back and forth.

2. With your feet at shoulder-width, raise your arms straight overhead with the palms facing forward. The elbows point forward.

3. A slightly bent elbow points forward, not to the side. Rotate your hand and forearm outward, so the palms face forward.

4. Flick your wrists directly back, not forward, nor to the sides. Let the wrists come forward

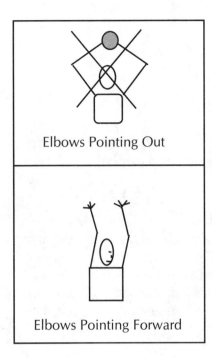

Elbows Pointing Out

Elbows Pointing Forward

without using effort. The arms remain motionless. The wrists sway back and forth like a wet noodle.

Troubleshooting

1. Initially, young players tire quickly, since their arms and wrists are weak. They often have difficulty lasting for one minute.

2. The hands and wrists remain loose.

3. Movement is forward and back, not sideways.

4. The elbows, if bent, point forward.

5. Young players make every possible mistake. The elbows bend outward; the wrist and hands freeze tight; the fingers squeeze together; the flick will be sideways or forward instead of back; etc. You need to work individually with each player.

Use of Assistants

Assistants look for bent elbows and tight hands.

Weekly Practice Everyday

Extensions

Practice this every day of the season, especially before shooting lessons. Players recognize the benefits immediately. Encourage players to repeat this before any game or shooting practice.

5.1 Flick Up

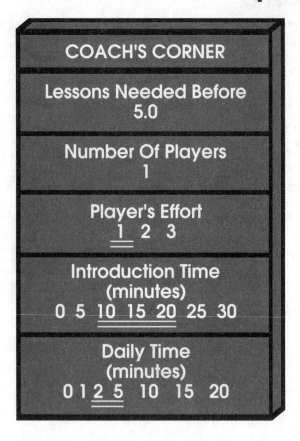

COACH'S CORNER
Lessons Needed Before 5.0
Number Of Players 1
Player's Effort <u>1</u> 2 3
Introduction Time **(minutes)** 0 5 <u>10</u> 15 <u>20</u> 25 30
Daily Time **(minutes)** 0 1 <u>2</u> 5 10 15 20

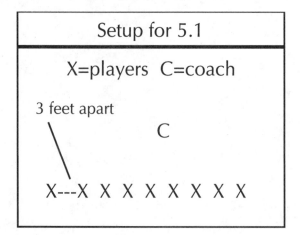

Setup for 5.1

X=players C=coach

3 feet apart

C

X---X X X X X X X X

Brief:

Players flick the ball upward and catch it on their fingertips.

Fundamental Notes

This is a significant shooting lesson. Players use their wrists and legs (in the extensions) to shoot, rather than their arms. They square up, aligning their body to the shot direction. You need to help each player properly align the body. Flicking and catching the ball on the fingertips also improves touch.

Setup

Players line up 4 feet apart, each with a basketball.

Directions for Players

1. The feet are shoulder-width apart; both arms are extended straight overhead at shoulder-width; the elbows are straight and pointing forward; the palms face forward.

2. Bend the wrists backward as far as possible; claw the hand. Balance the ball on the fingertips of the shooting hand.

3. Move the elbow of the shooting arm 2-3 inches inward, toward your face. Slightly rotate the forearm to the outside, if necessary. The shoulders and body remain facing forward.

•Players often misalign their bodies to get the elbows facing forward.

4. Flick the wrist so that the ball goes about one foot straight up.

5. Catch the ball on the fingertips, or ends, and continue flicking the ball straight up.

Troubleshooting

1. Each player squares up to shoot the ball; the arms are overhead with only the slightest bend of the elbows; the feet are parallel to each other; the shoulders face straight forward, not toward the side.

2. The hands are claw shaped; the wrist is bent back all the way; the wrist is flicked upward; the arms do not move. Do not mention or use the legs yet.

3. The players that have difficulty bending back the wrist, need to practice Lesson 5.0. The more the wrist is bent, the stronger the flick; players also use less arm movement–this is what we want.

4. Players have difficulty aligning their body and squaring up. Head, shoulders, feet, arms, etc., face the shooting direction, not necessarily the basket. Align each player's body parts individually, if necessary. Remember, only instruct players this way in this lesson, when working at the technique level. Do not teach squaring up this way when players actually shoot the ball.

5. Players flick the ball only 1-2 feet high.

Use of Assistants

Assistants watch for bent wrists, fingertip control of the ball, and squaring up.

Weekly Practice Everyday

Extensions

5.11 Opposite Hand Flick Up

Players use the wrist not only for shooting, but for passing and dribbling as well. So, we need to practice this with both hands. Repeat this lesson with the other hand.

5.12 Flick Up High

Use the legs in this lesson, not the arms, to add height to the wrist flick. Flick the ball 3-6 feet high. Players may catch the ball with two hands.

5.13 Shoot Up

Shoot the ball 5-20 feet straight up using the wrists and the legs, not the arms. Hold the ball and shoot it in a more normal way than you did in the previous lessons. Players must square up properly BEFORE doing this lesson.

5.2 One-Inch Shot

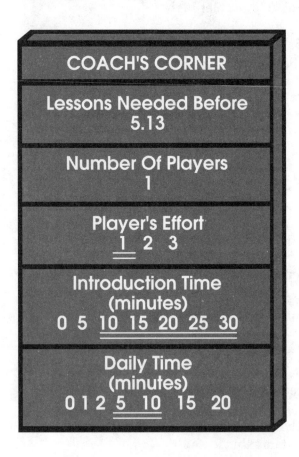

COACH'S CORNER

Lessons Needed Before
5.13

Number Of Players
1

Player's Effort
<u>1</u> 2 3

Introduction Time
(minutes)
0 5 <u>10 15 20 25 30</u>

Daily Time
(minutes)
0 1 2 <u>5 10</u> 15 20

Brief:
Players shoot the ball from a position directly under the basket.

Fundamental Notes

This technique level lesson forces players to extend their body, arms, and the ball to the maximum, because the basket is directly overhead. It is difficult to shoot the ball improperly, even though some players succeed. Take precautions to prevent players from stepping away from the basket. Squaring up to the actual shot direction or basket is introduced.

Setup

Ideally, each player needs to practice at a separate basket. However, in most situations you will need to use 3 lines (at the left, center, and right) at each basket; two or three players in each line. The nose of the first player in each line is directly under the rim of the basket. Mark these positions with masking tape. As with every other lesson in this book, make sure every player has a ball.

Directions for Players

1. Square up to the basket in the direction that you are going to shoot. In this lesson, you are not going to use the backboard. So, square up to the rim.

Squaring Up – Right and Wrong

arms → head → shoulders

squared up properly to direction shown

squared up wrong to this same direction

Setup for 5.2

view from above the basket

= players

Which players are squared up properly?

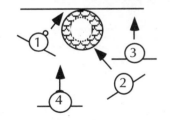

Write your answers here. or on another piece of paper. Answers below.

Answers
1 & 2 are squared up
1 to the backboard
2 to the rim
3 & 4 are not squared up

2. This is how to properly square up. Put your arms straight in front of you like a sleepwalker. Your arms make a right angle (90 degrees) with your shoulders. Your fingers point in the direction that you are going to shoot.

•Give a mini-lesson on squaring up. After showing the correct way to square up, demonstrate some incorrect ways: put the arms at an angle other than 90 degrees to the shoulders; rotate the body so that the angle is not 90 degrees. (See diagrams)

•Square up to the backboard. Then, square up to the rim as well as several other directions, where there is no basket. In each case, ask your players to point out the direction that you are squared up to shoot at, as well as if you are squared up properly.

3. Shoot the ball without stepping backward. Use the wrist and the legs only. It will be difficult at first. Take your time.

4. Move from the right of the basket, to the center, to the left and then back.

5. The ball does not hit the ground at any time during this lesson. No dribbling. Get your own rebound.

6. Practice flicking the wrists and the ball while waiting in line.

Troubleshooting

1. This is a shooting technique lesson. Do not take regular shots.

2. The ball does not hit the ground.

3. Players square up in the direction that they shoot.

4. This lesson puts all players, young and old, in an uncomfortable shooting position, too close to the basket.

5. Plan to be busy working with individual players.

6. Players often back off from the basket, unless you or a manager stand there.

7. Players who benefit the most from this lesson often have the greatest difficulty initially. They often show reluctance to do it.

Use of Assistants

Assistants stand behind players when they shoot, so players can not back off.

Weekly Practice Everyday

Extensions None

5.3 One-Foot Shot

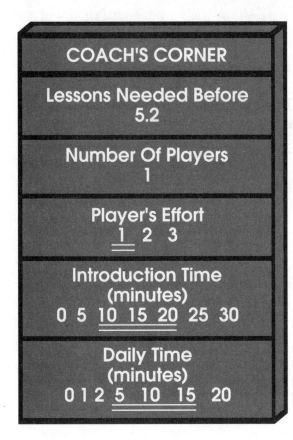

COACH'S CORNER

Lessons Needed Before
5.2

Number Of Players
1

Player's Effort
<u>1</u> 2 3

Introduction Time
(minutes)
0 5 <u>10 15 20</u> 25 30

Daily Time
(minutes)
0 1 2 <u>5 10 15</u> 20

Brief:

Players shoot one-foot shots from the right, center, and left of the basket.

Fundamental Notes

Players step back one foot from the basket and shoot a nearly regular shot. The shot is between the technique and practice levels. However, practice technique before doing this lesson. Every one-foot shooting lesson, and there are many of them, is similar in setup to 5.2, the previous lesson.

Setup

Ideally, one player per basket. Otherwise, use three lines–one at the left, center, and right, of each basket. Mark the one foot line with masking tape.

Directions for Players

1. Shoot a nearly normal shot from the one foot line. Square up to the backboard, move the ball high overhead, look to avoid other shooters, then shoot.

2. Use the backboard for each shot, even from the

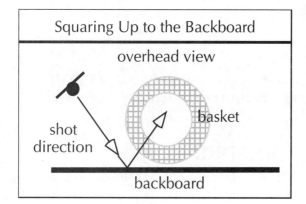

Setup for 5.3

Use Three Lines

Squaring Up to the Backboard

overhead view

shot direction

basket

backboard

center position. Pick a spot on the backboard to aim at. Square up to this spot, not the basket.

3. Shoot 5 shots from each position then rotate toward the left and then back again to the right. Continue till I say stop.

•With three players or more at one basket, shoot only one or two shots in a row before rotating positions. Players waiting in line can practice lessons 5.0 and 5.1.

4. The ball does not touch the ground. No dribbling. Rebound your shot.

Troubleshooting

1. Players square up to the backboard, then use it for each shot.

2. Players setup one foot from the basket, not two or three.

3. Players perform well if adequate time was spent on the previous technique lessons.

Use of Assistants

Assistants keep track of missed shots for each player. This is motivational. For each shot missed, require players to shoot 5 or 10 additional shots after practice.

Weekly Practice Everyday

Extensions

5.31 Regular One-Foot Shot

This lesson is the same as 5.3 except that the players shoot the ball more naturally. This is practice shooting.

5.32 One-Foot Shot + Dribbling

Lesson 4.3, a dribbling lesson, is needed before you do this one. Lesson 4.4 is also similar to this one. The only difference between 5.32 and 5.31 is that after the shot, each player dribbles back to the shooting line. If managers and players knock away balls from players dribbling with their heads down, then this lesson is the same as Lesson 4.4.

5.33 One-Foot Jump Shot

This lesson is the same as 5.31, except that players take a one-foot jump shot. The directions for the jump shot are simple– jump before you shoot. Little effort is exerted on the jump. Initially, it is better if players shoot on the way up. Note, that there are many ways to take a jump shot– fadeaways, shooting at the peak of the jump, jump hooks, etc. These variations are covered in lessons 6.31, 6.6, 6.61, and other lessons. Dribbling and defense are other options that can be added to this lesson.

5.4 The No-Step Layup 1-3

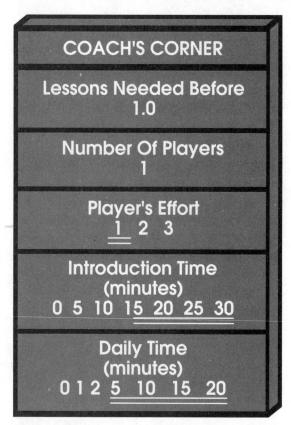

COACH'S CORNER

Lessons Needed Before
1.0

Number Of Players
1

Player's Effort
<u>1</u> 2 3

Introduction Time (minutes)
0 5 10 <u>15</u> <u>20</u> <u>25</u> <u>30</u>

Daily Time (minutes)
0 1 2 <u>5</u> <u>10</u> <u>15</u> <u>20</u>

Setup for Part 1

X=players C=coach

4 feet apart

C

X---X X X X X X X X

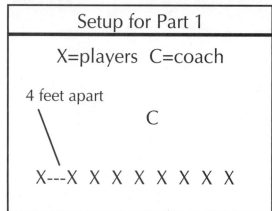

Layup Steps

Step 1   Step 2   Steps 3-4

Brief:
Novices master the mechanics of the layup in two steps, without dribbling or running.

Fundamental Notes

Novice players more readily learn the layup shot when it is taught separately. Too often young players require months, or even years, to correctly execute the layup off the proper foot. After 15 minutes you will notice remarkable improvement; in one week every player will be an expert. When players are directed to rebound their own shots, they are less likely to make common errors like broad jumping and floating too far underneath the basket before shooting. In Part 1, the movement is practiced without shooting. In Part 2, a layup is shot at the basket. Part 3 involves switching sides of the basket.

Setup

For Part 1, players set up 3-4 feet apart with a basketball. In Parts 2 and 3, players line up 2-3 feet from the basket. Initially, righties are on the right side of the basket and lefties are on the left side.

Directions for Players

Part 1

1. The ball starts at waist height, feet shoulder-width apart. Righties place the left foot one step forward, lefties the right foot, "not surers" put the left foot forward. You are righties now.

2. Twist the ball, so that the right hand is on top. Left hand for lefties.

3. Put your weight on and step on the forward foot. Simultaneously, move the ball up and the back leg forward and up. (You can make believe a string is attached from the shooting arm to the back leg.) Do not bring the back foot down.

4. When your arms are fully extended and the

back leg is forward (the thigh is horizontal, the foot is off the floor), repeat these maneuvers.

•Check each player, then repeat Part 1 at least 10 times.

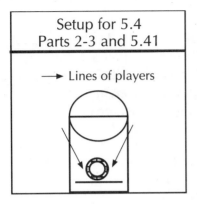

Setup for 5.4
Parts 2-3 and 5.41

→ Lines of players

Part 2

5. Use the painted rectangle, or any other blemish on the backboard, as a place to aim. Square up to the spot at which you aim.

6. The cues are: *foot forward, turn ball, ball up, back leg forward, shoot.*

7. Shoot one at a time. Get your own rebound, then without dribbling, return to the same line. The ball does not touch the floor. Right line start.

8. Practice Part 1 while you wait in line.

•Initially, making the shot is of little concern.

Part 3

•Players switch sides after 5-10 minutes. Righties shoot a left side layup the same way as they did on the right side. Lefties do not change the movements on the right side.

•After 5-10 minutes, move both lines to the center. Players use the backboard on the center layup.

•When players improve, run 2 or 3 lines (at the right, center, and left) at a basket, just like Lesson 5.3, the previous lesson.

Troubleshooting

1. Work with each player individually from a position under the basket.

2. Players square up to a chosen spot on the backboard where they aim.

3. Initially, young players usually square up improperly, especially on the opposite side of the basket; the left side for righties, the right side for lefties.

Use of Assistants

Assistants, if capable, work individually with players.

Weekly Practice   Everyday

Extensions

5.41 One-Step Layup

Players take a step with the left foot (right foot for lefties) and then shoot the layup. Gradually increase this step from a short one to a long one. Players shoot off the backboard from each position and return to the same line after each shot. Switch the lines after 5-10 minutes. When players are expert go to 5.42.

5.42 Layup Lesson

One step layups are shot from the three (3) positions–right, center, left–at the same time. To avoid collisions, caution players to pause before shooting to glance at the other shooters. Players rotate from right to center to left after each shot. No dribbling. The ball does not touch the floor.

5.43 Layup with Dribble

Players dribble back to the layup line in a setup like the previous lesson, 5.42. Instruct players to dribble to the sides, not through or between the lines. Players switch dribbling hand every 3 dribbles. They do not dribble in for the layup, they only dribble back to the lines. A dribbling Lesson, 4.2, is needed before this. Managers remind dribblers to keep there heads up and look around. This lesson is the same as 4.4 if managers knock balls away from dribblers who put their heads in the sand.

5.44 Layup with Passing

Lessons Needed Before 5.42, 9.1

Setup

Use two lines instead of the three used in the previous extensions. Rotate both lines every 2-5 minutes so that players have the opportunity to shoot from all three positions–right, center, and left. Position one player in each corner. Position two other players 15 feet down the sideline, one on each side. See the diagram. Use three balls in each line.

Directions (for one player)

1. After shooting the one-step layup and rebounding, a player throws an overhead pass to the corner and follows the pass to this position.

•Vary the pass.

2. The corner player passes up the sideline, then follows it.

3. The sideline player passes to the layup line and follows the ball.

•Wait until the players are ready before making each pass. No dribbling. The lines are independent of one another–the players in one line do not mix with players in the other line.

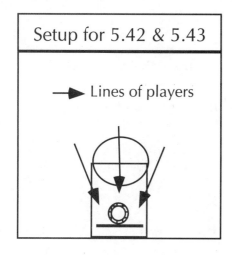

Setup for 5.42 & 5.43

→ Lines of players

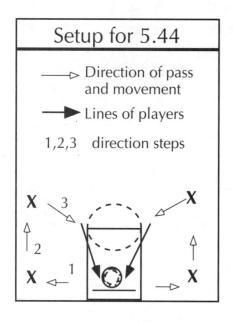

Setup for 5.44

⇢ Direction of pass and movement

→ Lines of players

1,2,3   direction steps

5.5 One Dribble Layup

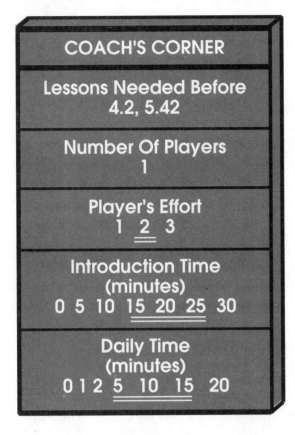

COACH'S CORNER

Lessons Needed Before
4.2, 5.42

Number Of Players
1

Player's Effort
1 2 3

Introduction Time
(minutes)
0 5 10 15 20 25 30

Daily Time
(minutes)
0 1 2 5 10 15 20

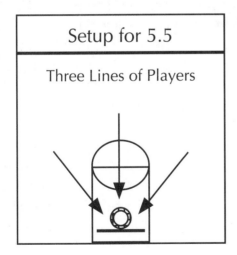

Setup for 5.5

Three Lines of Players

Brief:

Players dribble step before doing a one step layup. A dribble step is a step and a dribble at the same time.

Fundamental Notes

This lesson combines the layup with dribbling. After the dribble step, a one step layup is taken. The last step (and a half) before shooting is a slow step or a step used to slow down. After rebounding, players dribble back to the layup line as well. Managers knock away balls unprotected by players.

Setup

Use as many baskets as available. If you only have two, use 3 lines at each basket. Players move from the right to center to left and back again. Mark the starting point with masking tape or use a painted mark on the lane instead. Use only one basket, if you want to watch your players more closely.

Directions for Players

1. Start at the mark. Righties take one step with the right foot along with one low dribble. Lefties start with the left foot.

2. Grab the ball with both hands and take a one step layup.

•Demonstrate that the floating shot is much more difficult to make than going straight up. Floating is when a player takes a long jump to the basket and beyond, instead of a jump straight up. Floating also puts you behind the basket, so that you can't rebound a missed shot.

3. Rebound and dribble back to the next line.

4. Dribble in the half down position. Make sure the dribbles are low to the ground and your head is up. Go around the lines of players, not through them.

5. Switch dribbling hands every 3 dribbles.

6. While in line, continue dribbling with your head up.

7. Managers knock away the ball of any player looking at sneaker laces, or not paying attention.

Troubleshooting

1. Players stay in a half down position.

2. On the last step, players go straight up, not forward, so they do not float under the basket.

3. Players often want to take a 5 dribble, 5 step layup instead of just one. They need to stop dribbling for a second before starting.

Use of Assistants

Assistants knock away balls, to a far corner, of players looking down or not paying attention. They should go after the ball with less intensity than they do in Lesson 4.4.

Weekly Practice   Everyday

Extensions

5.51 Two Dribble Layup

The players move back one step and repeat Lesson 5.5. They take two dribble steps before completing a one-step layup. This lesson, in addition, is practiced with three dribble steps. Make certain that players are in the half down, ready position during the entire lesson.

5.6 Foul Shot Technique

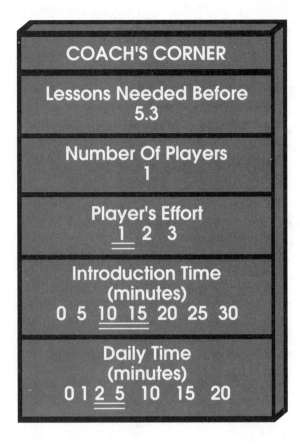

COACH'S CORNER

Lessons Needed Before
5.3

Number Of Players
1

Player's Effort
<u>1</u> 2 3

Introduction Time
(minutes)
0 5 <u>10 15</u> 20 25 30

Daily Time
(minutes)
0 1 <u>2 5</u> 10 15 20

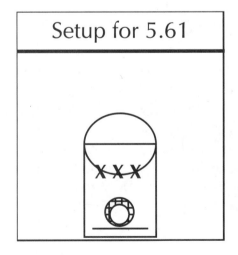

Setup for 5.61

Brief:
Preliminary steps and tips for game foul shot shooting are given.

Fundamental Notes

Fouls are always shot under great pressure in a game. Often the score is close. Invariably the game is momentarily stopped, so that every person in the gym focuses on the shooter. This lesson helps the player to relax and concentrate on the mechanics of the shot.

At every level, junior high to professional, players regularly miss foul shots in game deciding situations. The techniques presented here remedy most of the causes. One particular cause is that players do not shoot at their normal speed. Being more cautious, they slow down the movements of the arms, legs, and wrists to prevent mistakes. This becomes the mistake–you must shoot at a normal speed. Another reason why players miss foul shots at the end of the game is that they are tired and their muscles, especially the leg muscles, are stiff. As a result, they arm the ball–shoot with their arms–up to the basket, instead of shooting with the wrists and legs. This lesson shows you how to prevent these problems.

Setup

Players stand side by side, 5 feet apart, each with a basketball.

Directions for Players

1. Put the ball on the ground for a minute. The feet are shoulder-width apart.

2. Shake the wrists to loosen them.

3. Pick up the ball and dribble a few times with two hands. In the game you have very little chance to touch the ball. Handling it helps your touch and wrist movement.

4. Shoot the ball a few feet straight up at the **normal speed**, not at a slowed down pace, which throws off the normal shot. I have seen numerous players be overly cautious in win–lose situations and slow down, only to have their shot thrown off by this tactic. Slowing down from the normal shooting speed causes problems. Often I have seen entire teams do this, and shoot horrendously. Slow down before the shot, get yourself set, then shoot at the normal speed.

5. Bend the knees a few times to the half down position. This helps loosen up and reminds you to bend the legs while shooting.

6. Take a deep breath or two. This helps you to calm down. Hold your breath while you take the shot, just like a gun shooter does. This steadies your movement.

•Repeat this procedure 3 or 4 times. Use cue words– Wrists, Ball, Knees, Breath.

Troubleshooting

1. Make sure players know the cue words:
- Wrists-shake them.
- Ball-handle it. Dribble and shoot up.
- Knees-bend.
- Breath-take a deep breath before the shot.

2. Make sure players do not slow down the actual shot movements.

Use of Assistants None

Weekly Practice

Do this everyday when you practice foul shots. It only needs to be taught 2-5 times.

Extensions

5.61 Technique Short Shot

Comment

A foul shot is a long shot that often causes a novice's shooting technique to fall apart. This lesson uses a shorter shot, with the expectation that the longer shot develops during the season. Shooting fully rested in practice is also a waste. In a game, players shoot two fouls at a time while sweating and trying to catch their breath. This lesson tries to emulate this situation. Do this lesson last in practice to insure that the players are tired.

Setup

Players line up three feet from the basket on the line marking the boundary of the jump circle. If you only have

1 or 2 baskets, make players stand to the right or left of the first player. Managers stand under each basket to rebound and return the ball to the shooters.

Directions

1. Use the foul shooting technique cues: wrists, ball, knees, breath.

2. After 2 shots a player sprints, dribbling the ball, to the other end of the court (or anywhere) before shooting again.

3. Repeat this step as many times as possible within the 5-15 minute time limit of the lesson.

5.62 Technique Longer Shots

Repeat 5.61 stepping closer to the foul line, away from the basket, after each sprint. Instruct players to stay in normal shooting range. Watch closely for incorrect and strained shooting technique.

5.7 Foul Shot Practice

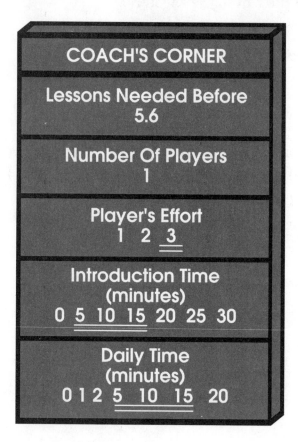

COACH'S CORNER

Lessons Needed Before
5.6

Number Of Players
1

Player's Effort
1　2　<u>3</u>

Introduction Time (minutes)
0　<u>5　10　15</u>　20　25　30

Daily Time (minutes)
0 1 2　<u>5　10　15</u>　20

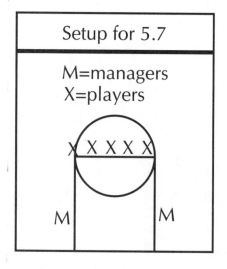

Setup for 5.7

M=managers
X=players

X X X X X

M　　　M

Brief:
This lesson gives players game-like foul shoot practice.

Fundamental Notes

This is the most difficult shooting lesson in the book. A big mistake is to do it prematurely. Wait for your players to have both the shooting and foul shooting techniques down pat at shorter distances.

Foul shoot practice often involves shooting 10, or even 20, shots in a row. Here are several reasons why this is not effective:

1. Players need to work on shooting technique, rather than shooting.

2. Players need to shoot closer to the basket and then gradually move to the foul line.

3. In a game a player is tired, out of breath, and under greater pressure and attention when shooting fouls.

To overcome these pitfalls, the practice foul shooting lesson addresses shooting technique as well as the game situation. It is best done near the end of practice, when players are more tired.

Setup

Players shoot from any position available on the foul line.

Directions for Players

1. Shoot twice at one basket and then sprint down court to the other basket.

•You may want players, depending on their age, to sprint back and forth down court several times.

2. Shoot before you catch your breath. Shoot from any position available on the foul line. Move to one side, if necessary. Do not wait for a center position.

3. Use the foul shooting technique–wrists, ball, knees, breath.

•The details are in Lesson 5.6.

4. Continue until the lesson ends.

Troubleshooting

1. This is the most difficult shooting lesson in the book. It is okay to be halfway through the season before you reach it.

2. Players must shoot before they catch their breath.

Use of Assistants

1. Assistants rebound the foul shots and pass the ball back to the shooter.

2. They also keep statistics on shots made and missed for each player.

Weekly Practice Everyday

Extensions None

5.8 Lateral Layup Lesson

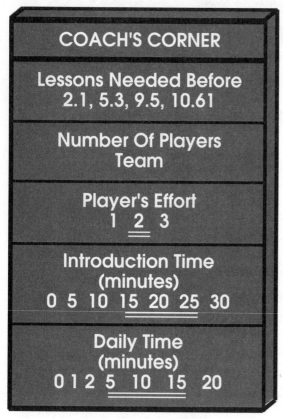

COACH'S CORNER
Lessons Needed Before 2.1, 5.3, 9.5, 10.61
Number Of Players Team
Player's Effort 1 <u>2</u> 3
Introduction Time **(minutes)** 0 5 10 <u>15 20 25</u> 30
Daily Time **(minutes)** 0 1 2 <u>5 10 15</u> 20

Brief:

This is the most common layup lesson used by teams in warm ups, as well as in practice.

Fundamental Notes

•This common layup lesson involves myriad skills: timing a cut to the basket, simultaneously catching the ball and shooting the layup, timing a cut for a rebound, rebounding, pivoting, and then throwing a timed pass to a cutter. Other lessons can provide better practice for each of these skills individually.

•When only one basket is available before a game this lesson is tolerable for experienced teams. When many baskets are available, this lesson is very inefficient. Most players stand around in line most of the time waiting to do something. Using 6 players at each basket, if you have more than one, is a more efficient use of time.

•This lesson may look good in pregame warm-ups, but I do not recommend it. I suggest that you use 5.3, 5.4, and/or 5.5 with as many basket-balls as possible for warm ups, as well as in practice. The Line Lesson, 1.3, and The Layup With Passing lesson, 5.44, are some better warm up lessons that develop similar skills.

Setup

1. Set up two lines with the same number of players 1-4 yards outside the left and right sides of the foul line extended. With older players, move the lines back toward midcourt.

2. The right side line starts as the shooting line; the left side line, as the rebounding line.

3. After 2-5 minutes, switch the layup line to the center and then to the left side.

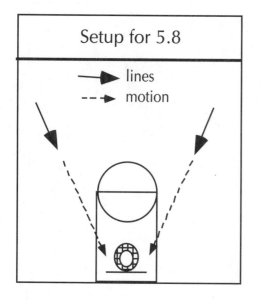

Setup for 5.8

→ lines
--→ motion

Directions for Players

1. Start when a player, the team captain or other designated player, under the boards with a ball says *go*.

2. The first players from each line run straight to the basket at the same speed.

3. The passer laterals the ball to the layup side cutter (the right side first) 3-5 feet from the basket near this mark (point it out) on the floor. Return to the shooting line via the baseline and sideline.

• Mark a spot for the lateral or use a marked spot on the floor. Other types of passes can be used.

4. The cutter catches the ball, slows down, and shoots a layup without dribbling. Always use the backboard. Then quickly run behind the basket to the opposite sideline, before running to the passing line.

5. The rebounder rebounds the ball without letting it hit the floor and then laterals it to the next cutter when they reach a similar position as the first cutter. Then, run out-of-bounds to the shooting line.

6. As soon as the rebounder controls the ball, the cutters start.

• Repeat the directions if necessary. After 5 minutes move the right line to the center. Players use the backboard from the center position as well.

• Five minutes later move the ball to the left line and the center line back to the right.

• Yell "center" for the first change and "left" for the second.

Troubleshooting

1. Righties, as well as lefties, shoot the layup the same way from all three positions. If players want to shoot with the opposite hand, they must practice it at all three positions–left, right, and center of the basket.

2. Players go straight up for the layup without any floating.

3. Novice players will have great difficulty doing this lesson. It is complex; it will probably do them more harm than good.

4. Players need to run quickly back to the opposite line from which they started, staying out of the cutting lanes.

5. Players have a tendency to change the starting point of each line. Usually, it moves toward the basket. Station a manager at the starting point, so that this does not occur.

6. Players also have a tendency not to slow down after they catch the ball. This makes the shot more difficult. Yell "slow down" after the ball is caught.

7. Both rebounder and shooter start their cut to the basket at the same time.

Use of Assistants

1. Assistants keep track of shots missed by each player.

2. Station a manager at the starting point of each line.

3. Managers, near the endline, remind shooters and rebounders to quickly move away from the cutting lanes.

Weekly Practice As needed.

Extensions

5.81 Bounce Pass Layup

Change the lateral pass in 5.8 to a bounce pass. This is more difficult.

Section 6
Moves

L E S S O N #	NAME	P L A Y E R S	C O U R T	B A L L	E F F O R T	LESSONS BEFORE	L E S S O N #	INTRO TIME	DAILY TIME
6.0	**Moves**	x	x	x	-	2.1, 5.3	**6.0**	5-15	0-20
6.1	Pivot Around Shoot	1	x	x	2	6.0	6.1	5-15	0-20
6.2	Pivot Backward Shoot	1	x	x	2	6.1	6.2	5-15	0-20
6.3	Step Fake Shoot	1	x	x	2	6.0	6.3	5-15	0-20
6.31	Fake Pivot Shoot	1	x	x	2	6.3	6.31	5-15	0-20
6.32	Fake Pivot Back Shoot	1	x	x	2	6.31	6.32	5-15	0-20
6.4	Pivot Fake Shoot	1	x	x	2	6.0	6.4	5-15	0-20
6.41	Pivot Fake Back Shoot	1	x	x	2	6.4	6.41	5-15	0-20
6.5	Hook Shot 1-2	1	x	x	2	6.0	6.5	5-15	0-20
6.51	Jump Hook	1	x	x	2	6.5	6.51	5-15	0-20
6.52	Hook with Fake	1	x	x	2	6.51	6.52	5-15	0-20
6.53	Step Hook	1	x	x	2	6.51	6.53	5-15	0-20
6.54	Fake Step Hook	1	x	x	2	6.52-3	6.54	5-15	0-20
6.55	Underneath Hooks	1	x	x	2	6.54	6.55	5-15	0-20
6.6	Jump Shot	1	x	x	2	6.0	6.6	5-15	0-20
6.61	Fake Jump	1	x	x	2	6.6	6.61	5-15	0-20
6.62	Fake Pivot Around Jump	1	x	x	2	6.61	6.62	5-15	0-20
6.63	Pump Fake	1	x	x	2	6.6	6.63	5-10	5-10

6.0 Moves

COACH'S CORNER

Lessons Needed Before
2.1, 5.3

Number Of Players
1

Player's Effort
1 2 3

Introduction Time
(minutes)
0 5 10 15 20 25 30

Daily Time
(minutes)
0 1 2 5 10 15 20

Setup-Section Six

The 3 positions used for most section 6 lessons

rotate in this direction

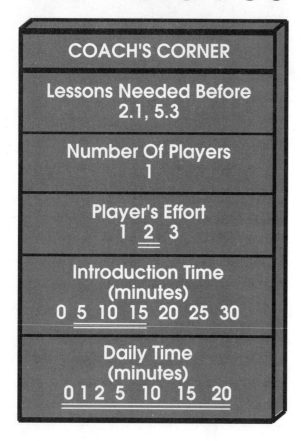

Center
X
Right   Left
X   X

Brief:

All section 6 lessons combine faking and pivoting with shooting. The information in this lesson applies to each lesson in this section. It is for coaches.

Fundamental Notes

Each player practices these lessons individually at a separate basket, not as a team. Even though players can execute these moves from anywhere on the court, practice them one foot from the basket. The various fakes introduced can be used in other than shooting situations. Teach these moves during the pre or post practice time to individuals or small groups of selected players whom you deem ready for them. This works well. After receiving this special attention, players eagerly practice any move on their own.

These things vary in each move:

1. Direction of the pivot–forward (same direction as walking) or backward (like walking backward)

2. The starting direction–facing the basket, with the back to the basket, or underneath the basket.

3. Three types of fakes are used.

•The ball body fake or ball fake involves faking toward the pivot foot with the ball and the body.

•If a step is taken away from the pivot foot with the ball fake, it is called a ball body step fake or just a step fake.

•When a pivot is used as a fake, it is a ball body step pivot fake or just a pivot fake.

4. The shots include regular one-foot shots, hook shots, jump hooks, jump shots, or underneath shots. At least 80 lessons are possible combining the shots with the fakes and other options; 160, if you practice with each hand.

Setup

See the individual lesson.

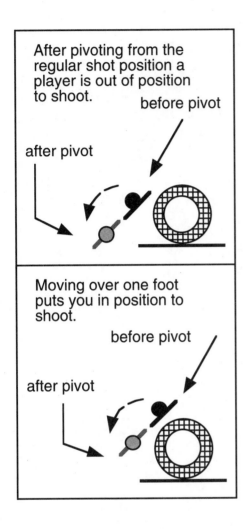

After pivoting from the regular shot position a player is out of position to shoot.

before pivot

after pivot

Moving over one foot puts you in position to shoot.

before pivot

after pivot

General Directions & Explanation

1. Players start in the half down position with the ball at waist height.

2. Five one-foot shots are taken from each of the three positions using the backboard, even in the center position. The positions (as they will be referred to) are right, center, and left of the basket.

3. The order of shooting is from right, to center, to left (opposite for lefties).

4. Use the left foot first as the pivot foot in each position and then the right foot.

5. Players shoot 30 shots per lesson; five shots at each of the 3 positions pivoting with the left foot and then 5 at each position using the right foot.

6. Players square up to the spot on the backboard where they aim. For hook shots, squaring up means that the shoulders and the ball are in line with the spot on the backboard where they aim. The lesson on hook shots explains this special type of squaring up in detail.

7. When starting with the back to the basket, players set up slightly to the right (the court right, not your right) when pivoting with the right foot or slightly to the left when using the left foot. This puts players in a normal shooting position after they pivot. See diagrams on this page.

8. Encourage players, even beginners, to practice some of these lessons with the opposite hand. Repeat each lesson completely with the other hand. Don't restrict practice to right handed on the right side of the basket and left handed on the left side. This limits, instead of expands, a player's moves.

9. *Backward* in directions always means that you move in the direction that your back is facing. It does not mean toward or away from the basket. *Forward* means that you move in the direction you face.

10. *Left* always means that you move toward the left side of the court. *Right* means move toward the right side of the court. These directions are absolute.

11. Lefties follow the same directions unless stated otherwise as in step 3 above.

Troubleshooting

Players often have a favorite pivot foot. Each lesson is executed first using the left foot and then repeated using the right foot. Practicing with only one pivot foot notice-ably detracts from a player's effectiveness.

Use of Assistants
See the particular lesson.

Weekly Practice As needed

Extensions See the individual lessons.

6.1 Pivot Around Shoot

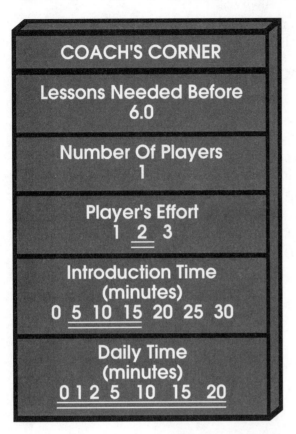

COACH'S CORNER

Lessons Needed Before
6.0

Number Of Players
1

Player's Effort
1 <u>2</u> 3

Introduction Time
(minutes)
0 <u>5 10 15</u> 20 25 30

Daily Time
(minutes)
<u>0 1 2 5 10 15 20</u>

Brief:

Starting with the back to the basket, a player pivots forward to face the basket and takes a one-foot shot.

Fundamental Notes

This shot is normally taken after both rebounding and picking up a loose ball under the basket. It is a template for many other moves, some farther from the basket, involving various fakes. It is an important offensive move. Practice this move slowly at the technique level.

Directions & Setup for Players

1. Start with the back to the basket on the right side, pivoting on the left foot. Move one step toward the left, so that after pivoting you are in position to shoot.

• See Diagrams. Use the same directions for left-

Pivot forward to face the basket. Left foot pivot.

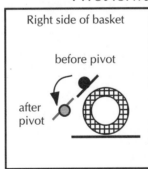

Right side of basket

before pivot

after pivot

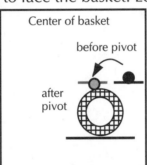

Center of basket

before pivot

after pivot

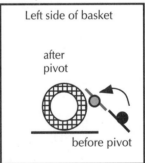

Left side of basket

after pivot

before pivot

Pivot forward to face the basket. Right foot pivot.

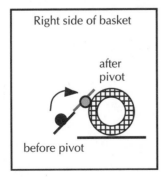

Right side of basket

after pivot

before pivot

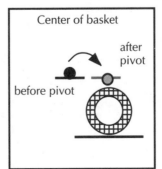

Center of basket

after pivot

before pivot

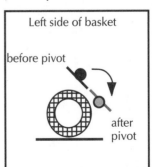

Left side of basket

before pivot

after pivot

ies, although they can start from the left side.

2. Raise the ball overhead and then pivot forward to face the basket. Square up, then shoot.

3. When pivoting on the right foot, set up one foot to the right to be in position to shoot after pivoting around.

Troubleshooting

1. Do this slowly at the technique level.

2. Players raise the ball overhead before they pivot. This is a slight exaggeration of the real motion, which involves turning and bringing the ball up simultaneously. However, bringing the ball up sooner prevents a player from becoming more easily tied up while the ball is low.

See 6.0 for more information.

Use of Assistants None

Weekly Practice As needed

Extensions None

6.2 Pivot Backward Shoot

Brief:

This is the same as Lesson 6.1, except the player pivots around in the backward direction.

Fundamental Notes

A player must be able to make a move in either pivot direction. Often when the ball is loose underneath the basket, it is the best to turn backward to score after picking it up. Lesson 6.1 covers pivoting forward (like walking forward), while this lesson covers pivoting backward (like walking backward).

Directions & Setup for Players

1. Start with the back to the basket. Set up one foot to the left, when pivoting with the left foot, and one to the right when pivoting with the right foot.

2. Push the ball overhead, then pivot backward

Pivot backward to face the basket. Left foot pivot.

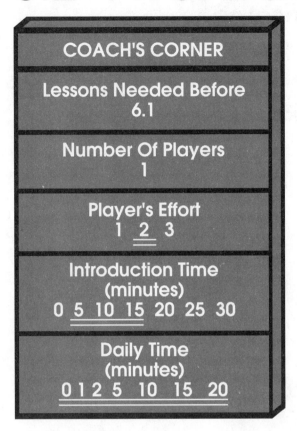 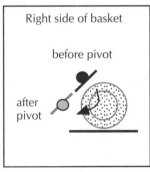 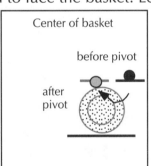

Pivot backward to face the basket. Right foot pivot.

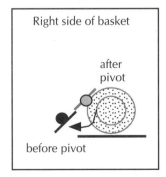 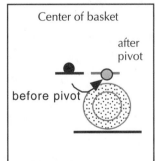 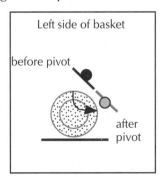 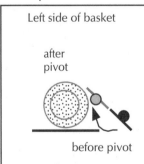

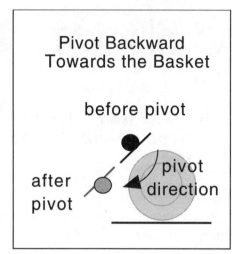

Pivot Backward
Towards the Basket

before pivot

after
pivot

pivot
direction

toward the basket.

3. Square up and shoot.

Troubleshooting

Set up just as you did in 6.1.

Use of Assistants None

Weekly Practice As needed

Extensions None

6.3 Step Fake Shoot

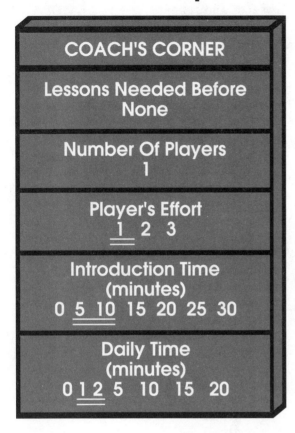

COACH'S CORNER

Lessons Needed Before
None

Number Of Players
1

Player's Effort
<u>1</u> 2 3

Introduction Time (minutes)
0 <u>5 10</u> 15 20 25 30

Daily Time (minutes)
0 <u>1 2</u> 5 10 15 20

Brief:

Facing the basket each player fakes, squares up, then shoots.

Fundamental Notes

This lesson introduces faking and shooting together. Use this move at any distance from the basket. The fake is used in many other lessons in this section. The step part of the fake is also called a jab step.

Directions for Players

1. Face the basket in the half down position with the ball at waist height.

2. The step fake entails slowly pushing the ball in a direction away from the pivot foot while simultaneously stepping in the same direction.

•Initially, keep the ball at waist height. Move it high or low on the fake when players are more expert.

3. After the fake, bring the feet back to shoulder

Step Fake Shoot. Left foot pivot.

⟶ Direction of step fake ● Pivot foot

Right side of basket	Center of basket	Left side of basket
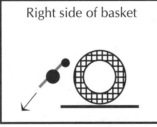	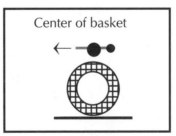	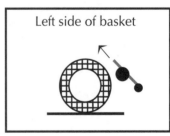

Step Fake Shoot. Right foot pivot.

Right side of basket	Center of basket	Left side of basket
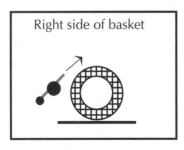	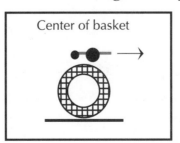	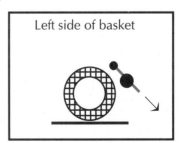

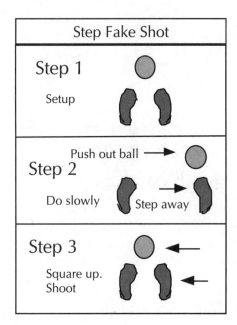

Step Fake Shot

Step 1

Setup

Step 2

Push out ball →

Do slowly

Step away →

Step 3

Square up.
Shoot

width while moving the ball overhead; square up and shoot.

4. Shoot 5 shots from the right, the center, and then the left. Switch the pivot foot and repeat.

Troubleshooting

1. The fake is slow. The move after the fake is at normal speed. Both are done slowly in this lesson. Speeding up this move makes learning more difficult. Players naturally speed up as their balance improves.

2. Shift the body weight to the stepping foot on the fake and then back to the pivot foot on the recoil. Distribute weight evenly on the shot.

Use of Assistants None

Weekly Practice As needed

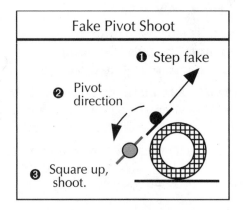

Fake Pivot Shoot

❶ Step fake

❷ Pivot
direction

❸ Square up,
shoot.

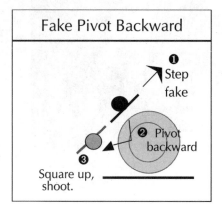

Fake Pivot Backward

❶ Step fake

❷ Pivot
backward

❸ Square up,
shoot.

6.4 Pivot Fake Shoot

Brief:

Facing the basket, a player pivots forward 180 degrees, a half turn, and then step fakes before pivoting back to the original position facing the basket.

Fundamental Notes

This lesson combines faking, pivoting, and shooting. This is a common sequence seen with college and professional players.

Directions & Setup for Players

1. Face the basket. Pivot forward 180 degrees so that your back is to the basket. Push the ball to the outside as you pivot. This looks like a step fake after you pivot.

2. Pivot backward to the original position facing the basket while holding the ball high.

3. Square up and shoot.

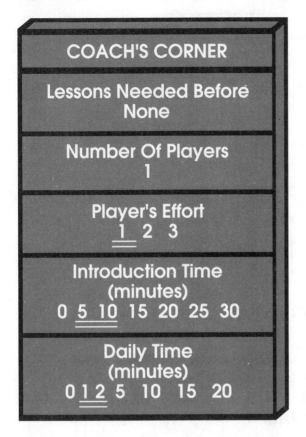

❶ Setup
   Left foot pivot
   Center position
❷ Pivot 180°
❸ Step fake
❹ Pivot back
   and shoot

Pivot Fake Shoot — left foot pivot foot center position

Pivot Fake Back Shoot — left foot pivot foot center position

Use of Assistants
None

Weekly Practice
As needed

Extensions

6.41 Pivot Fake Back Shoot

Perform Lesson 6.4 pivoting 180 degrees backward, instead of forward. Bring the ball high as you pivot back to the original position.

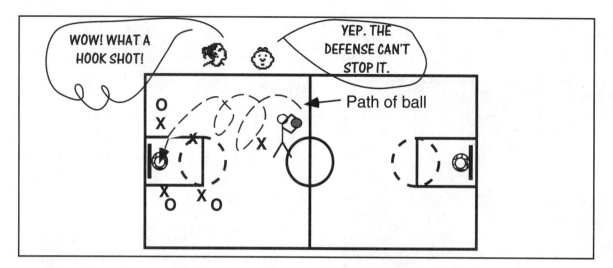

6.5 Hook Shot 1-2

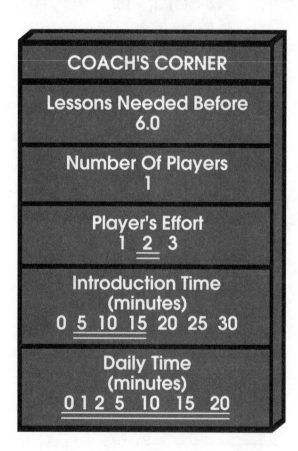

BRIEF:

Players learn how to square up for the hook shot in Part 1. In Part 2, players start with the back to the basket and then repeat this move facing the basket.

Fundamental Notes

Hook shots are not for novices for several reasons: one, to be effective, players need to be able to control the ball with one hand. Young players can't do this because they have small hands. Two, hook shots are used close to the basket when the defense is tight. With novices, tight defenses are seldom encountered.

•Hook shots, unlike other shots, are only used close to the basket under great defensive pressure. The power of the hook is that it neutralizes the defense. It allows players unimpeded 1-2 foot shots with the defense right in their faces.

•Two reasons stand out for the effectiveness of the hook. One, is that the body of the shooter protects the ball from the defense. The other is that the hook is a quick shot. Players need not even turn around to face the basket to shoot.

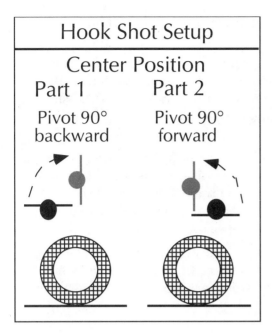

Hook Shot Setup

Center Position

Part 1	Part 2
Pivot 90° backward	Pivot 90° forward

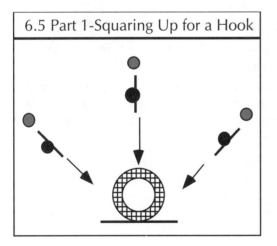

6.5 Part 1-Squaring Up for a Hook

•Besides shooting the hook from the left, right, and center positions, a player can execute a hook either facing the basket or with their back to the basket. The only difference in these shots is the direction of the pivot. Facing forward, the pivot is a half turn backward; with the back to the basket, the pivot is a half turn forward.

•Even though the hook is always shot off the same foot (right handers use the left foot, left handers the right foot) players standing on the opposite pivot foot take a step hook. (See 6.53) A right hander on the right foot (actually, the wrong foot in this situation) takes a step with the left foot. The shot is taken par normal off the left foot.

•All lessons are given for right handers. Left handers follow the same directions using the other pivot foot.

•As with the other shooting lessons, players line up one foot from the basket on the right , then center, and then left. Since the hook is most effective as a short shot, I recommend that you practice with each hand. This means twice as much practice.

•Two types of hooks are especially effective. One is the jump hook. (See 6.51) Because the ball is released higher and closer to the basket this shot is difficult to block. The other type of hook is taken from directly underneath the basket. (See 6.55) Using the hook from this position enables players to shoot without needing to take steps outward, turn around, and square up to the basket. Underneath hooks also catch the defense by surprise because players shoot from an awkward position. The net and the rim are also in the way of the defense. In general, the more awkward the position from which a hook is shot, the more effective a hook shot.

Directions & Setup for Players

Part 1

1. Start with the ball at waist height, left foot pivot foot. From one foot away on the right side face the basket.

2. Turn sideways so that the shooting arm and the ball are straight out to the side, not in front of the body. See the diagram. Both shoulders and the ball are in a straight line. The left elbow is forward and

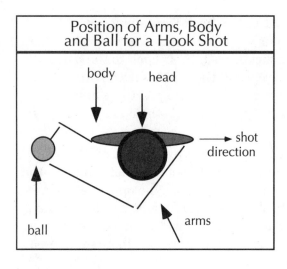

Position of Arms, Body and Ball for a Hook Shot

body   head

shot direction

ball   arms

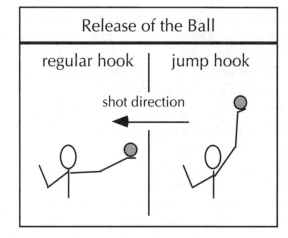

Release of the Ball

regular hook   jump hook

shot direction

Starting Positions for the Jump Hook

slightly up. The right elbow is back and slightly down.

3. Squaring up on a hook shot is accomplished by aligning the ball and the shoulders in a straight line with the point on the backboard that you aim at. See the diagram.

4. Hook the ball directly overhead using the wrist to flick the ball, just as other shots are performed; use the shooting arm as little as possible. A common error is to loop the ball in front of the body. In this position the ball is not protected by the body, so the defense can easily block the shot.

5. Repeat this and the other moves 5 times each. Move to the center position and then the left. Use the backboard from each position. Fifteen shots total.

Part 2

6. Start with your back to the basket, 1-2 feet to the left of your position in Part 1. Pivot 90 degrees, a quarter turn forward, square up, and shoot. Repeat 5 times from each position.

7. Start from a position facing the basket. Rotate a quarter turn backward, square up, and shoot. Repeat from each position.

Troubleshooting

1. The hook shot is taken directly from the side. The shoulders and ball are squared up to the spot on the backboard that you aim. The body protects the ball from the defense. Shooting from a position in front of your body shoves the ball right in front of the defensive player.

2. Flick the shot using the wrists. Avoid arming the ball overhead.

Extensions

6.51 Jump Hook

This lesson is identical to 6.5 Parts 1 and 2 except that:

1. The player jumps when shooting the hook.

2. Bring the ball up higher closer to the body and flick the hook without using the arm.

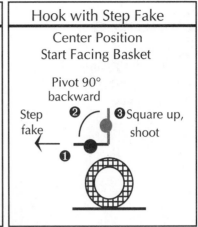

Hook with Step Fake	Hook with Step Fake
Center Position Start Back to Basket	Center Position Start Facing Basket

If you start with your back to the basket and then face the basket you shoot thirty shots. Righties always use the left foot as the pivot foot (right foot for lefties). Starting from the squared up position you only shoot 15 shots.

6.52 Hook (Jump Hook) with Step Fake

Both the hook and the jump hook can be practiced with the step fake explained in Lesson 6.4. The fake involves pushing the ball and stepping away from the pivot foot. Then, pivot a quarter turn, square up, and shoot. Do this move starting with the back to the basket and then facing the basket. The left foot is always the pivot foot (right for lefties).

6.53 Step Hook (Step Jump Hook)

It is difficult to take a hook off the right foot, if you are right handed. So, when the right foot is the pivot foot, a step needs to be taken to the left foot. The hook is then shot off the left foot as usual. This type of hook is called a step hook. Use these directions for a step hook or a step jump hook. For lefties, switch the words left and right in the directions.

1. With the back toward the basket, pivot a quarter turn backward on the right foot. Then step on the left foot, square up, and shoot. Shoot 5 shots from the left, center, and right. Shoot 15 shots total.

2. Facing the basket, pivot a quarter turn forward on the right foot, square up, and shoot. Again, shoot 5 shots from each position–right, center, and left. Fifteen (15) total.

6.54 Fake Step Hook

A fake makes the step hook, 6.53, a more effective move. Fake by moving the ball and the body in one direction and then stepping away in the other direction. The fake is in a different direction, depending on whether you start facing or with your back to the basket. In either case, the fake is toward your left away from the

Step Hook

❶ Right pivot foot center position

❷ Pivot 90° and step

❸ Square up and shoot

Back to basket

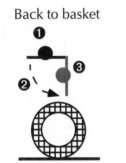

Facing the basket

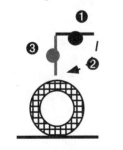

Step Hook with Fake

❶ Right pivot foot
Center position

❷ Step fake

❸ Pivot 90°
and step

❹ Square up
and shoot

Back to basket

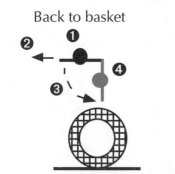

Facing the basket

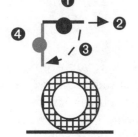

pivot foot. The right foot is always the pivot foot (left foot for lefties).

1. When you start facing the basket, step fake to the left, then pivot forward a quarter turn. Square up, and shoot.

2. When you start with your back to the basket, step fake to your left (the right of the court). Then pivot backward one quarter turn toward the basket. Square up and shoot.

6.55 Underneath Hook Shots

It is useful to have the ability to shoot a hook from directly under the basket. Picking up a loose ball or a rebound in traffic may not give you much time, or room, to move. These hooks can be shot in awkward and crowded situations. Use the backboard in each case. Practice each move at least 5 times in a row from as many directions as possible. Here are several moves to practice:

1. Stand directly behind the basket under the backboard facing the court. Using the left foot as the pivot foot, take a half step forward with the right foot toward the left, center, or right side of the basket. Do not bring your right foot down. Then take a hook shot off the backboard. This looks like a backward hook.

2. Repeat the previous move starting with the right foot as pivot foot. Then, take a step hook in any direction. This may be easier since the step enables you to get in a better position.

Underneath Hooks

Starting Under the Backboard

Step in any direction
with eiher foot

Starting Under the Basket

3. Stand directly under the basket facing the right sideline. Move toward the sideline or the center of the court. Take a hook, jump hook, or step hook. Facing the left sideline make the same move.

4. If you start facing the left sideline, the hook taken going forward resembles a scoop shot for right handers. Lefties scoop when moving toward the right sideline. Use the backboard for this shot.

6.6 Jump Shot

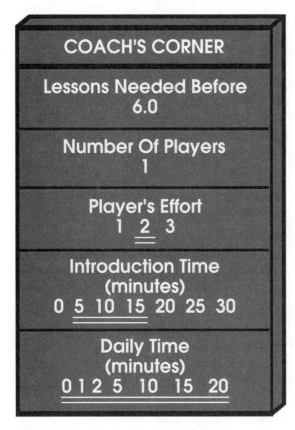

COACH'S CORNER

Lessons Needed Before
6.0

Number Of Players
1

Player's Effort
1 <u>2</u> 3

**Introduction Time
(minutes)**
0 <u>5 10 15</u> 20 25 30

**Daily Time
(minutes)**
<u>0 1 2 5 10 15 20</u>

Brief:

Players shoot a one-foot jump shot from the right, center, and left of the basket.

Fundamental Notes

In Lesson 5.33 the jump shot was introduced as a team lesson. Here it is as an individual lesson done in the format of all the lessons in this section: 5 shots from the right, center, and left. Switch pivot foot and repeat; 30 shots total. When players first learn the jump shot tell them just to jump and shoot. It's okay to shoot on the way up. Jump shots in games are released at every elevation and any instant–on the way up, at the top, and on the way down. On the way up is the most comfortable way to shoot a shot from a distance. Shoot at the top of the jump when the defense is close, or you are near the basket. The on the way down position is used when someone is "in your face." Along with the fade away, this is a more difficult shot. In the lessons below, stick with the jump shots released on the way up or at the top.

Directions & Setup for Players

1. Start with the left foot as pivot foot. Setup one foot from the basket on the right side.

2. Bring the ball overhead; square up; jump and shoot on the way up.

3. Shoot 5 shots on the right, center, and left. Switch pivot foot and repeat. Thirty shots total.

Extensions

6.61 Fake Jump Shot

Practice Lesson 6.3 using a jump shot. Set up facing the basket, step fake, square up and shoot. Use the left and then the right foot as pivot.

6.62 Fake Turn Around

This is the same as 6.4 and 6.41 except that you jump. Start with the back to the basket. Practice this move pivoting both forward and backward. It is very effective with tight defense.

6.63 Pump Fake

Pump or push the ball upward just before you are about to shoot it. Often you can pump it several times to get the defense in the air. After the defense jumps, take your regular shot, expecting to be fouled. This is primarily for older players. Practice it from the right, center, and left of the basket.

Note that quick shots usually work better than pump fakes. However, with very tight defense, pump fakes can be effective.

Section 7
Pressure Shooting

L E S S O N #	NAME	P L A Y E R S	C O U R T	B A L L	E F F O R T	LESSONS BEFORE	L E S S O N #	INTRO TIME	DAILY TIME
7.0	**Pressure Shot**	1	x	x	2-3	6.1 or 6.6	**7.0**	5-15	5-15
7.01	Pressure Shot with D	2	x	x	3	7.0	7.01	-	5-15
7.02	Pressure Shot Two	2	x	x	3	7.01, 10.3, 11.0	7.02	-	5-15
7.1	Run Stop Shoot	1	x	x	2-3	6.6	7.1	5-10	2-5
7.11	With D	2	x	x	3	7.1	7.11	-	2-5
7.12	Run Catch Shoot	2	x	x	3	7.1, 9.1, 10.6	7.12	10-20	5-15
7.2	Catch Up	2	x	x	3	5.51, 7.0	7.2	5-10	5
7.3	Defense in Face Shoot	2	x	x	3	5.3	7.3	5-10	2-5
7.31	Defense in Face Rebound	2	x	x	3	7.3, 11.3	7.31	-	2-5
7.32	Fouled Shooting	1	x	x	3	7.3	7.32	-	2-5

7.0 Pressure Shot

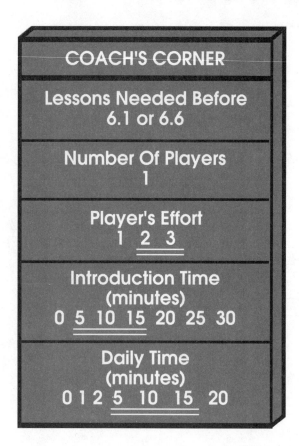

COACH'S CORNER

Lessons Needed Before
6.1 or 6.6

Number Of Players
1

Player's Effort
1 2 3

Introduction Time
(minutes)
0 5 10 15 20 25 30

Daily Time
(minutes)
0 1 2 5 10 15 20

Brief:

A player places a ball on the floor under the basket, then quickly picks it up and shoots.

Fundamental Notes

This lesson simulates shooting under game-type pressure. While grabbing the ball off the floor, a player positions the feet, as well as the body, to shoot. Demand that players do this part quickly, although the shot need not be taken too quickly. Try to excite players by yelling *hurry up* or *let's go* or anything that has the appropriate effect. This is an important part of the lesson. Game situations are a piece of cake after this because players will concentrate more readily and play better. I discourage coaches from doing this lesson with novices, because it may destroy their shooting technique.

Setup

One player starts under the basket facing any direction with a ball. The diagram on the next page shows several starting setups for this lesson. Other players line up 5 feet away. Use as many baskets as possible. Use 2 or 3 lines at each basket as needed.

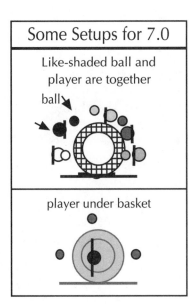

Some Setups for 7.0

Like-shaded ball and player are together

ball

player under basket

Directions for Players

1. Place the ball on the ground so that it does not roll. Stand up and only take one step back.

2. Quickly go for the ball, pick it up, and shoot. The shot need not be taken instantaneously.

• Harass players by yelling "go, go" or anything else. Managers can assist. This lesson is only effective if you attempt to excite players.

3. Rebound. Then place the ball on the floor right underneath the basket for the next player.

• Continue, as a group, or repeat this lesson 10 times as a solo lesson.

Troubleshooting

1. This is for more advanced players. It may destroy a novice player's developing shooting technique.

2. Pick up the ball and square up quickly. Shoot slowly.

3. Excite players. Try to make them shoot quickly and miss. If you are successful, and players shoot quickly, you must now instruct them not to respond to your harassment by shooting fast.

Use of Assistants

Yell and watch for walking.

Weekly Practice As needed

Extensions

7.01 Pressure Shot with D

A manager (or another player) harasses the shooter in Lesson 7.0. Harassing means that they bother the shooter, but do not interfere with the shot. Here are some harassing maneuvers:

1. Shout at the player.

2. Wave arms around.

3. Move body close to the shooter.

4. Wave arms to obstruct the vision of the shooter. Note that the shooter looks upward toward the basket, so the arms and hands of the defense must be slightly above the eyes, not at eye level. Caution your players and managers that moving the hands closer than six inches to the eyes is dangerous, as well as against the rules.

Setup for 7.1

The defense must place one hand in the offense's line of view.

line of view

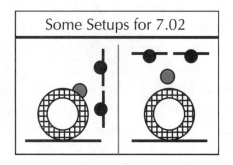

Some Setups for 7.02

7.02 Pressure Shot Two

Two players wrangle for the ball placed as in Lesson 7.0. They set up, side to side, with legs and elbows touching. The player that gets it is on offense; the other player is on defense. The job of the defense is to harass the shooter without fouling. Complete lessons 10.3 and 11.0 before doing this one.

7.1 Run Stop Shoot

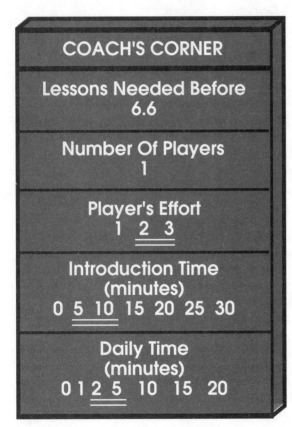

COACH'S CORNER

Lessons Needed Before
6.6

Number Of Players
1

Player's Effort
1 2 3

Introduction Time
(minutes)
0 5 10 15 20 25 30

Daily Time
(minutes)
0 1 2 5 10 15 20

Brief:

A player sprints to the basket for the ball, picks it up quickly, and then shoots slowly.

Fundamental Notes

When players sprint to the ball before shooting, they often shoot, and think they should shoot the ball, just as quickly as they ran for it. This results in many missed easy shots. This lesson slows players down to shoot, after a sprint to the basket.

Setup

Players line up at the top of the key facing the basket. Place the ball under the basket. Use as many baskets as possible.

Directions for Players

1. At the word "go" the first player in line sprints for the ball, stops and picks it up, then takes the shot in a relaxed, unhurried, way.

2. Get the rebound, place the ball on the floor near the basket, yell "go" to the next player, and then go back in line.

3. Continue.

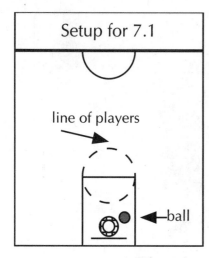

Setup for 7.1

line of players

ball

Troubleshooting

1. Yell "go, go" before the ball is picked up.

2. Yell "slow down" after players pick up the ball.

3. Ideally, you want players to slow down on their own, while you urge them to move faster.

Use of Assistants

They yell to urge players on and to slow players down.

Weekly Practice As needed

Extensions

7.11 Run Stop Shoot with D

The previous shooter in 7.1 waits under the basket to harass the next shooter before returning back in line.

7.12 Run Catch Shoot

Lessons Needed Before 7.1, 9.1, 10.0, 10.6

Setup

The cutting line is at midcourt. The passing line is 3 yards up court from one corner.

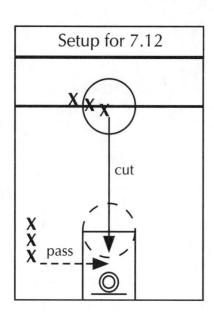

Setup for 7.12

cut

pass

Directions for Players

1. The passer throws the ball so that it meets the cutter at the basket. Follow the pass to the basket, harass the shooter and rebound the ball. Then, go to the cutting line.

2. The cutter sprints to the basket to catch the ball. Catch the ball, stop, square up, shoot, rebound, and then pass back to the passing line. Then follow the pass to the cutting line.

3. Stay out-of-bounds or out of the play area when returning to a line.

7.2 Catch Up

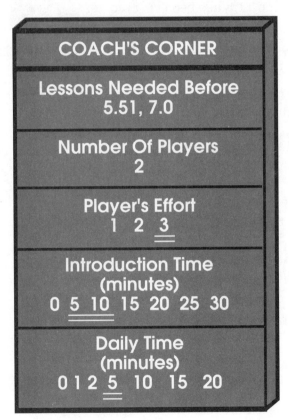

COACH'S CORNER
Lessons Needed Before 5.51, 7.0
Number Of Players 2
Player's Effort 1 2 <u>3</u>
Introduction Time (minutes) 0 <u>5</u> <u>10</u> 15 20 25 30
Daily Time (minutes) 0 1 2 <u>5</u> 10 15 20

Brief:

A defensive player sprints to catch the offensive player driving to the basket.

Fundamental Notes

The defense hustles to catch up to the offense, who starts one step ahead. The defense needs to sprint 2-3 yards past the offense before playing defense. Then, they force the offense to the opposite side of the basket. If the defense is beside, not ahead of the offense, then the only defensive tactic is harassment. Defense does not involve contact or charging into the offense. The offense dribbles to the basket with the defense at their heels (possibly in front). They slow down before shooting, even though the defense is breathing down their necks. If the defense catches up, the offense stops and shoots a short shot. Game situations are easier for the offense after this lesson. The defense learns not to commit flagrant and unnecessary fouls when they are not in position to stop the offense.

Setup

The team lines up in groups of two at midcourt. The offense starts near midcourt. The defense is 2

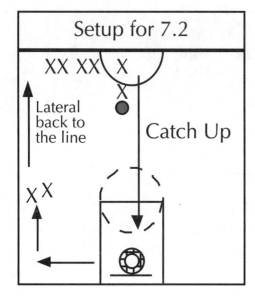

Setup for 7.2

XX XX X

Lateral back to the line

Catch Up

feet directly behind. One basket is used so you can observe the action.

Directions for Players

1. The offensive player has five seconds to take off to the basket, dribbling the ball.

2. After the offense takes one step, the defense takes off in pursuit.

3. The offense sprints to the basket and then shoots the layup slowly.

4. The defense needs to go 3 feet past the offense and then step in front to prevent the layup. If the defense is not able to go past the offense, then they can only harass from a distance.

5. Go for the rebound, whether or not the shot is missed.

• Box out, if Lesson 11.3 has been covered.

6. Every one goes back in line via the sideline, lateraling the ball back and forth. Next time up, offense and defense switch roles.

7. The next group starts as soon as the previous group rebounds and starts moving out-of-bounds.

Troubleshooting

1. The offensive player must slow down on the last step. If the offense is beaten by the defense, then the offense stops and takes a short shot rather than a layup.

2. The defense must not run right in front of the offense. To avoid blocking fouls and collisions, the defense must run at least 3 feet ahead of the offense, step in front, and then stop.

3. The defense may reach for the ball from the side, rather than exert the effort needed to run past the offense. Encourage the defense to catch up and, at least, get the rebound.

Use of Assistants

Keep track of missed layups.

Weekly Practice   Twice a week before the season

Extensions   None

7.3 Defense in Face Shoot

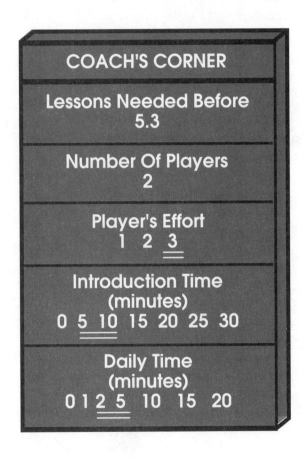

COACH'S CORNER

Lessons Needed Before
5.3

Number Of Players
2

Player's Effort
1 2 <u>3</u>

Introduction Time
(minutes)
0 <u>5</u> <u>10</u> 15 20 25 30

Daily Time
(minutes)
0 1 <u>2</u> <u>5</u> 10 15 20

Brief:

The offense shoots a one-foot shot (see 5.3) with the defense in their face.

Fundamental Notes

The offense shoots with up close defensive harassment. Initially, the defense neither touches the ball nor the offense. The defense must make an extra effort to maneuver out of the way of the shot, especially when the offense is a much shorter player.

Setup

One group sets up on each side of the basket, one foot away from the basket. Groups alternate shooting. Use as many baskets as possible.

Directions for Players

1. The offense takes a normal one-foot shot using the backboard.

2. The defense stands 3-4 inches away, directly between the shooter and the basket with hands outstretched harassing the shooter. One hand is in the face of the offense, no closer than six inches, impairing their vision of the basket. This hand can move. The other hand is outstretched

Defense in the Face

The defense must place one hand in the offense's line of view.

line of view

straight up to block the ball. This hand is stationary; do not slash forward at the ball. Yelling and talking about relatives enhances the harassment.

3. The defense does not block the shot. Move your hands at the last moment if necessary, so that the shot is not deflected.

4. Offense and defense switch roles after each shot.

Troubleshooting

1. The defense may jump with the offense.

2. The defense acts like it is going to block the shot, but does not.

3. One arm on defense is extended straight up.

4. No flailing of the arms.

Use of Assistants

1. Use assistants as defense.

2. Watch for flailing arms.

Weekly Practice As needed

Extensions

7.31 Defense in the Face Rebound

Both players go for the rebound after the shot in Lesson 7.3, whether or not the shot is made. Each player attempts to box out the other. Complete Lesson 11.3 first.

7.32 Fouled Shooting

Often fouls under the basket are not called. Players need to make these short shots, even if they are fouled; if the foul is called, so much the better. Let managers do the fouling, so players do not learn bad habits. The fouls are soft pushes on the shooting arm and shoulders. As the offense adjusts, the fouls can increase in intensity.

Section 8
Practice Shooting

L E S S O N #	NAME	P L A Y E R S	C O U R T	B A L L	E F F O R T	LESSONS BEFORE	L E S S O N #	INTRO TIME	DAILY TIME
8.0	**Practice Shooting**	-	x	x	-	-	**8.0**	-	-
8.1	Driving to the Basket	1	x	x	2	2.1, 5.51	8.1	10-15	5
8.11	Fake Then Drive	1	x	x	2	6.4, 8.1	8.11	5-10	5
8.12	Drive Opposite Foot	1	x	x	2	8.1	8.12	5-10	5
8.2	Full Court Shoot	1	x	x	2	4.24, 6.6, 8.1	8.2	5-10	5-15
8.3	Near to Far	1	x	x	2	5.62	8.3	-	5-15

8.0 Practice Shooting

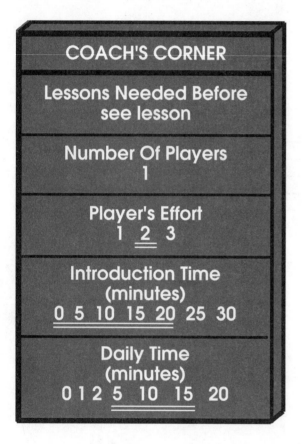

COACH'S CORNER

Lessons Needed Before
see lesson

Number Of Players
1

Player's Effort
1 <u>2</u> 3

Introduction Time
(minutes)
0 5 10 15 <u>20</u> 25 30

Daily Time
(minutes)
0 1 2 <u>5 10 15</u> 20

The practice shooting lessons give players a way to apply what has been previously taught. Only Lesson 8.11 presents a new move.

Lesson 8.1 involves driving to the basket; lessons 8.2 and 8.3 are the first ones that provide ways to practice shooting at a distance greater than one foot (finally!). Introduce these to one player or a small group in pre- or post-practice. Always suggest that they practice these lessons on their own. Players readily do this.

Novices should always shoot from 4 feet or less. Even experienced players need to spend most of their time on short shots and shooting technique.

8.1 Driving to the Basket

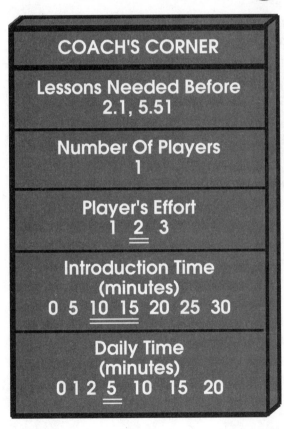

COACH'S CORNER

Lessons Needed Before
2.1, 5.51

Number Of Players
1

Player's Effort
1 <u>2</u> 3

Introduction Time (minutes)
0 5 <u>10 15</u> 20 25 30

Daily Time (minutes)
0 1 2 <u>5</u> 10 15 20

Brief:

From the foul line, a player drives left and right starting with either foot as the pivot.

Fundamental Notes

Players get their steps together for each drive like a hurdler getting steps together between hurdles. Righties always shoot off the left foot, and lefties off the right foot. For moments when righties use the left hand, they are considered lefties; lefties using the right hand are considered righties. Practice the four possible drives in this order (eight if you practice with both hands):

1. Left foot as pivot and go right.

2. Right foot as pivot and go right.

3. Left foot as pivot and go left.

4. Right foot as pivot and go left.

Do these at a moderate pace; no need to go fast. Encourage players to slow down if they encounter difficulty.

Setup

Each player starts at the foul line with a basketball.

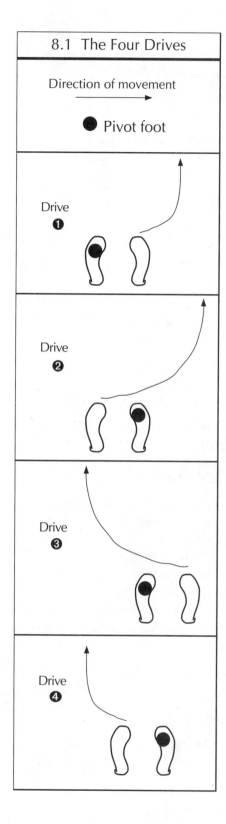

8.1 The Four Drives

Direction of movement

● Pivot foot

Drive ❶

Drive ❷

Drive ❸

Drive ❹

Directions for Players

1. There are four possible drives.

• Name the ones you plan to introduce.

2. Start from a half down position with the ball at waist height.

• Use these directions for each drive.

3. Push the ball low, far to the side of the drive.

4. The first step is a long one, so that you can get past the defense.

5. You must step around the defense, not through them, so move sideways before moving forward. Use a chair or another person as dummy defense to step around.

• Note that drives 2 and 3 involve a crossover step.

6. Dribble the ball with the first step.

7. Do not drag the pivot foot.

8. Right handers always shoot off the left foot on either side of the basket and left handers always off the right foot.

• Novice players take as many steps and dribbles as necessary to complete the move, whereas experienced taller players can limit the steps to between 2 and 4.

9. Use only 1 or 2 dribbles. Do each drive 10 times if it feels uncomfortable, five otherwise.

• Instruct experienced players to repeat this lesson with the opposite hand.

Troubleshooting

1. Watch each player if possible.

2. Instruct a manager to stand motionless as a defensive player; a chair works just as well. The driver steps around the defense on the first step. When past, reach around and out with the inside elbow to keep the defense behind.

3. Players tend to practice quickly, so slow them down. Speed naturally increases with repetition. Players need to move at a comfortable pace while practicing.

Use of Assistants

1. Stand stationary as a defensive player to step around.

2. Watch for a dragging pivot foot.

Weekly Practice   As needed

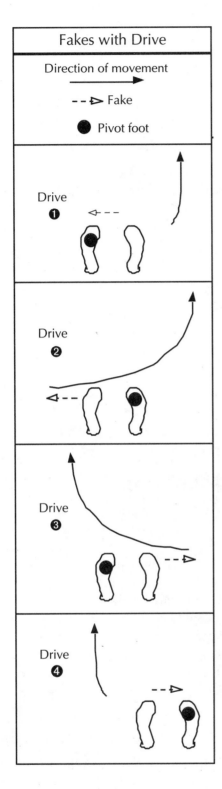

Fakes with Drive

Direction of movement

- - -▷ Fake

● Pivot foot

Drive ❶

Drive ❷

Drive ❸

Drive ❹

Extensions

8.11 Fake Then Drive

Players often fake before driving. The fake is executed slowly so that the defense has time to react. The defense can't react to a quick fake. Two types of fakes are used. Do each drive 5-10 times.

1. A **step fake** is used before the crossover step in drive 2 and 3 above. Slowly push the ball and the body away from the pivot foot as you step in that same direction. Bring the ball back, take the crossover step more quickly and drive to the basket. Do each drive 5 times.

2. Use a **ball body fake** for drives 1 and 4 above. Push the ball and turn the body in the opposite direction of the drive.

Then, step in the direction of the drive.

8.12 Drive Opposite Foot

This layup is taken off the wrong foot on purpose. The defense, especially tall players, are waiting for the offense to take one and a half steps before the layup. Because this opposite foot layup is shot one step sooner than expected, the defense is not ready to defend it; this is the main advantage of using it. The disadvantage is that practicing this layup undoes the fundamentals of novices and intermediate players. So, introduce this to experienced players only. Players drive to the basket like they do in Lesson 8.1. This layup is usually released one step farther from the basket than normal.

8.2 Full Court Shoot

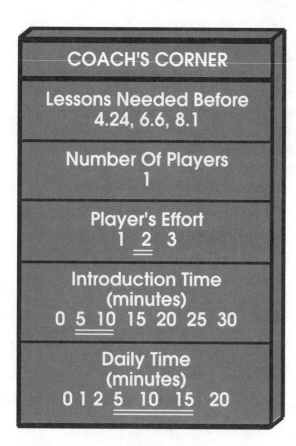

COACH'S CORNER
Lessons Needed Before 4.24, 6.6, 8.1
Number Of Players 1
Player's Effort 1 _2_ 3
Introduction Time (minutes) 0 _5_ _10_ 15 20 25 30
Daily Time (minutes) 0 1 2 _5_ _10_ _15_ 20

Brief:

A player dribbles back and forth from one basket to another, shooting at each basket.

Fundamental Notes

In a game, players shoot while out of breath after sprinting down court many times. Shots are not taken 10 in a row while players are nice, tidy, and rested. A good game shooter practices in a game-like way. This lesson gives players a way. Players run full court, shooting one shot at each basket. More time is spent dribbling in this lesson than shooting. So, do it right. Players switch hands on a regular basis. Try behind the back, between the legs dribbles often. This is also a good conditioning lesson if players run for at least 15 minutes.

Setup

A full court is needed. Other players, shooting at the baskets will not interfere.

Directions for Players

1. Run down one end and shoot, get the rebound, run down the other end and shoot. It is optional to follow it up if you miss. Pace yourself.

2. Switch the dribbling hand on a regular basis. Trick dribble between the legs and behind the back often. Keep the body and ball low, even though there is no defense.

3. Shoot from any distance, any place on the court: foul line, corners, top of the key, one-foot from the basket.

4. Run for 5-20 minutes.

Troubleshooting

1. This is particularly helpful to experienced players practicing long shots. Novice players work on short shots.

2. Novice players, in particular, need to dribble with the head up and the ball low to the ground. This is a dribbling lesson as well.

3. Warm up with another shooting lesson at the technique level before doing this. Work on the wrists, 3.0, and flick ups, 5.1, and other lessons like 5.2, 5.3, and 6.6.

8.3 Near to Far

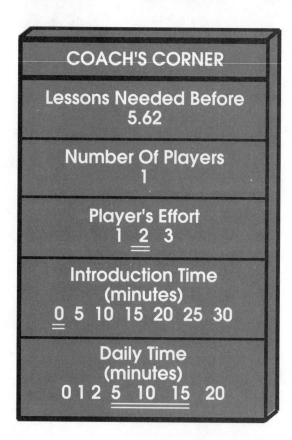

COACH'S CORNER

Lessons Needed Before
5.62

Number Of Players
1

Player's Effort
1 <u>2</u> 3

Introduction Time
(minutes)
<u>0</u> 5 10 15 20 25 30

Daily Time
(minutes)
0 1 2 <u>5 10 15</u> 20

Brief:

A player starts close to the basket and takes one step back after each shot made.

Fundamental Notes, Setup, Directions

This is a great way for novices, in particular, to increase their shooting range. Start shooting at the basket and step away one step at a time, after each shot made. This lesson allows players to find their current shooting range and then adjust to longer distances. Players must make adjustments for longer shots with the legs, rather than the arms. Players step backward only after a shot is made. If two shots in a row are missed, the player steps forward toward the basket.

This type of lesson is used by players at any level to improve foul shooting (5.62). It is also useful for improving shooting from the corner or three point range. Warm up with the wrists and other technique lessons.

Section 9
Passing

L E S S O N #	NAME	P L A Y E R S	C O U R T	B A L L	E F F O R T	LESSONS BEFORE	L E S S O N #	INTRO TIME	DAILY TIME
9.0	**Passing Technique**	1	-	-	1	2.0, 3.0	**9.0**	5	1-2
9.1	Overhead Short Pass	2	-	x	1-2	9.0, 10.0	9.1	5-10	5
9.11	Side Short Pass	2	-	x	1-2	9.1	9.11	-	5
9.12	Bounce Pass	2	-	x	1-2	9.1	9.12	-	5
9.13	Pivot Away Back Pass	2	-	x	1-2	2.1, 9.1	9.13	-	5
9.2	Baseball Pass	2	x	x	2	none	9.2	5-10	5
9.3	Baseball Pass Cut	2	x	x	2	7.1, 9.2	9.3	10-15	5-10
9.31	Midcourt Cut	2	x	x	2	9.3	9.31	-	5-10
9.32	Continuous Half Court	T	x	x	2	9.31	9.32	-	5-10
9.4	Continuous Full Court	T	x	x	2	7.2, 9.3	9.4	20-30	10-20
9.41	Full Court Pass	T	x	x	2	9.4	9.41	20-30	10-30
9.5	Pivot Pass & Communication	2	-	x	2	2.1, 9.1, 10.0	9.5	10-15	5-10
9.51	Pass Communication	2	-	x	2	9.5	9.51	10-15	5
9.52	Communication 2	2	-	x	2	9.51	9.52	-	5
9.6	D Overhead Side Pass	3	-	x	2-3	2.2, 9.51, 12.0	9.6	12-25	5-10
9.61	Defense Bounce Pass	3	-	x	2-3	9.6	9.61	-	5-10
9.7	Front Weave	3	x	x	2	5.8	9.7	15-20	10
9.8	Back Weave	T	-	x	2	1.1	9.8	10-15	5

9.0 Passing Technique

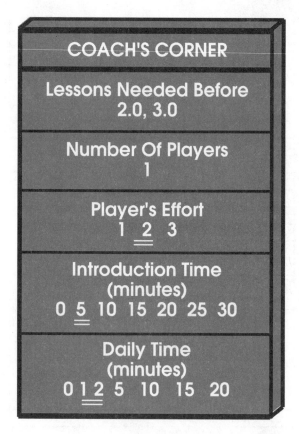

Brief:

Players flick wrists with their arms in several different passing positions.

Fundamental Notes

The key to passing, like the key to shooting and dribbling, is the wrist flick. Players flick passes with the arms outstretched from often awkward positions. The chest pass, a pass frequently taught, is infrequently used and then, only when the defense is loose. I do not practice it for this reason.

Setup

The players are in one row, 4 feet from each other.

Directions for Players

1. Start with your arms straight up overhead; elbows straight; palms facing forward.

2. Flick the wrists back and let them come forward naturally. Continue to do this while you follow the other directions.

3. Slowly move the arms to the right side keeping the elbows straight. The palms face forward. As the arms move down, bend the legs as well. Bend

Moving Through the Positions

up   half   full
      down   down

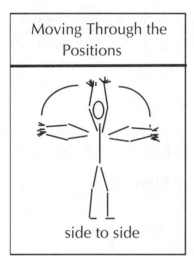

Moving Through the Positions

side to side

through the half down position. In the full down position the hands are inches from the ground.

4. Continue flicking the wrists as you move your arms. Move the arms back to the original position overhead. Then, move the arms to the left side as you bend the legs to the full down position.

•Repeat steps 3 and 4 several times.

Troubleshooting

1. Make sure that the palms are always facing forward.

2. The wrists need to be flicked backward, not forward.

3. The fingers need to be spread apart, not closed, in a claw-like position.

4. Watch players closely. It is difficult to flick the wrists on the sides as you bend and stretch. Throwing passes is even more difficult.

Use of Assistants

Assistants watch for bent elbows and improper flicking.

Weekly Practice   Everyday

9.1 Overhead Short Pass

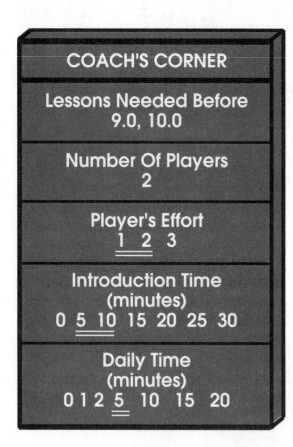

COACH'S CORNER

Lessons Needed Before
9.0, 10.0

Number Of Players
2

Player's Effort
1 2 3

Introduction Time
(minutes)
0 5 10 15 20 25 30

Daily Time
(minutes)
0 1 2 5 10 15 20

Brief:
Players flick short, two-handed overhead passes back and forth.

Fundamental Notes

Wrist motion is a key to passing. Telegraphing passes results when the arms are used without the wrists. Players must fully extend their arms to have the longest possible reach around the defense. Players also must look nearly straight ahead to cloak the direction of the pass, since good defense reads the eyes. Looking away or down often gives the pass direction away.

Setup

Use two rows, 3-6 feet apart, facing each other. The players are lined up opposite in groups of two. Each group has a ball.

Directions for Players

•Demonstrate an effective wrist pass that is not telegraphed like this: line the players up in one straight line, face them with the ball overhead in the passing position, look one way, and quickly flick the ball another way. A hard pass is okay. Do this several times. Ask players if they know it is coming. Show some telegraphed passes. These

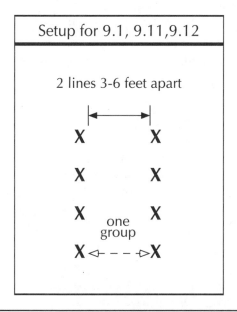

Setup for 9.1, 9.11, 9.12

2 lines 3-6 feet apart

X   X

X   X

X   one   X
      group

X ◁ – – – ▷ X

Side Pass Positions

Throw 5 passes each way.

● pivot foot

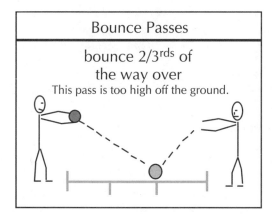

Bounce Passes

bounce 2/3rds of
the way over
This pass is too high off the ground.

have much arm movement. Telegraphers also often look where the ball is going. The defense can see this as well. So, tell players not to look in the direction of the pass or the opposite direction either. They need to act like they are not looking in any particular direction. This is another key to passing. (Good passers often look in one direction on purpose as a fake.) Effective passers do these things so that the defense does not have a chance to react.

1. Start with the ball overhead, elbows straight, hands clawed. Only the fingertips touch the ball.

2. Bend the wrists back as far as possible. As a fake, flick without passing. Then, flick the ball using the wrists without the arms.

3. Continue flicking the ball back and forth.

• Instruct players to switch the pivot foot after 2-3 minutes.

• As wrists become stronger, players move apart and throw harder passes.

Troubleshooting

1. Do not use the arms.

2. Give verbal instructions to coordinate novice groups: ball overhead, elbows straight, wrists back, flick.

3. Notice if players look directly where they pass. Not looking in any particular direction is a difficult skill to teach.

4. Expect weak passes, especially from novices.

Use of Assistants None

Weekly Practice Everyday

Extensions

9.11 Side Short Pass

1. Players set up in groups of two facing each other just as in Lesson 9.1.

2. Start with the left foot as pivot foot. Position the arms directly to the right side with the elbows as straight as possible.

3. Bend with the legs to the half down position. The back is nearly straight. This is an awkward position. It is even more difficult from the opposite side–left side for righties, right side for lefties.

Pivot Away Back Pass
❶ pivot backward 180°
❷ stretch to side
❸ pass

Right Foot Pivot

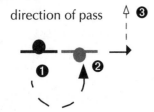
direction of pass

Left Foot Pivot

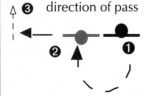
direction of pass

Fake with Back Pass
❶ step fake
❷ pivot backward 180°
❸ stretch to side
❹ pass

Right Foot Pivot

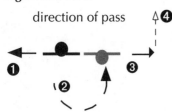
direction of pass

Left Foot Pivot

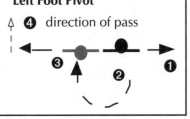
direction of pass

•Encourage older players to pass with the opposite hand in these positions.

4. Flick five passes from the right side and then five from the left.

5. Switch pivot feet and repeat.

9.12 Bounce Pass

Demonstrate the bounce pass as a side bounce pass. (There is no need to practice the chest bounce pass.) This pass bounces 2/3 of the way, not half way, to the catcher. Make or point out a mark on the floor where the pass should bounce. Emphasize that the elbows stay straight; just flick with the wrist. This is more difficult than the other passing lessons. The body is in the half down position, so the ball can be released closer to the floor. Throw five passes to each side. Start with the left foot as pivot foot, then switch.

9.13 Pivot Away Back Pass

If the defense is right on a player, it is often advantageous to pivot away, a half turn, before passing. This relieves the defensive pressure for an instant, but it also puts players with their backs in the direction of the pass. To pass they must twist the arms and head around and then extend the arms to the side. This is a difficult pass. More experienced players can use a step fake, Lesson 6.3, before pivoting.

Directions for Players

1. Set up to flick short passes as you did in the previous lessons. Use the side pass first. Start with the left foot as pivot.

2. The passer starts out facing the catcher. Pivot backward (or forward) a half turn, 180 degrees, so that your back is toward the catcher.

3. Stretch your arms to the side away from the pivot foot. This puts you in a position as far as possible from the defense.

4. Twist both your head and arms around. Make sure that your palms are also facing the catcher. Flick a pass. This is very difficult.

•Flick five passes this way and then repeat steps 1-4 using the right foot as pivot.

•Repeat this entire lesson using the bounce pass.

9.2 Baseball Pass

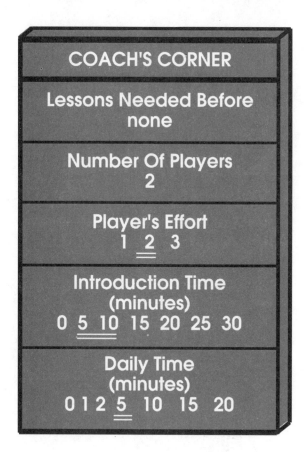

COACH'S CORNER

Lessons Needed Before
none

Number Of Players
2

Player's Effort
1 _2_ 3

**Introduction Time
(minutes)**
0 _5_ _10_ 15 20 25 30

**Daily Time
(minutes)**
0 1 2 _5_ 10 15 20

Brief:

Players stand on opposite sidelines firing one-handed baseball passes back and forth. Novices stand much closer initially.

Fundamental Notes

The one-handed baseball pass is more important than you think. It is the best way, and only way for novices, to throw a long pass. Long two-handed passes require more strength.

Setup

Players line up in groups of two, spread out as far apart as possible, facing each other on opposite sidelines.

Directions for Players

1. Throw a one-armed pass to your partner on the other side of the court. Try not to maim any of your teammates with errant passes.

•Initially don't worry about walking with novices.

•Eventually, instruct players to alternate the pivot foot.

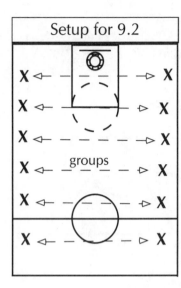

Setup for 9.2

groups

Troubleshooting

1. Initially, novices will not watch their pivot foot. This is okay.

2. At first novices have difficulty controlling the pass. Duck! Bring the lines of players closer together if necessary. Move the lines farther apart as the players' control improves.

Use of Assistants

Watch for walking, catch errant passes, retrieve loose balls.

Weekly Practice As needed

Extensions None

9.3 Baseball Pass Cut

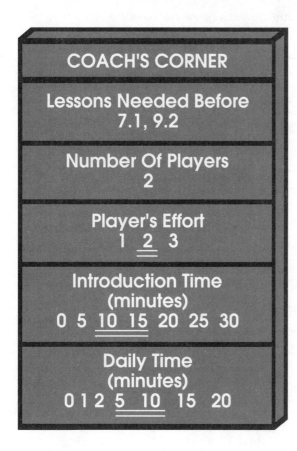

COACH'S CORNER
Lessons Needed Before 7.1, 9.2
Number Of Players 2
Player's Effort 1 <u>2</u> 3
Introduction Time (minutes) 0 5 <u>10</u> 15 20 25 30
Daily Time (minutes) 0 1 2 <u>5</u> <u>10</u> 15 20

Brief:

One player throws a half court baseball pass to another player cutting to the basket.

Fundamental Notes

This baseball pass lesson involves cutting, catching, communication, dribbling, and shooting as well. Use it as part of a continuous motion lesson. Even though many passes will go astray, it is a great lesson for youngsters.

Setup

There are two lines: the passing line is located at the midcourt center jump circle; the cutting line initially is on the right sideline, halfway between the end and midcourt lines. Use 2 or more basketballs.

Directions for Players

1. As soon as the passer controls the ball, make eye contact with the cutter. This signals the cut.

2. The cutter runs down the sideline. A few yards before the endline, fake one step outside, and then cut inward toward the basket. This is like the move an end on a football team makes.

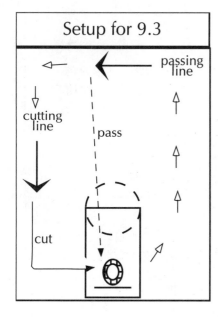

Setup for 9.3

passing line

cutting line

pass

cut

3. Time the pass so that the cutter and the ball meet at the basket. Go to the cutting line after the pass.

4. At the basket, catch the ball and then come to a complete stop. Take a one-foot shot, not a layup.

5. Rebound your shot. Immediately move to the left sideline, out of the way of the next cutter. Dribble to the passing line. Give the ball to the next passer.

6. Start the next cut when (not after) the previous group rebounds the ball.

•After 5 minutes switch the cutting line to the left side of the basket. The cutter runs down the left sideline and then cuts to the basket.

Troubleshooting

1. The pass and the cutter meet at the basket.

2. After a quick cut, a one-foot shot is taken without hurry.

3. After rebounding, players must move out of the way quickly.

4. Players make eye contact before the cut. This is not a 10-minute look. This contact should take place immediately after the rebound.

Use of Assistants

1. Several managers stationed behind the basket gather errant passes.

2. One manager reminds players to quickly move out of the way immediately after rebounding.

Weekly Practice As needed

Extensions

9.31 Midcourt Cut

The starting positions in Lesson 9.3 are changed, and no shot is taken. This can be used in place of Lesson 9.3 or, more importantly, it can be used with Lesson 9.3 for the continuous motion lesson that follows.

Setup

1. The passing line is 3 yards to the left of the basket.

2. The cutting line is on the left sideline halfway to mid-court.

Directions

1. After making eye contact with the passer, the cutter runs to midcourt, steps outside, and then cuts inside to the center

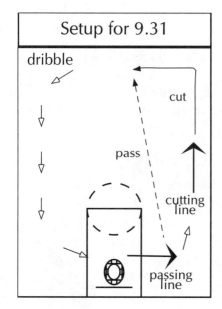

Setup for 9.31

dribble

cut

pass

cutting line

passing line

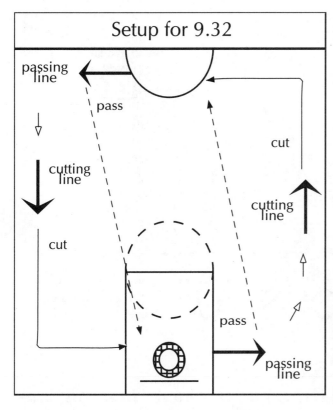

Setup for 9.32

passing line

pass

cutting line

cut

pass

cut

cutting line

passing line

cutting line

pass

passing line

of the court.

2. After catching the pass, dribble back to the passing line via the right sideline.

3. The passer throws the pass so that the cutter and the ball meet two yards after the cut inward. Then, go to the cutting line.

•Move the passing and cutting lines to the right side of the court after five minutes.

9.32 Continuous Half Court

This lesson combines lessons 9.3 and 9.31 to make a worthwhile continuous motion lesson. Passing, cutting, and shooting skills are involved.

Setup

Use the initial setups for lessons 9.3 and 9.31. There are two cutting and two passing lines. Move the passing line at midcourt 2-3 yards closer to the right sideline, so that cutters and passers are farther apart.

Directions for Players

•Here are the combined directions starting after the shot.

1. After rebounding, dribble toward the left sideline to the passing line. Make eye contact with the cutter on the left side, and then throw a pass that meets the cutter two steps after cutting to the center of the court.

2. Advance to the left side cutting line. Make eye contact with the passer and cut. Catch the pass two steps after cutting to the center of the court. Dribble toward the right sideline to the other passing line.

3. Make eye contact with the cutter on the right side. The pass meets the cutter at the basket.

4. The cutter stops, takes a one-foot shot, rebounds, and then dribbles to the left sideline passing line.

•After 5-10 minutes, instruct the players to rotate in the other direction around the gym. The left side cutters cut to the basket. The right side cutters run to midcourt. Rotate the passing lines toward the opposite sideline.

•Initially, do this lesson without any dribbling, using the rule that no ball hits the ground.

•Do this lesson using the full court as well. See the next lesson.

9.4 Continuous Full Court

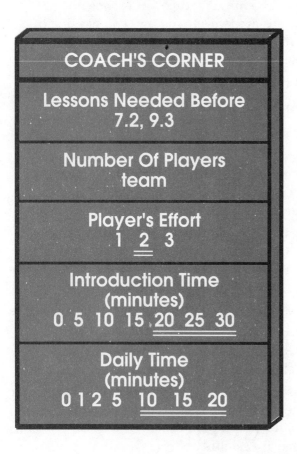

COACH'S CORNER

Lessons Needed Before
7.2, 9.3

Number Of Players
team

Player's Effort
1 <u>2</u> 3

Introduction Time
(minutes)
0 5 10 15 <u>20</u> <u>25</u> <u>30</u>

Daily Time
(minutes)
0 1 2 5 <u>10</u> <u>15</u> <u>20</u>

Brief:

Using the full court in a continuous motion lesson, half court baseball passes are thrown to players cutting to the basket.

Fundamental Notes

This baseball pass lesson involves cutting, catching, communication, and shooting as well. Use it as part of a conditioning lesson. Much is going on, so don't try it without completing lessons 9.3 to 9.32. The next lesson, 9.41, is simpler because it eliminates many of the lines.

Setup

The setup is similar to 9.32 but doubled.

1. There are four cutting lines. Each is located on the sideline midway between the endline and the midcourt line. See the diagram.

2. The players initially move counter clockwise around the court, from the right side of the basket to the left side.

3. The four passing lines are located on sidelines where they meet with other lines. Two are at the intersection of the midcourt line on the left and right side of the court. The other two are opposite

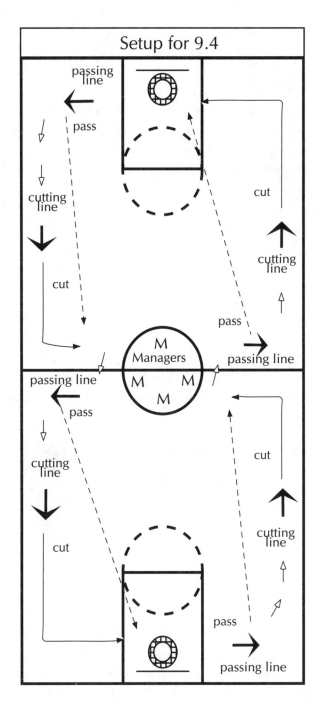

Setup for 9.4

passing line

pass

cutting line

cut

cut

cutting line

pass

M Managers M M M

passing line

passing line

pass

cutting line

cut

cut

cutting line

pass

passing line

each other at the corners to the left of the basket. (Move these to the right side corners when players move in the other direction, clockwise, around the court.) See diagrams.

Directions for Players

1. We will follow one player around the court starting with the passing position at midcourt. The directions are the same for players on either side. As soon as you control the ball, dribble to the sidelines while attempting to make eye contact with the cutter. This signals the cut.

2. Time the pass so that it meets the cutter at the basket.

3. Go to the cutting position halfway down the sideline and wait till the passer makes eye contact.

4. Run toward the endline. A few yards before the endline, step outside before cutting inward toward the basket.

5. At the basket, catch the ball, come to a complete stop, and then take a one-foot shot, not a layup.

6. Rebound your shot. Dribble toward the sidelines while looking to make eye contact with the next cutter.

7. Pass the ball so that it meets the cutter near the midcourt line, two steps in from the sideline.

8. Go to the next cutting line on the sideline, halfway between midcourt and the endline.

9. After making eye contact with the passer, cut to the midcourt line and then inward two steps to catch the ball.

10. Now you have made a half circuit. The other half is the same.

• Walk through it first.

• Repeat sequence, rotating in the other direction.

Troubleshooting

1. The cut from the midcourt line is 2-3 steps inward, so that collisions are avoided with players on the other side.

2. Players must operate with their heads up to avoid collisions. Players should look, not only to make eye contact and pass, but also to avoid cutting into or passing into another player.

3. Players need not go at full speed during this lesson, since it is part of a 30-minute conditioning lesson.

4. With novices, you will need a few days of practice to execute this properly. Teach each cut and pass separately as in the preceding lessons.

5. Players step fake outward before cutting toward the center of the court for the ball.

6. Initially, players are not aware enough of the positions of other players. This lesson is action packed. Cutters must recognize open spaces just like in a game, and passers need to make accurate passes that meet the cutter at a point. Otherwise, there will be foul ups.

Use of Assistants

Station at least two managers facing opposite directions at dead center midcourt to prevent any collisions and to catch errant passes.

Weekly Practice Several days in a row initially.

Then, as needed.

Extensions

9.41 Full Court Pass

This is the same as Lesson 9.4, except that the passes are full court in length.

Setup

This simplifies the set up in Lesson 9.4 because 4 lines are removed. What is left are two passing lines at the corners opposite each other (move these lines 2-6 yards down court) and two cutting lines near midcourt on the sidelines.

Directions

•These directions follow one player through this lesson starting at the shooting position at the basket.

1. Catch the ball, stop, and shoot a one-foot shot. Rebound and move to the left side of the court.

2. While dribbling to the left sideline and slightly up court, make eye contact with the cutter.

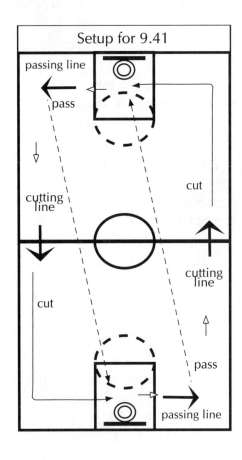

Setup for 9.41

3. Time the pass so that the cutter catches the ball at the basket.

4. Go to the cutting line at midcourt along the sideline. Make eye contact with the passer. Cut down the sideline. Three yards from the endline fake a step outward and cut inward toward the basket.

5. Catch the ball at the basket and stop. You are back in the starting position.

•Repeat this lesson, moving around the court in the opposite direction.

Time to introduce 20-30 minutes

Daily Time 10-30 minutes

9.5 Pivot Pass & Communication

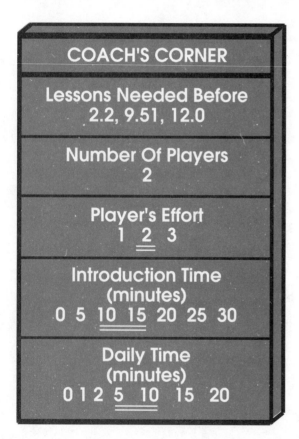

Brief:

Players catch, pivot, and then pass in groups of two. In the extensions, passer and catcher communicate before passing.

Fundamental Notes

Pivoting to pass is probably the most commonly used move in basketball. Players execute it nearly every time they take possession of the ball. Note that you need to teach the basic catching technique from Lesson 10.0 first. Passing and communication go hand-in-hand. Not only do players expect other players to pass or cut at the right moment to the right spot, but they actually communicate these ideas in non-obvious ways. Experienced players do this at an unconscious level; not so with novices. In Lesson 9.51 the catcher communicates where they want the pass. In Lesson 9.52 the passer communicates to the catcher where the ball will be thrown.

Setup

Use two lines facing each other, 4-6 yards apart. The players in one line face their partners in the other.

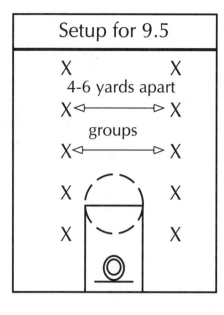

Setup for 9.5

X   X

4-6 yards apart

X ⟷ X

groups

X ⟷ X

X   X

X   X

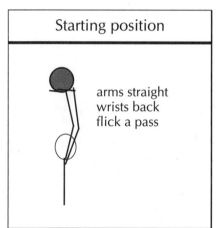

Starting position

arms straight
wrists back
flick a pass

Directions for Players

1. Start with the ball in the overhead position, elbows straight, wrists bent back as far as possible. The left foot is the pivot foot.

2. Flick an overhead pass.

3. Catch the ball using the left foot as the pivot foot. Do not catch the ball and then switch pivot feet. Pivot around once with the ball overhead before passing.

4. After each catch and pass, alternate the pivot foot.

• Switch the type of pass thrown every 1-2 minutes. Start with the overhead pass, then do the side and bounce passes.

Troubleshooting

1. Players flick passes without using the arms.

2. Watch for walking. Players prepare to catch the ball on the proper pivot foot.

3. Players tend to use the same, a favorite, pivot foot, so remind them to switch.

Use of Assistants

Watch for walking, moving arms, and bent elbows.

Weekly Practice   Everyday

Extensions

9.51 Pass Communication

Players communicate many ways before making the pass. One way involves the catcher pointing with the hands where they want the ball thrown. This resembles a baseball catcher making a pocket for the pitcher to aim at. The passer, as well, can point with hands or ball. Another way for a catcher or passer to communicate involves pointing with the head, eyes, or the nose. Besides left and right, and high and low, the ball can be passed forward or toward the back. If the signals are obvious at first, don't worry. You want players to get the idea. In little time they will learn how to be very tricky.

Directions

The catcher communicates to the passer where to pass in Lesson 9.51. To avoid collisions, make sure the pass is only one yard in the communicated direction. Move the groups farther apart from their positions in Lesson 9.5, so there is less chance of interference among the groups.

1. The catcher communicates to the passer where to throw the ball.

2. Use the hands for one minute before instructing players to use the other methods, including the nose and eyes. Change the type of communication each minute.

3. Vary the type of pass and pivot foot used to pass as well. Allow players to catch the ball on either foot.

9.52 Communication 2

The passer does the directing in this lesson. Two methods are used:

1. Point with the hand or the ball in the direction of the pass.

2. Point with the head, eyes, or the nose.

9.6 D Overhead Side Pass

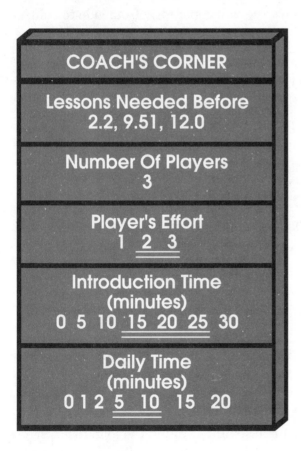

COACH'S CORNER

Lessons Needed Before
2.2, 9.51, 12.0

Number Of Players
3

Player's Effort
1 <u>2</u> 3

Introduction Time
(minutes)
0 5 10 <u>15 20 25</u> 30

Daily Time
(minutes)
0 1 2 <u>5 10</u> 15 20

Brief:
Players make an overhead or side pass with defense covering them.

Fundamental Notes

Passing with the defense directly in your face is difficult. However, players pass like this in a game. So, passing must be practiced this way, after the basic technique is learned. The defense covers the passer, not the catcher. The catcher and passer communicate as they did in Lesson 9.51. Since the defense moves directly from one passer to the other, this is a hustle lesson as well.

Setup

The setup is the same as the previous lesson with the addition of the defensive player on the passer. The passer and the catcher are 3-6 yards apart. Move the groups as far apart as possible.

Directions for Players

1. The defensive position is one foot from the passer. Aggressively attempt to block the pass and the vision of the passer. Slowly count out loud to five to start and end play.

2. The passer has five seconds to get the pass off.

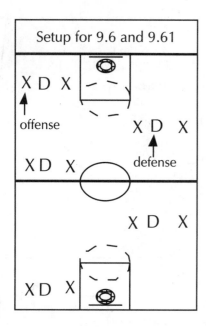

Setup for 9.6 and 9.61

X D X

offense

X D X

X D X   defense

X D X

X D X

Use either an overhead or side pass, no bounce passes. Alternate the pivot foot.

3. The catcher communicates to the passer where to pass the ball. After catching the ball, pivot around once and then pass. Don't wait for the defense.

4. The defense immediately runs to the other passer and starts counting again. This looks a little like monkey-in-the-middle.

5. Offense and defense switch on my cue, or after about 1 minute.

6. Tips for the passer:

a. Do not wait for the defense.

b. Pivot with the ball in a position to pass.

c. Move the ball constantly from side to side.

d. Use ball and step fakes (see 6.3).

e. Move the ball and your arms beyond the body and hands of the defense before you let the ball go. This prevents the defense from stopping the pass.

f. Fake high and then push the ball under the outstretched arm of the defense.

Troubleshooting

1. Players have great difficulty with this lesson because they must apply many skills.

2. The defense does not flail their arms at the ball.

3. Players tend to use the same pivot foot each time. This severely hampers their ability to execute skills in a game. Make sure players alternate or switch every minute.

Use of Assistants

Position assistants around the gym to catch stray passes, to watch for walking, and to keep the groups a safe distance apart.

Weekly Practice   As needed

Overhead Side Pass in Steps

Ball and step fake to either side then push the ball past the defense under the arm pits.

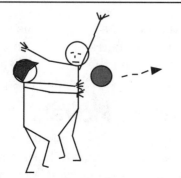

Release the ball when it is past the body and arm of the defense.

Extensions

9.61 Defense Bounce Pass

Players use a bounce pass in Lesson 9.6. Fake high, and then push the ball both down and past the outstretched hands and body of the defense. Releasing the ball beyond the defense makes it difficult for the defense to interfere with the pass. Make sure the pass bounces two-thirds of the way to the catcher.

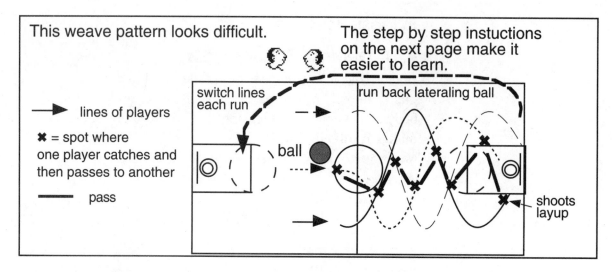

This weave pattern looks difficult.

The step by step instuctions on the next page make it easier to learn.

→ lines of players

✖ = spot where one player catches and then passes to another

—— pass

switch lines each run

ball

run back lateraling ball

shoots layup

9.7 Front Weave

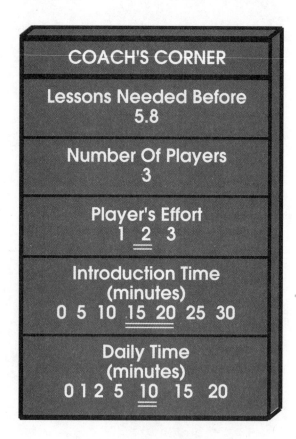

COACH'S CORNER

Lessons Needed Before
5.8

Number Of Players
3

Player's Effort
1 <u>2</u> 3

Introduction Time (minutes)
0 5 10 <u>15 20</u> 25 30

Daily Time (minutes)
0 1 2 5 <u>10</u> 15 20

Brief:

Three players weave the ball from midcourt to the basket.

Fundamental Notes

This super lesson improves passing, cutting, and especially timing skills. Players also enjoy it and get a great workout. Novices may need several days to learn this lesson. You may find it easier to teach this lesson using two players, instead of three. Use it also as a pregame warm-up.

Setup

Players start at midcourt in three lines. One line is in the center and the others are five yards to either side. The first player in each line is in the same group. The second in each line form a second group and so on. Each player in the center line has a ball.

Directions for Players

1. Each player runs a zigzag pattern across the court from the left, to the right, and back again, until the basket is reached. The player with the ball at the basket shoots the layup. Let's walk through it first. (See the diagrams.)

2. Start the weave with the ball in the center.

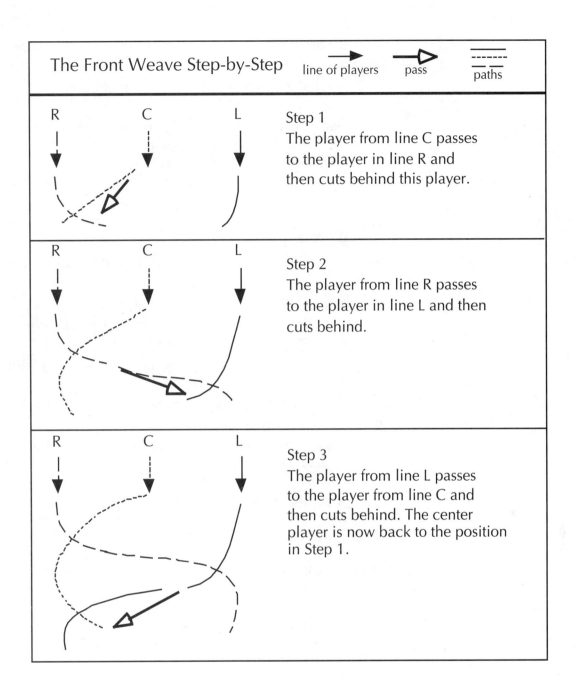

The Front Weave Step-by-Step   line of players   pass   paths

Step 1
The player from line C passes to the player in line R and then cuts behind this player.

Step 2
The player from line R passes to the player in line L and then cuts behind.

Step 3
The player from line L passes to the player from line C and then cuts behind. The center player is now back to the position in Step 1.

• Instruct the player on the right.

3. Cut three yards in front of the player with the ball to receive a pass. Catch the ball slightly to your side of center.

4. Take 2-3 steps after catching the ball, before passing to the player from the left side, three yards ahead of you.

• Tell the player on the left side where to move.

5. After passing, continue to move diagonally toward the side-line. Turn when 3-5 yards left of center and cut toward the center ball again. Cut in front of the player with the ball and receive a pass, just to the left of the center.

6. Continue this zigzag pattern until you reach the basket.

7. Shoot, rebound, run down the sidelines, and reposition yourself in different lines.

8. The second group starts just as the previous group shoots the layup.

9. If a bad pass is thrown, continue running. The player closest to the ball sprints after it and then passes to a teammate, who is probably near the basket by this time.

•When players are more expert, direct them to use bounce passes.

Troubleshooting

1. It is a good idea to demonstrate this lesson at full speed with players who know how to do it.

2. Walk through this initially with your players.

3. Players run 3-5 yards toward the sidelines after the pass, and then turn and cut to the center for the ball.

4. Players need to hustle down the sidelines back to a different line position (left, center, or right).

5. Inform novices that this may take several days to learn, so they will not be disappointed.

6. Always cut diagonally in front of the player with the ball.

7. Don't worry about *walking* initially.

Use of Assistants None

Weekly Practice As needed

Extensions None

9.8 Back Weave

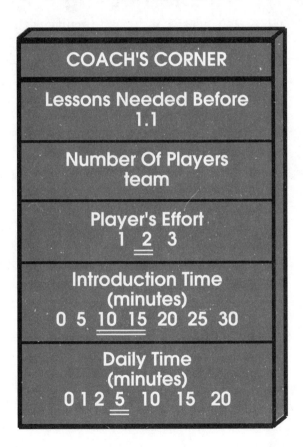

Brief:

Players weave the ball back and forth between two lines.

Fundamental Notes

This is the safe way to hand off the ball, if the defense is playing a tight person-to-person defense. Players without the ball cut behind (away from the basket) the player with the ball. Both before and after lateraling, the passer picks the defense on the catcher. This is for more experienced players.

Setup

Use two lines, one on either side of the court. Each starts 5 yards up court from the corner. A player with the ball stands at the top of the key facing the left sideline.

Directions for Players

1. A cutter from the left side runs directly toward the ball. When 1-3 feet away, grab the lateral and move slightly toward midcourt, avoiding a collision with the passer. It is okay to bump into, or rub shoulders with, the passer.

2. The player giving up the ball pivots to block the path of the defensive player on the catcher by

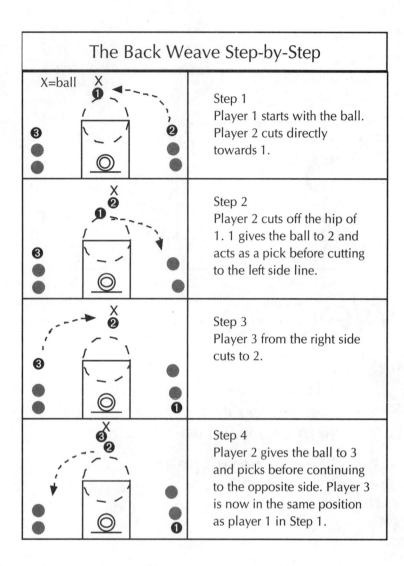

The Back Weave Step-by-Step	
X=ball	**Step 1** Player 1 starts with the ball. Player 2 cuts directly towards 1.
	Step 2 Player 2 cuts off the hip of 1. 1 gives the ball to 2 and acts as a pick before cutting to the left side line.
	Step 3 Player 3 from the right side cuts to 2.
	Step 4 Player 2 gives the ball to 3 and picks before continuing to the opposite side. Player 3 is now in the same position as player 1 in Step 1.

turning their back partially to the cutter. Be careful not to step into the defense. You want this defensive player to *wipe off on you* or step away from the ball. You are a pick or screen with the ball.

3. After giving up the ball, hesitate for two seconds as a pick, then go to the line on the left side.

4. A player from the opposite side cuts to the ball and the weaving is continued.

5. To keep the weave moving, cut to the ball just before the previous lateral is made.

Troubleshooting

1. Novices will have difficulty with the timing.

Use of Assistants
Initially, managers can act as the defense. After teaching Lesson 13.0, Picking 1-2, use players on offense and defense.

Weekly Practice As needed

Extensions None

Section 10
Catching and Cutting

L E S S O N #	NAME	P L A Y E R S	C O U R T	B A L L	E F F O R T	LESSONS BEFORE	L E S S O N #	INTRO TIME	DAILY TIME
10.0	**Catch Cut Technique**	1+	-	x	1	1.0, 9.0	**10.0**	10-20	5-10
10.01	Catching Technique 2	2	-	x	1	10.0	10.01	-	5-10
10.1	Go Fetch It	1+	-	x	1-2	10.0	10.1	5-20	2-10
10.11	Coming to the Ball	1+	-	x	1-2	10.1	10.11	5-10	5-10
10.2	Jump to Ball	2	-	x	1-2	10.0	10.2	10-15	5-10
10.3	Loose Ball Lesson	2	-	x	3	1.1, 11.2	10.3	5-10	3-5
10.31	Go for It	2+	-	x	3	10.3	10.31	-	3-5
10.4	Catching Bad Passes	1+	-	x	2	10.2	10.4	3-8	2-5
10.5	Cut Fake Technique	1	-	-	1	none	10.5	10-20	5-15
10.51	Cutting Off a Pick	3	-	-	1	10.5	10.51	10-20	5-15
10.6	Cut to the Ball	2	-	x	2	10.2, 10.5	10.6	10-20	5-15
10.61	Cut Communication	2	x	x	2	10.6	10.61	10-20	5-15
10.7	Three Second Lesson	1	x	-	1	10.2, 10.5	10.7	3-6	3-4
10.71	Cut into Lane	2	x	x	2	10.2	10.71	10-15	5-10
10.8	Overplay the Catcher	2	x	x	3	9.5, 10.6, 12.5	10.8	10-20	5-20
10.81	Front the Catcher	3	x	x	3	9.5, 10.6, 12.4	10.81	10-20	5-20
10.82	D on Catcher, Cut	3	x	x	3	10.8	10.82	-	5-15
10.9	D Pass, Overplay Catch	4	x	x	3	9.6, 10.82	10.9	5-20	5-15
10.91	D Passer, Front Catch	4	x	x	3	9.6, 10.81	10.91	5-10	5-15
10.92	D on Catcher,PasserCut	4	x	x	3	10.82-10.91	10.92	5-20	5-15

10.0 Catch Cut Technique

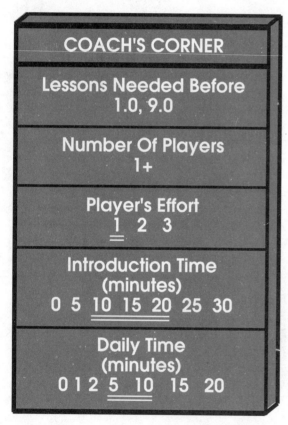

COACH'S CORNER

Lessons Needed Before
1.0, 9.0

Number Of Players
1+

Player's Effort
1 2 3

Introduction Time
(minutes)
0 5 10 15 20 25 30

Daily Time
(minutes)
0 1 2 5 10 15 20

Brief:
With outstretched arms and hands, players jump toward the ball just before it reaches them.

Fundamental Notes

Lessons 10.0 and 10.1, as well as many other lessons in this section, are for novices. However, catching a ball is not as simple as it looks. You jump just before catching the ball so that you can rearrange your feet to land balanced without walking. The position of the hands and arms are important as well. Spread the fingers apart to make the hand claw-like. Fully outstretch the arms in the direction of the pass. Most importantly, you need to be moving forward full steam until after the catch. Novices will have difficulty. In this lesson you work one-on-one with them.

Setup

Players line up, one behind the other, five feet away from you.

Directions for Players

1. Stand with the right foot forward, hands clawed, and arms outstretched.

2. In this position, jump just before you catch

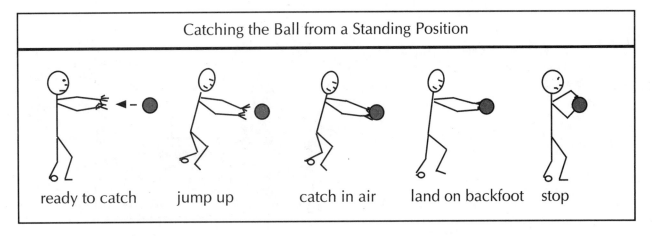

Catching the Ball from a Standing Position

ready to catch   jump up   catch in air   land on backfoot   stop

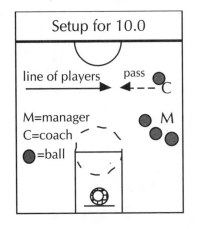

Setup for 10.0

line of players   pass   C

M=manager   M
C=coach
● =ball

the ball. Catch the ball while in the air. Land on the back foot, the pivot foot, first.

• When players run to the ball they land on the front foot.

3. The jump is just high enough to arrange or rearrange your feet after you catch the ball.

4. Pass the ball back to me and go to the end of the line.

• Repeat twice, then switch the pivot foot to the right foot. In this case the left foot is forward.

Troubleshooting

1. The hands are clawed in a ready position to catch the ball. The arms are fully extended.

2. The jump should take place when the ball is almost in the hands.

3. Expect novices to have difficulty initially. After two or three practices, they will catch the ball more naturally.

Use of Assistants

An assistant can run another passing line. Players can switch back and forth between lines. Instruct players having difficulty to remain in your line.

Weekly Practice   Everyday

Extensions

10.01 Catching Technique 2

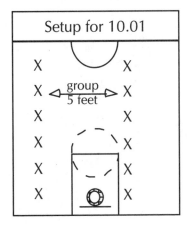

Setup for 10.01

X   X
X   group   X
X   5 feet   X
X   X
X   X
X   X
X   X

Players, in groups of two, flick overhead passes to each other and catch them as they did in 10.0. Players set up five feet apart and alternate the pivot foot.

10.1 Go Fetch It

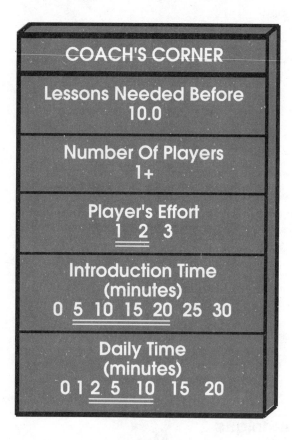

COACH'S CORNER

Lessons Needed Before
10.0

Number Of Players
1+

Player's Effort
1 <u>2</u> 3

Introduction Time
(minutes)
0 <u>5</u> 10 15 <u>20</u> 25 30

Daily Time
(minutes)
0 1 <u>2</u> <u>5</u> <u>10</u> 15 20

Brief:

Players run after a ball thrown in a direction away from them, pick it up, pivot, and pass.

Fundamental Notes

This lesson is a diagnostic test for catching without walking. Players hustle after the ball and slow down after they grab it. It is very worthwhile for novices.

Setup

One line, in single file, of players facing you. Stand near the center of the court. A manager is five yards away in position to catch the return passes.

Directions for Players

1. I am going to throw a grounder 2-5 yards to the left or right of you.

2. Go after the ball, grab it, and then slow down. Pivot around and throw it back to the manager. Then go back in line.

3. The "hitch" is how you pick up the ball. Just before picking it up, jump slightly to arrange your feet properly as in Lesson 10.0.

4. Say "Jump, grab, one, two" (or just "jump, one,

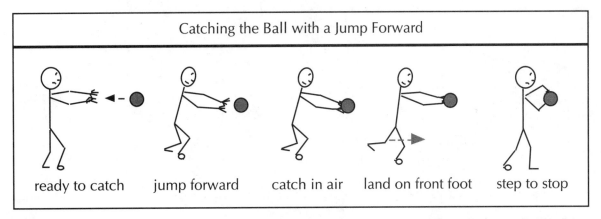

Catching the Ball with a Jump Forward

ready to catch   jump forward   catch in air   land on front foot   step to stop

Setup for 10.1

X=players

C=coach
M= manager

passing
directions

X X X XX
X
X
XX

C
M

two") when you pick up the ball. The *one* is a step on the pivot foot. The *two* is a step to stop.

Troubleshooting

1. This lesson is for novices of all degrees, so the velocity of the ball, how far away it is tossed, and the speed the player needs to run should be varied accordingly.

2. Players slow down only after the ball is grabbed, not before. Many players will slow down to catch the ball.

3. Players often have trouble with the "one, two." They walk like a player on a tight rope ready to fall off. Instruct them to take a few extra steps and count, "1,2,3" or, "1,2,3,4" initially so they do not lose their balance.

4. Players who have trouble need individual attention.

Use of Assistants

1. Work one-on-one with a player.

2. Managers catch return passes from the players. This frees you to throw more passes.

3. An able assistant can run their own line. This line should be far away from your line. Players rotate from one line to the other.

Weekly Practice   Everyday

Extensions

10.11 Coming to the Ball

Coming to the ball is the key to catching the ball. Otherwise, the defense comes to the ball ahead of the offense and catches it. The setup is the same as the one in Lesson 10.1. This lesson is applicable to players with more varying degrees of skill than 10.0 is.

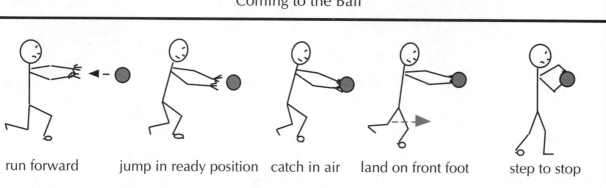

Coming to the Ball

run forward   jump in ready position   catch in air   land on front foot   step to stop

Directions

1. The players run directly toward you.

2. Slowly throw or roll the ball directly toward the player.

3. Initially, instruct players to run slowly to the ball. Eventually they sprint to the ball.

4. Players jump to arrange their feet just before grabbing the ball as in the previous lesson. Players say, "jump, grab, one, two" or just, "jump, one, two" as they catch the ball.

5. Players must grab the ball and then slow down. Make sure they do not slow down before the grab.

6. Since they are running toward the ball, the first foot down after the catch is the pivot foot. The second foot is the stop. Note that some novices may need to take a third and fourth step to slow down initially. This is okay. It may take a day or two for them to stop balanced. Insist players take more steps initially, if they are ready to fall over after the catch.

7. After the catch, pass the ball to the manager, and then return to the line.

10.2 Jump to the Ball

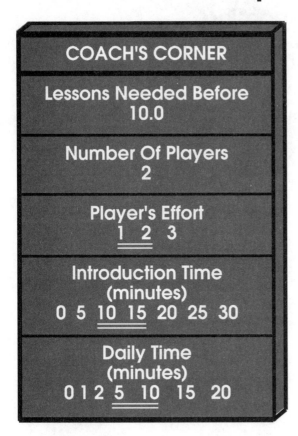

Brief:

Players long jump to the ball as they catch it.

Fundamental Notes

In this last step before catching the ball, a player long jumps forward toward the ball. This prevents the defense from jumping in front to interfere with the pass. The passer and the catcher communicate, so that the jump forward and the pass are timed properly.

Setup

Players line up in groups of two about five yards apart. Each group is three yards apart.

Directions for Players

1. The passer fakes an overhead pass and then throws one.

2. The catcher stands sideways. The foot closer to the ball is the pivot foot. The fake signals the catcher to pivot around forward. Move the back foot ahead of the pivot foot; then long jump forward toward the passer as far as possible with arms outstretched and fingers spread.

3. Catch the ball before landing; "catch one two"

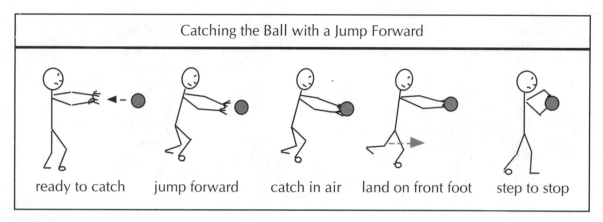

Catching the Ball with a Jump Forward

ready to catch   jump forward   catch in air   land on front foot   step to stop

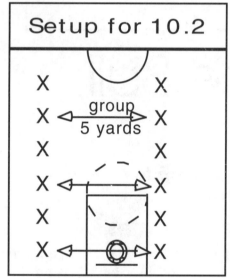

Setup for 10.2

X   X

X ← group → X
   5 yards

X   X

X ←   → X

X   X

X ←   → X

10.2 in Steps

❶ Overhead ball fake
❷ Pivot forward
❸ Pass
❹ Jump to the ball

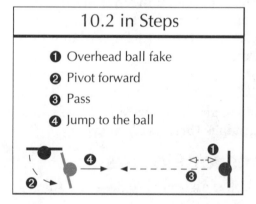

again. The passer and catcher need to work out the timing.

4. The passer and catcher switch roles.

5. Catchers alternate the side they face before jumping forward. Passers alternate the pivot foot.

Troubleshooting

1. The catcher makes a pocket or target with the hands for the passer.

2. The jump forward is a long jump, not a high jump.

Use of Assistants   None

Weekly Practice   Everyday

Extensions

Lesson 11.3 adds faking and cutting to this lesson.

10.3 Loose Ball Lesson

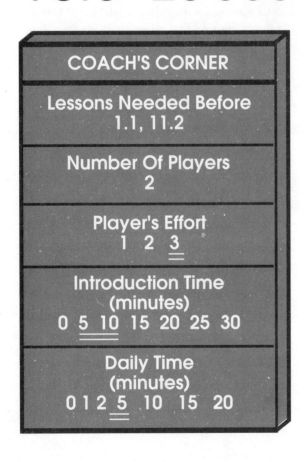

COACH'S CORNER

Lessons Needed Before
1.1, 11.2

Number Of Players
2

Player's Effort
1 2 <u>3</u>

Introduction Time
(minutes)
0 5 <u>10</u> 15 20 25 30

Daily Time
(minutes)
0 1 2 <u>5</u> 10 15 20

Brief:
Two players go for *a loose ball.*

Fundamental Notes

The key to retrieving a loose ball is to prevent the other player from getting there first. This is similar to actions taken to rebound. Watch each group individually, instead of refereeing many group collisions simultaneously. This measure also prevents flagrant fouling. Expect a moderate amount of pushing.

Setup

Two players line up, side to side, elbow to elbow, leaning against each other. Place the ball two feet away.

Directions for Players

1. When I yell *go*, step in front of the other player. Attempt to push your foot and arm first, and then your body in front of them. This is called *getting position.*

2. Get position first, then go for the ball.

•Repeat. One group at a time.

Starting Positions

Troubleshooting

1. The purpose is to get position, not to shove away the other player.

2. Players watch the ball, not the other player. By contact with the arm and body, players sense the actions of their opponent.

3. Players learn quickly.

Use of Assistants

A qualified assistant watches another group.

Weekly Practice As needed

Extensions

10.31 Go for It

Toss the ball slowly in any direction, even toward the players, instead of just placing it on the floor as in Lesson 10.3.

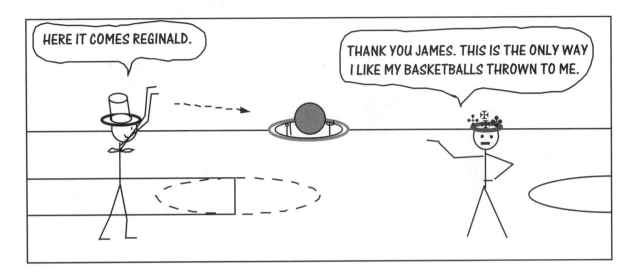

10.4 Catching Bad Passes

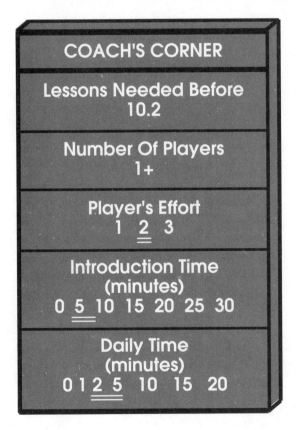

COACH'S CORNER

Lessons Needed Before
10.2

Number Of Players
1+

Player's Effort
1 2 3

Introduction Time
(minutes)
0 5 10 15 20 25 30

Daily Time
(minutes)
0 1 2 5 10 15 20

Brief:
Players catch intentionally thrown bad passes.

Fundamental Notes

Players often receive passes that are off the mark or timed improperly during a game. There are many reasons for this: the defense is tight; another defensive player deflects the ball; a simple miscue. In any case, this is a poor excuse to let the pass go. Each player needs to go after bad passes. This lesson teaches a player how to catch a bad pass, as well as emphasizes the need to go after it.

Setup

One line of players, one behind the other, facing the coach, who is 3-7 yards away. One manager stands behind the coach to keep track of the balls. Another stands farther away to catch passes from the players.

Directions for Players

1. When you jump forward for a pass, I will throw you a bad one. Catch it, or at least stop it.

2. Pass the ball to a manager and then return to the line.

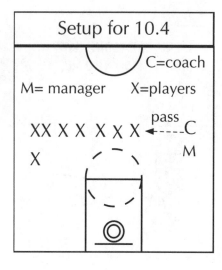

Setup for 10.4

C=coach

M= manager   X=players

XX X X X X X ←- - - -C
                pass
X   M

•Initially, throw passes that bounce right in front of the player. Then throw passes that are off to one side. The speed of the passes depends on the level of the player. Usually, only slow to medium speed passes are needed.

Troubleshooting

1. Some players expect perfect passes all the time or *forget it*. This lesson fosters a positive attitude toward bad passes by making them a challenge to catch.

2. After the coach throws bad passes, all players know that they have the responsibility to catch all bad passes from other players (or die trying!).

Use of Assistants None

Weekly Practice As needed

Extensions None

10.5 Cut Fake Technique

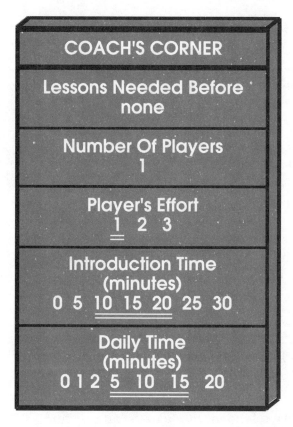

COACH'S CORNER

Lessons Needed Before
none

Number Of Players
1

Player's Effort
<u>1</u> 2 3

**Introduction Time
(minutes)**
0 5 <u>10 15 20</u> 25 30

**Daily Time
(minutes)**
0 1 2 <u>5 10 15</u> 20

Brief:
Before cutting, a player makes one of several fakes.

Fundamental Notes

Faking without the ball is a skill that is often overlooked by coaches. Cutting and faking go together, hand in hand. It is difficult to think of a situation where faking is not essential before cutting. Several fakes are often used together, or one right after the other. In each case, the fake only needs to slow down the defense by one step. This maneuver enables the offense to be open for an instant. Overtly faking a cut, on the other hand, is used to keep the defense close. This move allows other players to operate more freely.

Setup

Players line up, side by side on the midcourt line. The coach stands at the foul line.

Directions for Players

The Sleep Fake

1. The first fake is one that is accomplished only too readily. It is the sleep fake. Relax. Appear to be uninvolved. Turn away from the action slowly. Actually, pay close attention to everything. You are waiting for the right moment to cut.

2. Do this fake while I am talking to you. When I hold up three fingers, sprint forward to the top of the key.

•Do not make it easy for the players to see your fingers. Hold up 2 and then 4 as many times as needed before holding up 3.

•Watch each player's fake. Instruct players how to make it more convincing.

•Repeat this 3 or 4 times.

The Step Away Fake

3. The step away fakes works well with the sleep

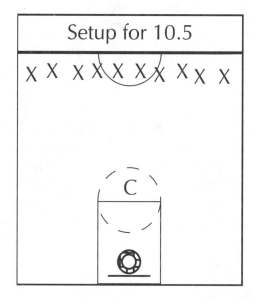

Setup for 10.5

X X X X X X X X X

C

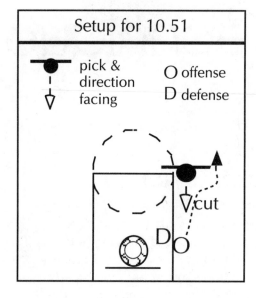

Setup for 10.51

pick & direction facing

O offense
D defense

V cut

D O

fake. Take several lazy steps in the opposite direction that you plan to cut.

•Repeat step 2.

The Step Behind Fake

4. The best fake involves sleepily stepping behind the defense; step between the defense and your basket. You want the defense to forget about you. In any case, they can not see you and the ball at the same time. This works best against zones.

5. Every other player starting at the far right is the defense. Stand in the half down defensive position facing me. Do not move in this lesson. This is not the way to play defense. You never let a player walk behind you.

6. The offense starts beside the defense. Sleepily step behind. When the defense turns to look, sprint toward me to the top of the key.

•Repeat step 2. Switch offense and defense.

Troubleshooting

1. Make sure players look like they are sleeping.

2. The fakes are very slow, whereas the cut is a sprint. Starting a cut is like the start of a 50-yard dash.

3. Players have a tendency to fake too quickly and sprint too slowly.

Use of Assistants

It is advantageous to have lots of assistants. Instruct them to play defense for the step behind fake.

Weekly Practice   Several times during the season.

Extensions

10.51 Cutting off a Pick (or Screen)

A cutter uses a pick to rub off a defensive player. This lesson concentrates on the cutter. Players jog. The defense cooperates, unless the cutter uses the pick poorly. Lesson 9.8 is similar. Lesson 13.0 teaches how to set up as a pick; Lesson 13.01 teaches how to defense the pick.

Setup

The cutter and defense line up in groups of two under the basket. The cutter starts at the left side low post.

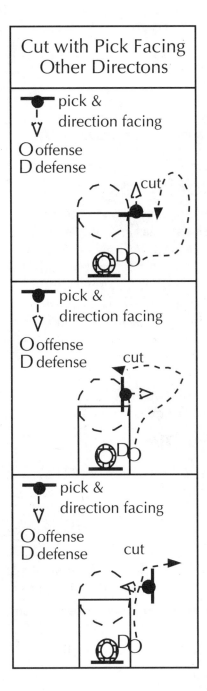

Cut with Pick Facing Other Directons

pick & direction facing

O offense
D defense

cut

pick & direction facing

O offense
D defense

cut

pick & direction facing

O offense
D defense

cut

The defense is right beside. Use a manager as a pick. The pick sets up at the left side high post, initially facing the basket.

Directions for Players

1. The pick freezes during this lesson. Hold your arms across your chest for protection from the defense.

2. The cutter runs by the pick in the same direction that the pick faces. In this case, you are cutting out for the ball. Rub or bang shoulders with the pick as you pass by, so the defense does not slide in between.

3. Both the offense and the defense jog, not run, so there are no fatal collisions. Return back to the line and switch roles.

•After each player uses the pick, tell the pick to face the left sidelines.

4. If the pick faces the left sideline, slowly cut diagonally outward toward the left sideline keeping the defense with you. Then cut from the left to the right, so that you face the pick as you run by.

5. Rub shoulders with the pick as you cut by.

•Use the pick from several other directions. The cutter first maneuvers the defense to the optimal position, then cuts. Remind players to both face and rub shoulders with the pick.

10.6 Cut to the Ball

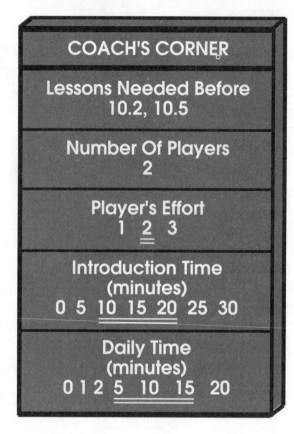

COACH'S CORNER

Lessons Needed Before
10.2, 10.5

Number Of Players
2

Player's Effort
1 <u>2</u> 3

Introduction Time (minutes)
0 5 <u>10 15 20</u> 25 30

Daily Time (minutes)
0 1 2 <u>5 10 15</u> 20

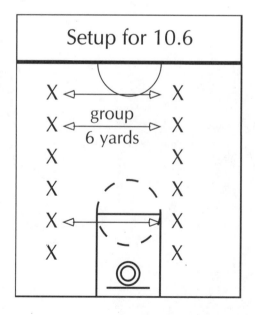

Setup for 10.6

X ←→ X
X ←→ X
group
6 yards
X   X
X   X
X ←→ X
X   X
◎

Brief:
Players fake, and then cut to the ball.

Fundamental Notes

To catch a pass, players cut either to the ball or to the open space. In this lesson a player cuts directly forward to the ball. Presses, especially full court presses, can readily be beaten with this skill. This fact makes this lesson of particular importance to novices and their coaches. Initially, run this lesson at the practice level before speeding it up.

Setup

Players are in groups of two about six yards apart. Separate each group as much as possible.

Directions for Players

1. The catcher fakes and then cuts to the ball. Use the step away sleep fake.

2. Stop running only after you catch the ball. Think– *jump, catch, one, two*. Stop on the *one, two*.

3. The passer throws the ball after the fake at the start of the actual cut. Use an overhead pass.

4. Repeat steps 1-3 switching roles. Alternate the pivot foot in each role.

•Use side and side bounce passes as well.

Troubleshooting

1. The catcher catches the ball, takes two steps, and then stops.

2. The catcher has the arms outstretched, hands ready, and fingers spread as they cut.

3. Remind players that it is important to alternate the pivot foot when both catching and passing.

4. Players not ready for this lesson have a tendency to stop before they catch the ball. If this is

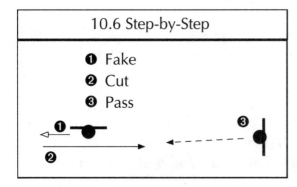

10.6 Step-by-Step

❶ Fake
❷ Cut
❸ Pass

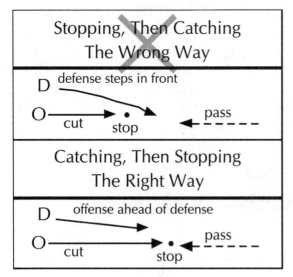

Stopping, Then Catching
The Wrong Way

D   defense steps in front

O —— cut ——→ • stop   pass ←— — — —

Catching, Then Stopping
The Right Way

D   offense ahead of defense

O —— cut ——→ • stop   pass ←— — — —

the case, go back and work on a previous Lesson, 10.11, Coming to the Ball.

Use of Assistants None

Weekly Practice Everyday

Extensions

10.61 Cut Communication

This is the same as Lesson 10.6 except that the passer and catcher decide on two things before each pass.

1. The signal to start

2. Where the ball and the catcher will meet.

The signal is usually given by the passer. A look or a ball fake are commonly used signals. Cutters often use a fake as a signal.

The ball can be thrown short, even a lateral is okay, or long to one side or another. Instruct one player to point nonchalantly with a finger or other body part.

Initially encourage players to discuss what signals to use. The defense often determines this, but in this lesson the offensive players do. Eventually, they will intuitively respond to each other like more experienced players.

10.7 Three Second Lesson

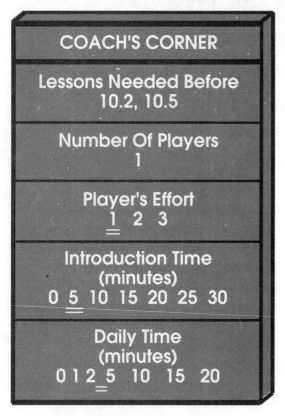

COACH'S CORNER

Lessons Needed Before
10.2, 10.5

Number Of Players
1

Player's Effort
<u>1</u> 2 3

Introduction Time
(minutes)
0 <u>5</u> 10 15 20 25 30

Daily Time
(minutes)
0 1 <u>2</u> 5 10 15 20

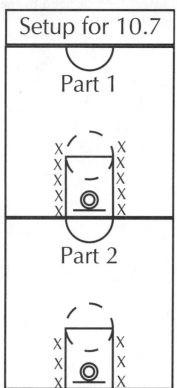

Setup for 10.7

Part 1

Part 2

Brief:

A player cuts into the lane and stays there for the maximum amount of time before getting out.

Fundamental Notes

Often novice players go into the lane on offense without counting. The result is a three second violation. This lesson teaches players to count as well as jump into the lane for a pass. At most, it only needs to be practiced a few times. There are two parts to this lesson.

Setup

See directions

Directions for Players

Part 1

1. Line up on both sides of the lane, as close as possible to the low post. Do not stand on the line.

2. Start counting when you step into the lane. Count out loud–*one one thousand, two one thousand, out.* As you say "out" step out of the lane.

3. Repeat this 10 times. It should take about 1 minute.

Part 2

4. Three players line up on each side of the lane, six altogether. The others stand back.

5. Jump into the lane ready to catch a pass. The arms are outstretched and the body is in the half down ready position. Count as you did before and then jump out of the lane.

6. Repeat this 10 times with each group of 6. It should take about one minute per group.

Troubleshooting

1. For Part 2, players jump into the lane ready to catch the ball.

2. If the ball arrives after the jump, players must jump to the ball again.

The Ready Position

Cut into Lane Step-by-Step

❶ passer fakes

❷ cutter jumps into lane
passer passes

❸ cutter catches ball and shoots
passer follows ball to basket

❶ X passer

❷ ❸

cutter X → ❷

❸

Use of Assistants None

Weekly Practice 1-3 times per season

Extensions

10.71 Cut into Lane

This is like Part 2 above, except that each player receives a pass in the lane, then turns and shoots.

Setup

The cutting line sets up at the low post; the passing line is at the top of the key. Use as many baskets as are available.

Directions for Players

1. The overhead fake by the passer is the signal to the low post player to jump into the lane. Throw an overhead pass, so that the player and the ball meet at the basket.

2. Catch the ball, pivot, shoot, rebound, and then go to the passing line with the ball.

3. The passer follows the ball to the basket for the rebound, then goes to the cutting line.

• Halfway through the lesson, switch the cutting line to the other side of the basket.

10.8 Overplay the Catcher

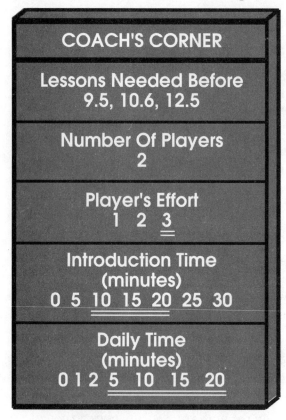

COACH'S CORNER

Lessons Needed Before
9.5, 10.6, 12.5

Number Of Players
2

Player's Effort
1 2 <u>3</u>

Introduction Time
(minutes)
0 5 <u>10 15 20</u> 25 30

Daily Time
(minutes)
0 1 2 <u>5   10   15   20</u>

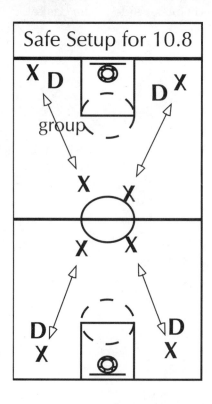

Safe Setup for 10.8

group

Brief:

The catcher catches a pass while being overplayed by the defense.

Fundamental Notes

At last, the first realistic passing lesson. You think your players can pass and catch! Worse, your players think that they can! Wait till they do this. In a game situation your team has a big lead, then the defense full court presses you to smithereens. Guess what! Your players need practice. By now the players know the techniques. Expect them, especially novices, to have problems with this lesson. If a pass makes it to the catcher, your players may want to celebrate. This is extremely difficult. However, the reward are commensurate with the difficulty–no team will ever successfully press you again. Do it.

Setup

Two offensive players are 7 yards apart. The defense overplays the catcher. The groups are arranged with the catchers as far apart as possible. A safe setup puts the passers near the center of the gym, and the catchers with defense near the out-of-bounds lines.

Directions for Players

1. The defense sets up to overplay the catcher. The passer signals the start of the lesson by faking an overhead pass. Then count slowly, and loudly, to five.

•Halfway through the lesson, instruct the defense to overplay on the other side of the offense.

2. The catcher fakes, and then attempts to catch the ball as far as possible from the passer. The worst scenario has the passer picking for the catcher on the lateral.

3. If the ball is not passed at the count of five, the lesson ends.

4. Rotate positions from passer to catcher to defense and repeat.

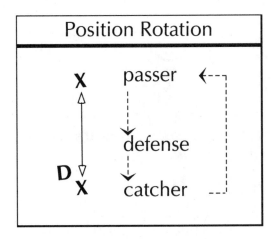

Position Rotation

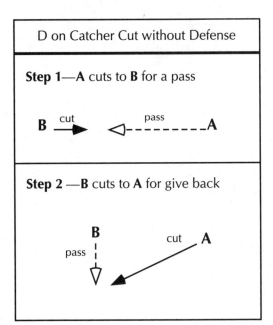

D on Catcher Cut without Defense

Step 1—A cuts to **B** for a pass

Step 2 —B cuts to **A** for give back

Troubleshooting

1. Go back to previous lessons, if you see a need.

2. Encourage communication between the offensive players.

Use of Assistants

Station assistants between groups to keep them far apart.

Weekly Practice   Everyday

Extensions

10.81 Front the Catcher

The defense fronts, instead of overplaying the catcher. Lesson 12.4 teaches fronting. Fronting involves facing up to the defense without watching the passer. Use it in presses and out-of-bounds plays. The defense moves, watching the midsection of the offense and also watching the eyes for telltale signs of a pass.

10.82 D on Catcher, Cut

After the pass in lessons 10.8 or 10.81, the passer cuts to the ball. The defense endeavors to obstruct the pass back. The defense either overplays or fronts, you decide. This is a *give and go* (pass off and cut for the ball) type play for the passer.

10.9 D Pass, Overplay Catcher

COACH'S CORNER

Lessons Needed Before
9.6, 10.82

Number Of Players
4

Player's Effort
1 2 <u>3</u>

Introduction Time (minutes)
0 <u>5</u> <u>10</u> <u>15</u> <u>20</u> 25 30

Daily Time (minutes)
0 1 2 <u>5</u> <u>10</u> <u>15</u> 20

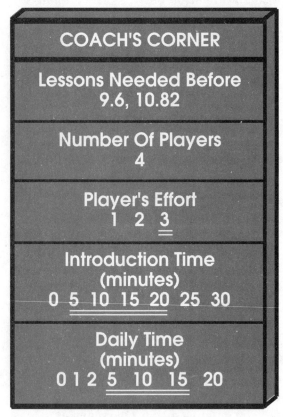

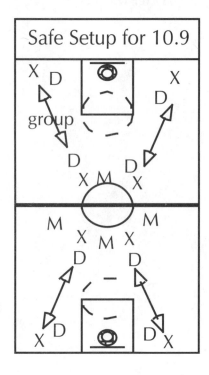

Safe Setup for 10.9

Brief:

Two offensive players pass against a pressing defense.

Fundamental Notes

A defensive player covers the passer in Lesson 10.8. They play two-on-two. The offense needs to communicate before, or during, the play. This difficult lesson reaps big reward just as the previous lesson, 10.8. Only its difficulty may be the drawback.

Setup

The same as for Lesson 10.8. The initial passers are toward the center of the court. The initial catchers are toward the out-of-bounds lines. Play toward the out-of-bounds lines. The defense sets up to overplay the catcher. If the court looks crowded, instruct the groups to alternate.

Directions for Players

1. The passer signals the cut. The cutter fakes, then cuts to a spot or the ball. Communicate to decide.

2. Try each lesson twice without changing positions. The first switch involves the offense and defense. The next involves the initial catching and passing positions.

3. The defensive players count to five loudly. If the pass is not made by five the play ends. Unsuccessful tries count.

Troubleshooting

1. Offensive players plan a strategy.

2. Players need to alternate pivot feet.

3. Switch players in each group everyday, as well as the players working together, so that each player has an opportunity to communicate with every other player on the team.

4. Expect success to come slowly in this very difficult lesson.

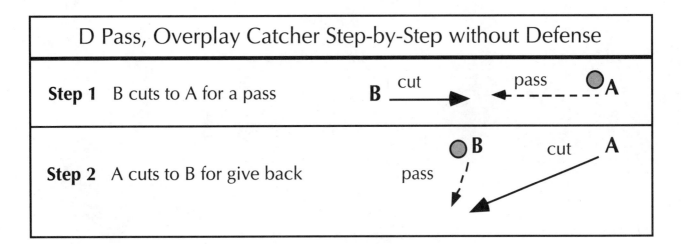

D Pass, Overplay Catcher Step-by-Step without Defense	
Step 1 B cuts to A for a pass	
Step 2 A cuts to B for give back	

Use of Assistants

Assistants stand near midcourt in order to prevent collisions between groups.

Weekly Practice Everyday

Extensions

10.91 D Passer, Front Catcher

The defense fronts instead of overplaying the catcher in Lesson 10.9.

10.92 D on Catcher, Passer-Cut

This is the same as Lesson 10.9 or 10.91 with the passer cutting to the ball. The defense covers the cutter. Instruct the defense to either overplay or front. This is called a *give and go* because the passer gives up the ball (passes) and then goes (cuts) to the ball. The objective for the offense is to get the ball out-of-bounds.

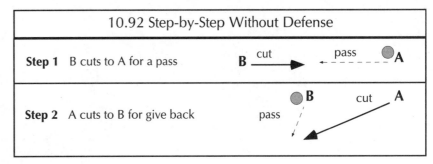

10.92 Step-by-Step Without Defense	
Step 1 B cuts to A for a pass	
Step 2 A cuts to B for give back	

(Notes)

The Basketball Coach's Bible

Section 11
Rebounding

L E S S O N #	NAME	P L A Y E R S	C O U R T	B A L L	E F F O R T	LESSONS BEFORE	L E S S O N #	INTRO TIME	DAILY TIME
11.0	**Rebound Grab Ball**	2	x	-	1	1.1, 2.1	**11.0**	5-10	2-5
11.1	Watching the Ball	1	-	-	1	none	11.1	5-10	5
11.11	The Ready Position	1	-	-	1	11.1	11.11	3	1
11.12	Move to Rebound	1	-	-	1	11.1	11.12	5	5
11.2	Step in Front Box Out 1-2	2	x	x	3	10.3, 11.12	11.2	10-15	5-10
11.3	Blocking Boxing Out 1-2	2	x	x	3	11.2, 12.5	11.3	15-30	10-20

11.0 Rebound Grab Ball

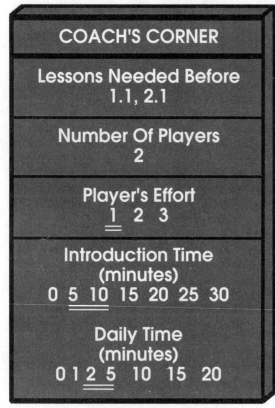

COACH'S CORNER

Lessons Needed Before
1.1, 2.1

Number Of Players
2

Player's Effort
<u>1</u> 2 3

Introduction Time (minutes)
0 <u>5 10</u> 15 20 25 30

Daily Time (minutes)
0 1 <u>2 5</u> 10 15 20

Setup for 11.0

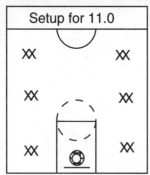

1-jump & grab

2- pull ball & pivot away

Brief:
One player holds the ball high overhead; the other grabs the ball and pulls it away like a rebound.

Fundamental Notes
This is the first step, and also the easiest, in learning how to rebound.

Setup
Each group positions itself five yards apart.

Directions for Players
1. One player holds the ball high overhead. It is okay to make your partner jump slightly for it.

2. The other player grabs the ball using the fingertips for control.

3. Pull it away, and then pivot away holding the ball overhead in a passing position.

4. Alternate holding the ball. Grab five rebounds each.

Troubleshooting
1. Players both pull the ball away, and pivot away at the same time.

2. Do not allow tall players to tease shorter ones by holding the ball too high overhead.

Use of Assistants
Assistants can be permanent ball holders.

Weekly Practice   Everyday for one week

Extensions   None

11.1 Watching the Ball

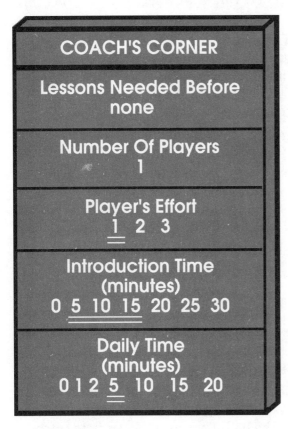

COACH'S CORNER
Lessons Needed Before none
Number Of Players 1
Player's Effort <u>1</u> 2 3
Introduction Time (minutes) 0 <u>5 10 15</u> 20 25 30
Daily Time (minutes) 0 1 2 <u>5</u> 10 15 20

The Ready Position

Brief:

Players watch the shot arc to predict where the ball rebounds.

Fundamental Notes

The best rebounders quickly and accurately predict where a ball will rebound, and then go for it. It's no coincidence that these players are always around the ball. The skill of watching and predicting is seldom practiced (except in horse racing). It is the key to rebounding, especially offensive rebounding. Five minutes of watching noticeably improves a player's rebounding.

Setup

The players form a semicircle eight feet from the basket.

Directions for Players

1. Yell the instant you know where the ball will rebound. Use words like *short, left, center, right, far* as soon as you can. It is okay to yell more than one direction.

2. *Short* means that the ball will not reach the basket. In this case, going for the ball leads you directly under the basket.

3. If you think the ball is going to the left, center, or right of the basket, yell that direction.

4. You also need to predict and then position yourself at the proper distance from the basket. Long and hard shots rebound farther from the basket than short and soft shots. If you expect a big bounce go 4-6 feet or more from the basket; 2-4 feet for regular shots. In this lesson do not go for the ball, just yell.

• Shoot all varieties of shots–hard, soft, high arc, low arc, short, far–from different places on the court. Try to miss. This may be easy.

• Shoot 10-15 shots. It is okay for players to change positions.

Troubleshooting

1. Instruct only 2 or 3 players to yell at a time, so you can identify the predictors. The others can point where the ball will rebound.

2. Explain some laws of physics to your players. Exclude relativity. The harder the shot, the longer the rebound. Softer shots yield short rebounds. The angle that the ball hits the rim equals the angle the ball bounces off the rim, etc.

3. Watch and predict where the ball contacts the rim. This reveals the rebound direction–up, straight back toward you, down, left or right.

Use of Assistants

1. Use assistants to get the actual rebound, pass the ball back, and maintain a stash of shooting balls for you.

2. Players pass rebounds that inadvertently bounce to them to the managers.

Weekly Practice 3-4 days or as needed

Extensions

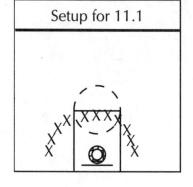

Setup for 11.1

11.11 The Ready Position

It is a difficult task to determine exactly when a rebound will bounce your way. Even after the rebound, players often need to scramble on the floor for the ball. They must be ready to catch, or grab, the ball at any moment. The ready position is just that– the best position to be in at any time on the court. To get into the ready position, the forearms need to be bent up (or back) all the way. The wrists are bent back; the fingers are spread and clawed. The body is in the half down position. Practice this by saying "ready" to your players in whatever position they are in.

Do this in Lesson 11.1 as well.

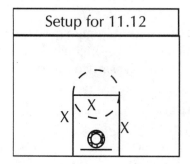

Setup for 11.12

11.12 Move to Rebound

Players start in the ready position. Three players at a time put their money where their mouth was in Lesson 11.1. They follow their own predictions to the rebound. The objective is to get best position first. Players need not jump for the rebound. The player in the best place gets the rebound; no fighting for the ball. Players stay in the ready position throughout the lesson. Repeat this lesson 2-5 times with each group.

11.2 Step in Front Box Out 1-2

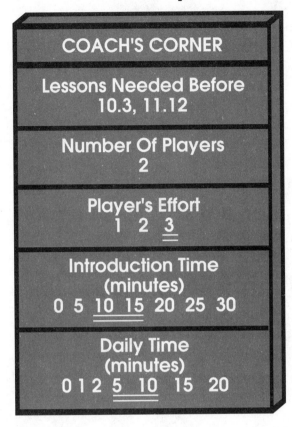

COACH'S CORNER

Lessons Needed Before
10.3, 11.12

Number Of Players
2

Player's Effort
1 2 <u>3</u>

**Introduction Time
(minutes)**
0 5 <u>10</u> <u>15</u> 20 25 30

**Daily Time
(minutes)**
0 1 2 <u>5</u> <u>10</u> 15 20

Setup for 11.1

Brief:
Starting shoulder-to-shoulder, two players work for the inside position.

Fundamental Notes
This lesson is similar to Lesson 10.3 except that the players go for the rebound. They have the additional responsibility of watching the flight of the ball as well as the shooter. This skill is used with both offensive and defensive rebounding. The skills practiced in this lesson are easier than real boxing out because players are in similar starting positions; there is no offense or defense.

Setup
Three groups of players, two in a group, work at each basket. The groups start 2-3 yards from the basket on the left, center, and right sides. The players in each group start shoulder-to-shoulder.

Directions for Players

Part 1-Step in Front
1. Start in the ready position. Stay in it throughout the lesson.

2. Watch the shooter and the ball, not your opponent. Stay in contact with your opponent using your arms and body. From this contact you can determine their whereabouts and movements.

3. Step in front as soon as you go for the ball. You want your opponent to bang into you. This stops their momentum.

4. Avoid collisions with other groups on the court.

•Shoot from different positions. Again, it should be no problem to miss the shots.

5. If I make the shot, play the ball like it is a miss.

6. After the rebound, pass the ball to a manager on the endline, switch partners, and setup in the ready position for the next rebound. Right side players rotate right.

Part 2–Box Out

7. Start eight feet from the basket in the same position as you did in Part 1. One player, the defense, is in the inside position.

8. The inside player keeps the other player boxed out for five seconds by doing the following:

> **a.** Spread the elbows out and toward the back. Try to keep your opponent between your elbows.

> **b.** Take up more space by bending slightly lower than the half down position. Move your legs further apart and stick your behind out.

9. The outside player, the offense, cooperates initially by pushing gently on the back of the other player.

10. When the defense, or opponent, becomes more expert, the offense goes directly to the basket. Do not use much finesse. Try to push around or through your opponent.

11. Start when I say *go*.

•You can shoot the ball from this setup when players are more expert.

Troubleshooting

Remind your players of the following:

1. Start shoulder-to-shoulder in the ready position–Part 1.

2. Step in front immediately as you go for the ball–Part 1.

3. Watch and predict where the ball will go. Play your opponent by contact.

4. When boxing out a player, spread your body by moving your legs and elbows apart.

5. Keep your opponent on your back between your elbows. Your behind needs to be out and back.

11.3 Blocking Boxing Out 1-2

Brief:

The defense blocks offensive players charging for the basket and then boxes them out.

Fundamental Notes

A player running unimpeded to the basket for a rebound is nearly impossible to stop. Stopping the charge to the basket is a key to boxing out. This lesson is difficult because the players start 10-15 feet from the basket. The offense is blocked and then boxed out closer to the basket.

Setup

The offense starts at the high post left side. The defense overplays the offense. Players stay in two lines near the top of the key. When players are more expert, position them on both sides of the high post. In Part 1, place the ball at the foul line. Shoot the ball in Part 2.

Directions for Players

Part 1

1. The offense charges down the outside of the lane toward the basket. Neither make tricky moves around nor charge through the defense.

•Initially, instruct players to run at half speed.

2. Initially, the defense overplays the offense and watches the ball placed at the foul line.

3. When I yell *shot* the offense charges directly toward the basket. The defense stops directly in front of the offense, causing a collision. Block the offense with one forearm.

4. Then, pivot around, which ever way (left or right) is easier, so that you can stay in contact with the offense. Keep the offense on your arms and back. This is boxing out.

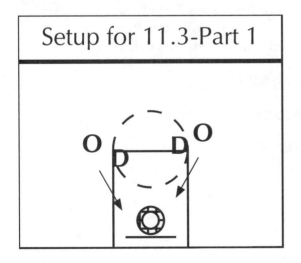

Setup for 11.3-Part 1

Steps in Blocking Boxing Out

Defense ⬤— Offense O

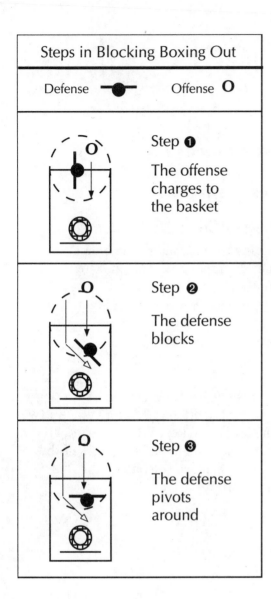

Step ❶

The offense charges to the basket

Step ❷

The defense blocks

Step ❸

The defense pivots around

Setup for 11.3-Part 2

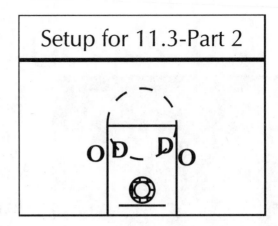

Part 2
•Move the offense to the mid post position and repeat this lesson with shooting and rebounding. Use two groups, one on each side of the lane.

Troubleshooting
1. Before the shot, the defense rotates their hips and runs sideways toward the basket; do not allow players to tread backward.

2. It is okay for the defense to both block and box out too assertively at first.

3. The defense looks at the ball during this lesson, not the offense.

4. Initially, the offense goes directly for the basket. As the defense acquires skill, the offense goes more for the ball and/or to box out the defense.

Use of Assistants None

Weekly Practice 3-4 times per season

Extensions None

Section 12
Defense

L E S S O N #	NAME	P L A Y E R S	C O U R T	B A L L	E F F O R T	LESSONS BEFORE	L E S S O N #	INTRO TIME	DAILY TIME
12.0	**Defensive Position**	1	-	-	1	4.0	**12.0**	10-20	2-4
12.1	Move in D Position	1	-	-	1	12.0	12.1	10-30	5-25
12.2	Force Left & Right1-5	2	-	-	1-2	12.1	12.2	5-10@	2-5@
12.21	Three Yard Lesson	2	-	-	2-3	12.2	12.21	15-30	5-15
12.22	Mirror Lesson	2	x	x	3	12.21	12.22	-	5-10
12.3	Trapping 1-3	3	-	-	2-3	12.21	12.3	15-25	10-15
12.31	Trapping Game	3	-	-	2-3	12.3	12.31	-	10-20
12.4	Front Keep Out of Lane	2	x	-	3	12.1	12.4	10-20	10-15
12.41	Front and Box Out	2	x	-	3	11.3, 12.4	12.41	10-15	10-15
12.5	Overplaying 1-6	2	x	-	1-3	10.7, 12.2	12.5	~5-30	~5-15
12.6	Defense the Low Post	2+	x	-	1-2	12.5	12.6	20-30	10-15
12.61	Low Post with Passing	2+	x	-	2-3	12.6	12.61	-	10-20
12.7	D on Shooter	2	x	x	2	5.3, 11.3	12.7	10-15	3-8
12.71	D on Driver	2	x	x	2-3	12.7, 12.21	12.71	10-20	5-10
12.72	2 on 1	3	x	x	3	12.7, 9.52+	12.72	10-20	5-10

12.0 Defensive Position

COACH'S CORNER

Lessons Needed Before
4.0

Number Of Players
1

Player's Effort
<u>1</u> 2 3

Introduction Time (minutes)
0 5 <u>10</u> 15 20 25 30

Daily Time (minutes)
0 1<u>2</u> 5 10 15 20

Brief:
This lesson teaches the basic defensive body position.

Fundamental Notes

The easiest skills to teach are the defensive skills. Unlike offensive ones like shooting and dribbling, which require adroitness, defensive skills require mostly sweat. Players master defensive lessons quickly and learn hustle as well. In addition, the defensive position is very similar to the dribbling position. It is no coincidence that good dribblers are also good defensive players (the reverse need not be true). Practicing one benefits the other. Defensive lessons also improve conditioning.

The defensive body position is designed so that a player can readily sprint in any direction. With slight modification, players tailor it to any defensive situation.

Setup
The players line up side by side, five feet apart.

Directions for Players
1. Start in the half down body position.

2. The feet are slightly more than shoulder-width apart.

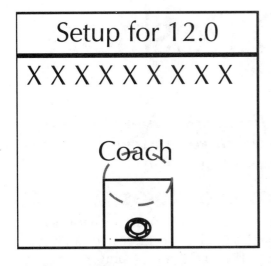

Setup for 12.0

X X X X X X X X X

Coach

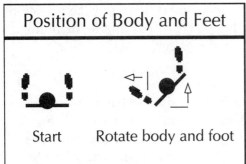

Position of Body and Feet

Start   Rotate body and foot

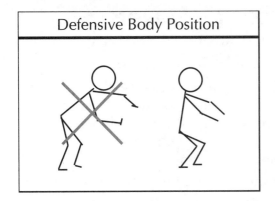

Defensive Body Position

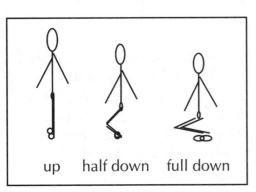

up   half down   full down

3. Put the right foot forward and rotate the left foot slightly (45 degrees) to the left. See the diagram.

4. Extend the right hand forward and slightly upward, to block the pass and the view of the offense. The palm faces the defense; the fingers are fully separated, clawed and stretched upward.

5. Extend the left hand sideways, low to the ground, to cover the ball. Rotate the hand so that the palms face the ball; the fingers of the clawed hand point downward.

6. Body weight is on the ball of each foot. You are now in the defensive body position.

•Check the position of each player.

7. Tap dance by moving each foot one inch off the ground. This looks like a football drill. With each tap, count out loud by ones up to 20. Do it.

8. Put the left foot forward and switch arm positions. Put the right arm down, the left arm up. Repeat tapping to 20.

•Repeat 1-4 times.

•Repeat steps 1-7.

Troubleshooting

1. The knees, not the back are bent. Instruct any player bending the back to do this lesson in the full down position.

2. Tap on the ball of each foot.

Use of Assistants   None

Weekly Practice   Everyday for about a week

12.1 Move in D Position

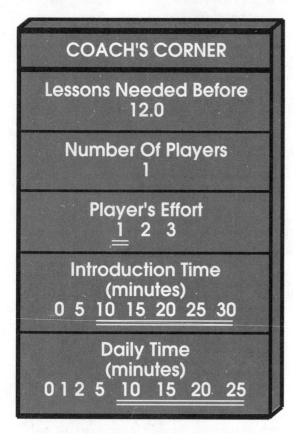

COACH'S CORNER

Lessons Needed Before
12.0

Number Of Players
1

Player's Effort
<u>1</u> 2 3

Introduction Time
(minutes)
0 5 <u>10 15</u> 20 25 30

Daily Time
(minutes)
0 1 2 5 <u>10 15 20 25</u>

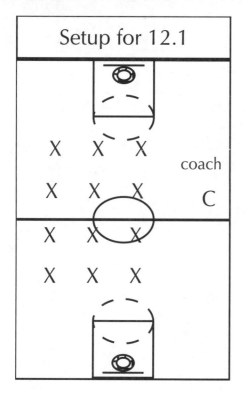

Setup for 12.1

Brief:
Players first walk, then jog, and then sprint in each direction from the defensive position.

Fundamental Notes
Defensive movement starts from the defensive position practiced in Lesson 12.0. With a pivot and slight rotation of the hips, a player can quickly sprint in any direction. As with all defensive lessons, this one involves hustle, dribbling position, and conditioning.

Setup
Players set up in defensive position, five yards apart in 2-4 columns and 2-4 rows. See the diagram. The right foot is forward. Center the players in the gym to avoid collisions with the walls.

Directions for Players
1. Tap dance counting to 20. Start now.

•Repeat as many times as needed.

2. Take 4 steps in the direction that I tell you. The first step is always a push off step in the opposite direction. Initially, walk through the directions. Always start with the right foot forward. See the diagrams.

3. To go forward, push off with the back foot (step 1), take one step forward with the right foot (step 2), step with the left foot (step 3), and then the right (step 4).

•Repeat this 2 more times. Then repeat these steps 3 times with the left foot forward.

4. Right foot forward. To go backward, push off with front foot (1), swivel the body to face backward, step with back foot, the left foot (2), then with the right (3), and then the left (4). Swivel forward again. See the diagram.

•Repeat this two more times. Then repeat with the left foot forward.

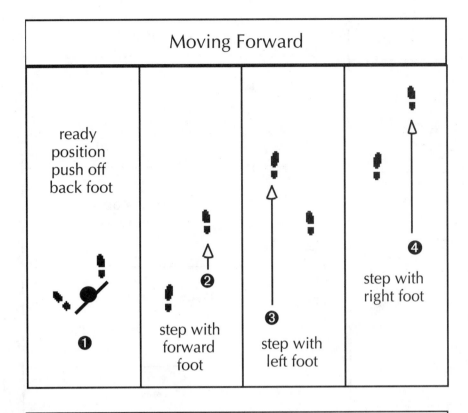

Moving Forward

ready position push off back foot ❶

step with forward foot ❷

step with left foot ❸

step with right foot ❹

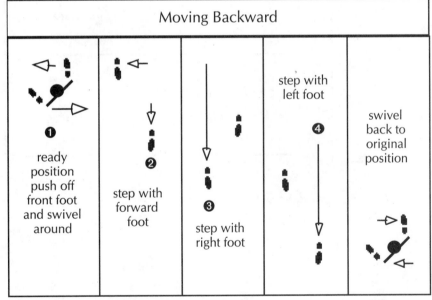

Moving Backward

ready position push off front foot and swivel around ❶

step with forward foot ❷

step with right foot ❸

step with left foot ❹

swivel back to original position

• Combine the forward and backward movements. Players tap dance between directions. Continue to step 5 when players can execute this at a fast pace.

5. To move left, push off with the front right foot (1), step to the left with the left (2), step over with the right (3), and then the left (4). See the diagram.

• Repeat this 2 more times. Then, repeat 3 times with the left foot forward.

6. To move right, push off with the back left foot (1), step right with the right (2), step in front with the left foot (3), and then with the right (4). See the diagram.

• Repeat this 2 more times. Then repeat with the left foot forward.

• Repeat the left and right movements, gradually speeding up the lesson.

• When players are ready, combine the left, right, forward, and back movements. Players tap dance between directions. Step 7 is a set of combined directions.

7. *Right foot forward, tap dance, forward, back, left, right, back, back, left, forward, forward, right, switch, left foot forward,....* Continue.

• Great vigilance prevents peeling players off the walls, each other, or gym equipment.

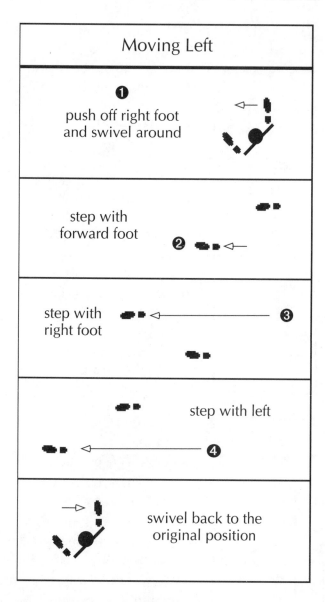

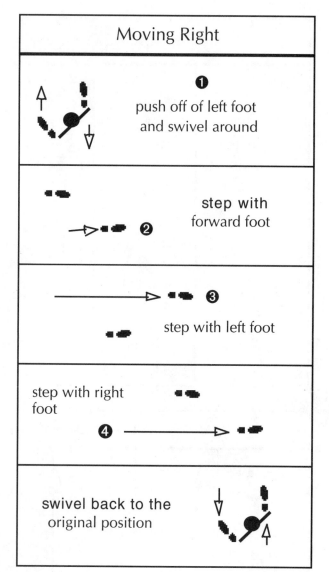

Moving Left

① push off right foot and swivel around

step with forward foot ②

③ step with right foot

step with left ④

swivel back to the original position

Moving Right

① push off of left foot and swivel around

step with forward foot ②

③ step with left foot

step with right foot ④

swivel back to the original position

Troubleshooting

1. Players tap dance between commands.

2. Players stay in the half down position during this lesson. Watch for bent backs and straight knees.

3. Gradually increase speed from a walk to a sprint as players learn this lesson.

Use of Assistants

Position an assistant on each sideline to warn players of impending collisions.

Weekly Practice Everyday

Extensions None

12.2 Force Left & Right 1-5

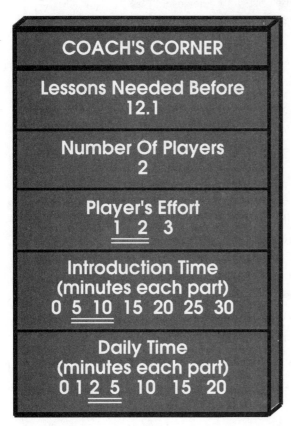

COACH'S CORNER

Lessons Needed Before
12.1

Number Of Players
2

Player's Effort
1 _2_ 3

Introduction Time
(minutes each part)
0 _5_ 10 15 20 25 30

Daily Time
(minutes each part)
0 1 _2_ 5 10 15 20

Brief:

The defense stays a constant distance from the offense, forcing them to dribble left or right.

Fundamental Notes

The key to defensing a player with the ball is to stay a constant distance away. As the offense moves closer to the basket, this distance decreases. Three yards is used for most lessons, because at this distance players can easily recover from a mistake. Players readily shorten this distance when tighter coverage is called for.

Tap dancing on the balls of the feet, keeps a player ready to move in any direction. Jump steps, not slides, keep players most ready to move.

Most right handers prefer to dribble with the right hand, few like to use the left; lefties usually prefer to dribble with the left hand. Positioning the defense slightly to the right of a player forces the offense to both move and dribble left. See the diagram. Positioning to the left forces a player right. Forcing makes it more difficult for the offense to dribble up court, drive to the basket, or execute any ball movement. Forcing often hampers novices from dribbling.

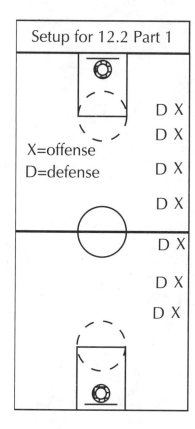

Setup for 12.2 Part 1

X=offense
D=defense

This lesson has five parts which can be taught on successive days.

Setup

Use managers on offense, so more players can work on defense. The offense lines up on the sideline, 3-5 yards apart, facing the court. The defense initially sets up one foot away.

Directions for Players

Part 1 Tap Dance–Force Positions

1. Defense: set up in defensive position, left foot forward, one foot away from the offense. Place your left foot one foot to the left of the offense. You are on the right of the offense. Offense,

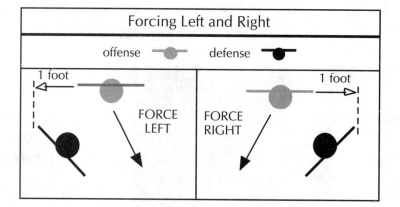

raise your right hand to convince doubters. If the offense goes right, they bump into you. If they go left, it is clear sailing. This is the *force left* position. Usually, you force righties this way.

•Check the position of each player.

2. The *force right* position places the right foot forward, one foot right of the defense. Switch to the force right position. This is the way to force left handers.

3. Tap dance on the balls of the feet. Continue while I give you directions to move to the force left and right positions.

•Instruct the players to switch back and forth several times.

•Repeat steps 1-3 switching the offense and defense. Managers stay on offense.

Part 2 Tap Dance, Jump Step, Force

4. The defense tap dances in the force left position. Back off until you are three yards away.

•Novices are not often able to judge distance well. Instruct them to move one yard, then two, then three, and back again until they estimate well.

5. The offense slowly walks forward for 2-4 seconds. The defense continues to maintain the three-yard distance by jump stepping or sliding backward. Take small quick steps. When you take a jump step, do not bring your feet close together. Do not just slide your feet all the way together either. If you take this step quickly it resembles a jump. Continue to tap dance during this lesson. (You may want to forget this last instruction initially)

6. Offense–walk back toward the original position. Defense– maintain the three-yard separation. Offense– continue to walk back and forth.

•Instruct the players to force left, and then right, and then left again. Offense and defense switch. Repeat. Continue when players are more expert.

Part 3 Force While Walking

7. Offense–walk back and forth at will. Walk only–no jogging. Faking is okay. The defense must watch the midsection of the offense, not the limbs (or ball), to avoid being faked out. Continue to tap dance and force left.

•Instruct the players to force left and then right for 20 seconds intervals.

8. Offense and defense switch.

•Repeat.

Part 4 Force Moving Faster

9. Offense, jog back and fourth, not to the sides.

•Repeat force left and right instructions, then the offense and defense switch.

Part 5 Force One Yard

10. Defense, move one yard from the offense. Continue.

•Instruct players to force left and right. Then offense and defense switch.

Troubleshooting

1. The defense toils for less than 1 minute in each part. Make sure each player forces both left and right.

2. Players move in the half down position, jump stepping back and forth.

3. Watch that players maintain the correct distance from the offense during each part of the lesson.

Use of Assistants

Use assistants as offense as well as to help keep groups a safe distance apart.

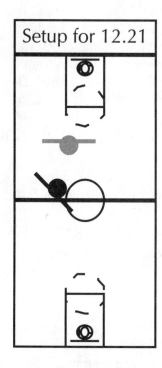

Setup for 12.21

Weekly Practice Everyday

Extensions

12.21 Three Yard Lesson

Do Lesson 12.2 with only two players on the court at a time. The offense can operate at full tilt. It lasts 25 seconds. Time it. The offense not only moves back and forth, but also left and right. The distance between offense and defense is three yards. Players alternate forcing left and then right according to your yelled instructions. Offense and defense switch roles. This is difficult.

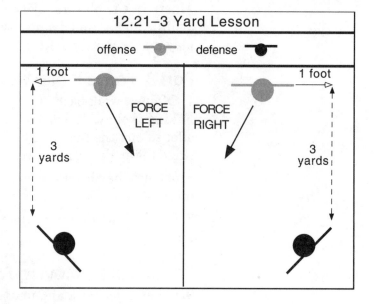

12.21–3 Yard Lesson

offense ——●—— defense ——●——

1 foot | FORCE LEFT | FORCE RIGHT | 1 foot

3 yards | 3 yards

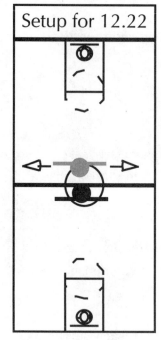

Setup for 12.22

12.22 Mirror Lesson

The offense in Lesson 12.21 lines up, head to head, with the defense. Move side to side only. The defense attempts to stay in front of the offense. This is difficult. Instruct the offense to increase the speed as the defense becomes more expert.

12.3 Trapping 1-3

Brief:
Two defensive players prevent an offensive player from dribbling forward.

Fundamental Notes

Trapping retards an offensive player from advancing the ball in both half and full court presses. It often stops the dribble and hampers passing as well. Two defensive players normally trap one offensive player with the ball. A smart defensive player alone can use the sideline, instead of another player, to trap the offense. With two players' trapping, one player must force left while the other forces right. This lesson involves forcing, communication and teamwork, hustle, and conditioning.

Setup

Part 1 –Each group of three sets up 10 yards apart.

Part 2 –One group sets up at the foul line.

Directions for Players

Part 1 Trapping

1. The defensive players set up one yard away

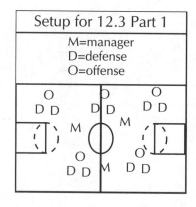

Setup for 12.3 Part 1

M=manager
D=defense
O=offense

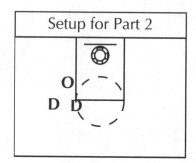

Setup for Part 2

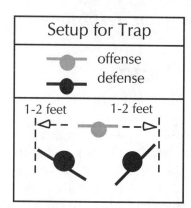

Setup for Trap

offense
defense

1-2 feet   1-2 feet

from the offense with their inside feet slightly inside the feet of the offense. The outside feet are both outside the feet of the offense and forward toward the offense. This necessitates that the offense move backward.

2. The offense tries to walk by, through, or around the defense. No running.

3. The defense prevents this walking by moving with the offense, keeping the offense in the same relative position between the two offensive players. Coordinate your efforts. Block the offense if they try to go through or around.

•Each play lasts 5-15 seconds.

4. Ready. Go... Stop. Rotate positions.

•Repeat till each player is on offense at least twice.

Part 2 Full Speed

•As the defense learns how to trap, speed up the offense. Go full speed with only one group on the court.

Part 3 Finishing Off the Trap

5. It is important to finish off the trap properly. The objective is not necessarily to steal the ball. Tying a player up for 5 seconds, or causing a bad pass, is just as good. Fouling a trapped player is a costly mistake after exerting much effort. Instead of flailing your arms, slowly move closer to the offense. Let them give you the ball.

6. Set up in groups of three, about five yards apart.

7. Two defensive players try to tie up the offense, no fouls.

8. The offense pivots away high-low like lesson 2.22. Keep your head up. Count slowly to five.

9. Switch roles each time. Each player pivots twice.

Troubleshooting

1. Initially, allow the defense to block the offense.

2. In a game, the offensive player has a ball, so the defense keeps their arms extended outward and hands low to stop the dribbling.

Use of Assistants

Part 1–Assistants stay between groups to prevent collisions.

Weekly Practice 3-6 times per season.

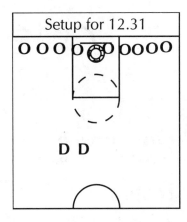

Setup for 12.31

Extensions

12.31 Trapping Game

Two defensive players stand at the top of the key, waiting to trap the offensive player that takes off from the baseline. The rest of the team is on the endline. Secretly give each team member a number. When you call the number of a player they take off. The defense has 6 seconds to trap this player. Count out loud. As soon as one player is finished, call another number before the defense has a chance to set up. Repeat this five times with each defensive group. Kids like it.

12.4 Front-Keep Out of Lane

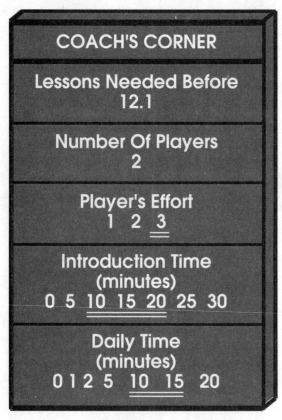

COACH'S CORNER

Lessons Needed Before
12.1

Number Of Players
2

Player's Effort
1 2 <u>3</u>

Introduction Time
(minutes)
0 5 <u>10 15 20</u> 25 30

Daily Time
(minutes)
0 1 2 5 <u>10 15</u> 20

Defensive Movement in The Lane

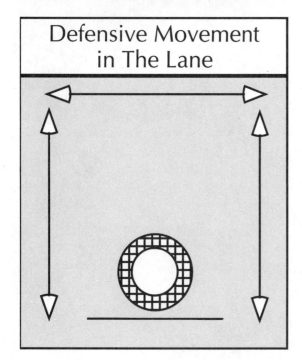

Brief:

The defense prevents the offense from entering the lane area by stepping in front and blocking.

Fundamental Notes

Lessons 12.4 to 12.6 primarily teach how to cover a player without the ball. They also help with *on ball* coverage. Fronting means that the offense plays the defense, face to face, without distraction. The defense does not look for the ball. Fronting has one major game application in out-of-bounds plays. This lesson, on the other hand, has several other defensive applications: one-on-one play, blocking and boxing out. It also reduces both the fear of contact and the excessive fouling that occurs with more contact between players. Hustle is also involved.

Setup

Position two lines, one for the offense and one for the defense, at the top of the key. The first offensive player starts at the foul line. The first defensive player stands inside the lane facing the offense. See the diagram.

Directions for Players

1. Offense—get past the defense into the lane. Walk initially.

2. Defense—block the offense with the arms and body. If the offense charges into the lane, push them off with your hands. Push their upper arms and shoulders, rather than their stomach and face. Mom and dad will appreciate it. The offense should initiate the contact, if you are positioned properly.

3. Start in the half down ready position.

• The lesson lasts 5-10 seconds; time it. Offense and defense then switch.

4. Ready... Go... Stop. Switch (or Next)

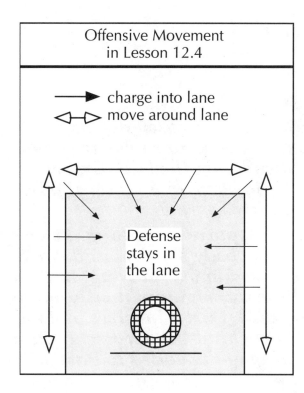

Offensive Movement
in Lesson 12.4

→ charge into lane
◁—▷ move around lane

Defense stays in the lane

Troubleshooting

1. Remind players that when fronting, never look for the ball. Keep your eyes on the player's midsection (and eyes if a pass is expected).

2. The offense must work hard, so that the defense obtains practice.

Use of Assistants None

Weekly Practice 2-3 times

Extensions

12.41 Front and Box Out

Shout "shot" at the end of Lesson 12.4. At this point the offense goes straight for the basket. The defense blocks, pivots, and then boxes out the offense. Lesson 11.2 or 11.3 is needed first.

12.5 Overplay 1-6

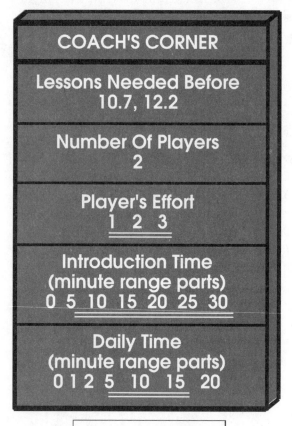

COACH'S CORNER

Lessons Needed Before
10.7, 12.2

Number Of Players
2

Player's Effort
1 2 3

Introduction Time
(minute range parts)
0 5 10 15 20 25 30

Daily Time
(minute range parts)
0 1 2 5 10 15 20

Part	Intro	Daily
1	20-30	10-15
2	5-15	5-10
3	5-15	5-10
4	5-15	5-10
5	10-15	5-10
6	10-15	5-10

Times for Each Part (minutes)

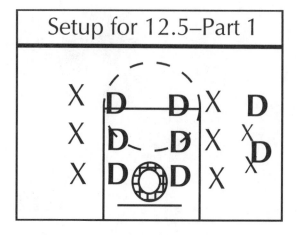

Setup for 12.5–Part 1

Brief:

These 6 lessons teach defense, emphasizing coverage near the basket, away from the ball. Experienced players can do several parts in one day.

In Part 1, players are taught as a group the body position and movements used in overplaying. In Part 2, players work individually on the same skill. Part 3 involves a player cutting behind the defense. In Part 4, boxing out is added to Part 3. In Part 5, the defense covers the offense after losing contact. Part 6 involves an offensive player cutting into the lane, right in front of the defense, from the high post.

Fundamental Notes

These lessons are the key to both individual and team defense. Overplaying prevents the offense from catching a pass where they want–close to the basket. It also prevents cuts into the low post, or any other area, as well as offensive rebounds–because it's easy to box out from the overplaying position. As a team skill, overplaying enables strong- and weak-side help. These lessons are more important than defense *on the ball*, because they teach defense *near the basket* where teams both shoot best and score the most points. Good defense alters this.

Setup

Overall–The offense starts in the low post area. The defense is inside the lane, next to the offense. See each part for other particulars.

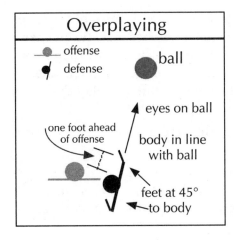

Overplaying

offense
defense
ball

eyes on ball

one foot ahead of offense

body in line with ball

feet at 45° to body

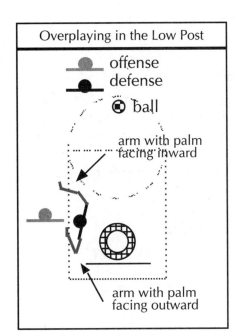

Overplaying in the Low Post

offense
defense
ball

arm with palm facing inward

arm with palm facing outward

Directions for Players

Part 1 Overplay

Setup

Three offensive players set up on each side of lane. Spread out as much as possible. The defense sets up in the lane next to offense. Other players can set up next to any line as though it were the lane. Place the ball at the top of the key.

Directions

1. The defense has the foot closest to the offense one step ahead. The right foot is ahead on the left side; the left on the right side. The behind or back foot is almost in a straight line with the other foot.

2. If you put your arms straight out, the front arm points forward downcourt; the other points toward the endline. Bend both elbows slightly downward. The palm of the front hand faces inward. The hand is in a ready position to deflect a pass. Rotate the back hand inward and down so that the palm faces outward (away from the lane) and the forearm points downward. The hand is in position to touch the offense. Move it back and forth to sense offensive movement.

•See the diagrams.

3. Move both arms toward the offense so that you are touching them. Touch them with your back hand and your front elbow. Feel where the offense moves. Offense, slowly move 2-3 steps up and down the lane.

4. Defense, keep your eyes on me while you do this. Move, so that you stay in the same position relative to the offense.

5. If the offense attempts to step in the lane in front of you, they should bump into your forearm and body. Offense, try stepping in the lane.

6. If they attempt to step behind you into the lane, they should bump into your back arm and body. Offense, try it.

7. Offense and defense switch.

•Repeat steps 1-6.

•Groups change sides, then repeat steps 1-6.

Part 2 Individual Practice

•Repeat this lesson with one group on each side of the lane at a time. Time the length of each play to 10-20

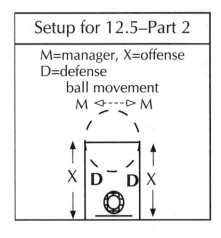

Setup for 12.5–Part 2

M=manager, X=offense
D=defense
ball movement

M ◁---▷ M

X D D X

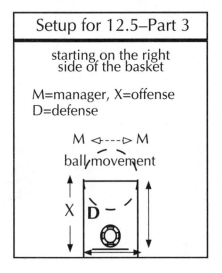

Setup for 12.5–Part 3

starting on the right
side of the basket

M=manager, X=offense
D=defense

M ◁---▷ M
ball movement

X D

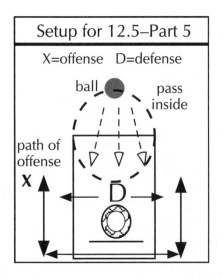

Setup for 12.5–Part 5

X=offense   D=defense

ball   pass
inside

path of
offense
X

D

seconds. Each player needs to work on both sides of the lane. Speed up the offense as the defense catches on. The defense watches the ball, not the offense. Place the ball at the top of the key, or let managers have a catch, back and forth, there. Go on to Part 3 only when the defense can overplay the offense moving at full speed.

8. The offense tries to get into the lane in front of, or better, behind the defense.

9. The defense keeps the offense out of the lane. Keep your eyes on the ball at all times. Play the offense by touch. Let the offense move into your arms. Any gentle contact clues you to offensive movements.

Part 3 Overplay Both Sides
•Only one group works at a time.

10. The offense first tries to cut in front of, and then goes behind, the defense. Keep going to the other side of the lane.

11. Defense, prevent the offense from stepping into the lane. When the offense goes behind the basket, not just behind you, allow the offense to cross over to the other side of the lane. Continue to play the offense on the other side of the lane. Keep your eyes on the ball. Locate the offense by touch.

•Offense and defense switch.

Part 4 Overplay and Box Out
•Boxing out, Lesson 11.3, is added to Part 3. Use two groups.

12. After 3-6 seconds I will yell "shot." The offense then goes for the basket. The defense boxes them out.

Part 5 No-Touch D
•This lesson teaches the defense how to react if they lose their offensive assignment. Offense and defense set up in the low post. A player at the top of the key attempts to pass the ball to the offense. Do this one group at a time.

13. Defense, purposely lose contact with the offensive player. This happens in games.

14. Stay in the middle of the lane. Watch the ball only. Do not turn around to look for the offense. If you watch the passer, a pass cannot be thrown into the lane.

15. The passer tries to hit an open player in the lane. Pass the ball within six seconds. Count out loud.

•In a game players locate their coverage at the first opportune moment–when a pass cannot be thrown into the lane.

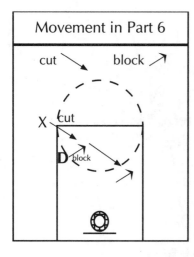

Movement in Part 6

cut   block

X cut

D block

Part 6 Overplay Cutter

•One group at a time.

16. Offense, cut from the high post on one side to the low post on the other side.

17. Defense, stay ahead of the cutter. Prevent the cutter from making a straight cut by stopping in front. Making contact all across the lane slows the cutter. Passers also have difficulty timing passes to cutters being bumped and impeded. When 3-4 feet from the basket, move to or stay in front of the cutter.

Troubleshooting

1. Start each part with a demonstration.

2. The offense walks very slowly at first. As the defense develops each skill, increase the speed of the offense. The offense should go slower, rather than faster, than needed.

3. The defense looks at the ball at all times and plays the offense by touch.

12.6 Defense the Low Post

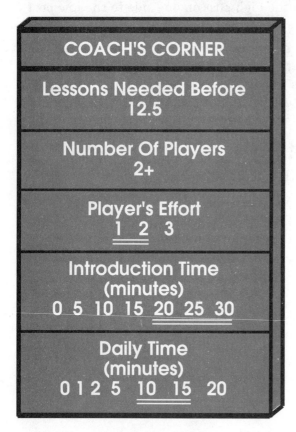

COACH'S CORNER

Lessons Needed Before
12.5

Number Of Players
2+

Player's Effort
<u>1</u> 2 3

Introduction Time
(minutes)
0 5 10 15 <u>20</u> 25 30

Daily Time
(minutes)
0 1 2 5 <u>10</u> <u>15</u> 20

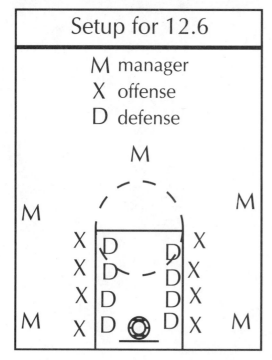

Setup for 12.6

M manager
X offense
D defense

Brief:

On the strong side, the defense overplays and steps in front of the low post player. On the weak side, the defense opens up to the ball and keeps the offense on their back.

Fundamental Notes

In the overplaying lesson, 12.5, the ball remains in a fixed position. In this lesson, as in a game, defense is played while the ball moves from side to side. Strong-side and weak-side defense are played differently. On the strong side, the same side of the court as the ball, the defense plays aggressively to prevent a pass to the low post. On the weak side, the side away from the ball, the defense stays in a position to both help out on defense as well as prevent a pass inside. In either case, the defense stays close enough to box out after a shot. Be aware that offenses go to the right side in games more than to the left. Do this lesson as a group initially. Players also need strong- and weak-side defensive practice on both sides of the basket. When you repeat this lesson switching offense and defense roles, it takes less time than it did initially.

Setup

Half the team lines up on the lane as offense. The other half is defense. If the lane area is crowded, move players outside the lane as close to the low post as possible. Position managers in a semicircle around the periphery to pass the ball around. The ball directions in the lesson are for the managers. Demonstrate the lesson with one group near the foul line.

Directions for Players

1. The strong side of the court is the side that the ball is on; the weak side is the other side. The strong and weak sides are separated by an

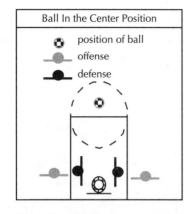

Ball In the Center Position
- ◉ position of ball
- offense
- defense

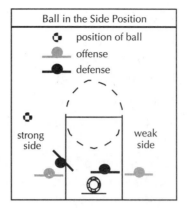

Ball in the Side Position
- ◉ position of ball
- offense
- defense

strong side   weak side

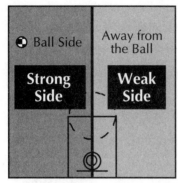

◉ Ball Side   Away from the Ball

Strong Side   **Weak Side**

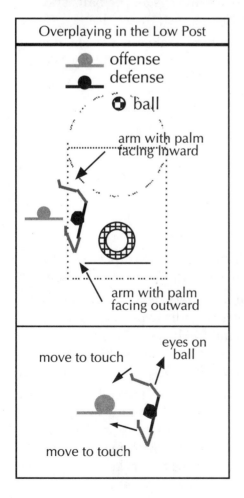

Overplaying in the Low Post
- offense
- defense
- ◉ ball

arm with palm facing inward

arm with palm facing outward

move to touch   eyes on ball

move to touch

imaginary line down the center of the lane to the basket. (Point this out.) Strong-side and weak-side defense are played differently. When the ball is in the center of the court everyone plays strong-side defense.

•Pass the ball around the periphery. Point out the strong and weak side players after each pass.

2. Players on the weak side are not immediate scoring threats like those on the strong side. So, you can rotate away from the offense toward the center of the court to help cover strong-side players. This is called helping out.

•Move the ball to the center position.

3. Overplay the offense now. Shoulder to shoulder your body points to the ball. Your forward foot is slightly ahead of the offense; the back foot is slightly behind. Your eyes are on the ball. Play defense by touch.

•Move the ball to the right side of the free throw line extended.

4. The right side is the strong side. Shoulder to shoulder, strong-side players point to the ball. Weak-side players pivot around on the back foot to squarely face the ball. This is called opening up to the ball. This is too open. You will find it is more difficult to prevent cuts and cover the offense this way. Rotate half way back to the original position. This is the halfway opened up position we want. Shoulder to shoulder, your body points slightly to the center of the ball position.

•Work with each weak-side player. Move the ball to the corresponding left side position and repeat.

5. Move the ball to the right corner position. Strong-side players pivot on your front foot to step in front of the offense with your back foot. You are directly facing the ball. The inside arm is straight up; the outside arm is straight back. Often you can stay in this position until the ball comes out of the corner. If the ball is shot, squirm around the offense toward the inside hand that is straight back. If not, pivot on the outside foot, so that you overplay the offense from the basket side. When the ball comes out of the corner, move back the same way (unless the ball is on the other side of the court). Step in front with the back foot. Then step to the side, pivoting on the forward foot.

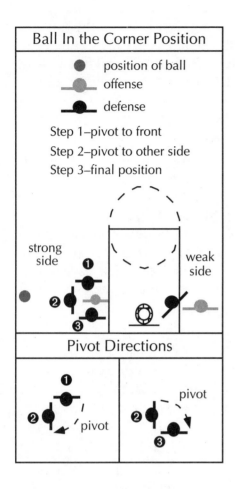

Ball In the Corner Position

- ● position of ball
- ○ offense
- ● defense

Step 1–pivot to front
Step 2–pivot to other side
Step 3–final position

strong side

weak side

Pivot Directions

• Repeat this double pivot move several times.

6. Weak-side players open up slightly more. If the offense cuts behind the basket to the strong side, open up more to keep them on your back.

• Check the position of each player.

• Then, move the ball to the left corner and repeat steps 5 and 6.

7. Do not stand so close to the defense that their body blocks you out. You need room to move for the ball. Stay at least one foot away.

• Move the ball around the periphery one pass at a time. Check each player before progressing.

• Offense and defense switch. Repeat steps 1-7.

• Repeat again with players switching sides. This does not take much time.

Troubleshooting

1. The defense is in the half down defensive position throughout this lesson.

2. The eyes of the defense are always on the ball. The position of the offense is determined by touch.

3. Strong-side players are aligned, shoulder to shoulder, with the ball. Weak-side players open up halfway to the ball.

Use of Assistants

Assistants pass the ball around the periphery.

Weekly Practice   As needed

Extensions

12.61 Low Post with Passing

1. One offensive player is in each low post position. The defense applies the defensive skills learned in Lesson 12.6.

2. The other players and managers pass the ball around the periphery. As the defense gains expertise, allow the offense both to move around freely as well as pass to the low post. Execute this lesson at several baskets with defense on the passers. Run this lesson for 10-30 seconds.

Note that there are two ways to move around a player in the low post. One is to move in front and the other is to move behind. Novices should always move via the front of the offense. Don't worry about lobs. With more experienced players, use whichever method works.

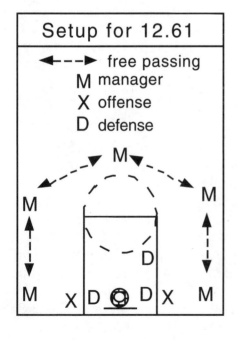

Setup for 12.61

- ◄--► free passing
- M manager
- X offense
- D defense

In some situations, the defense may be able to effectively overplay the offense from either side. The rule that applies in every situation is: use what works best. If you teach one simple way, not three, to players, it will be easier than you thought to adjust to game situations.

12.7 D on Shooter

COACH'S CORNER

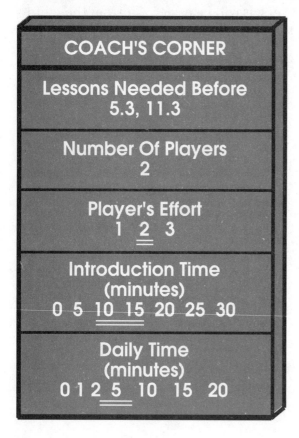

Lessons Needed Before
5.3, 11.3

Number Of Players
2

Player's Effort
1 <u>2</u> 3

Introduction Time (minutes)
0 5 <u>10</u> 15 20 25 30

Daily Time (minutes)
0 1 2 <u>5</u> 10 15 20

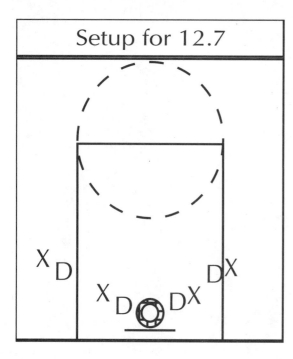

Setup for 12.7

Brief:
The defense harasses the shooter without committing a foul.

Fundamental Notes

This is similar to Lesson 7.3. The key to covering a shooter effectively, without fouling, involves the movement of the arms. Any attempt to snuff the ball (down the throat of the offense) usually has adverse results. Often, a foul is called even if there is no contact. Referees call fouls when they see arms flailing around. If there is a successful block, the offense usually picks the ball off the floor and then scores unopposed while the defense basks in the full glory of the snuff.

The primary objective of the defense is to alter the shot of the offense and then box them out. This lesson shows many ways to alter the shot. Players practice boxing out as well. Offensive skills are also practiced; one is shooting under pressure; another is going for the rebound after shooting.

Setup

The offense takes a two-foot shot with the defense right on them. Groups set up on the left and right of the basket. The groups shoot alternately.

Directions for Players

1. The defense sets up directly in front of the offense. The left arm and hand are fully extended upward, slightly to the right side of the shooter. If the shooter is left handed, the right arm is extended and slightly to the left. Do not move this arm in any direction–side to side or back and forth. Especially, do not bring the arm downward to snuff the ball in the shooters face. Excessive motion results in a foul call, whether or not there is any contact. Let the offense shoot the ball into your hand if you want an effective snuff.

2. The other hand should be about six inches or

Position of Arms

The defense must place one hand in the offense's line of view.

line of view

more from the face. Attempt to obstruct the vision and distract the shooter. Wave your fingers; open and close your hand; any motion can distract the shooter.

3. Use your voice as well. Make funny noises. Yell, "fire; help; yikes, your laces are loose; your underwear is showing" or anything else that might distract the shooter. No abusive or derogatory statements concerning heritage.

4. Do not jump or make an excessive attempt to block the shot.

5. After the shot, block and then box out the shooter.

6. Offense, go for the ball after the shot.

•One option is to continue play until the shot is made. Whoever gets the rebound is on offense; the other player is on defense.

7. Offense and defense switch after each shot.

Troubleshooting

1. The object is to alter the shot, not to block it.

2. Box out the shooter. Otherwise, the shooter just waltzes in for a follow-up layup.

3. Players tend to swing their arms wildly to "put it in your face." To correct the slashing habit, repeat this lesson 10-15 times with a culprit making this mistake under your personal supervision.

Use of Assistants None

Weekly Practice As needed

Extensions

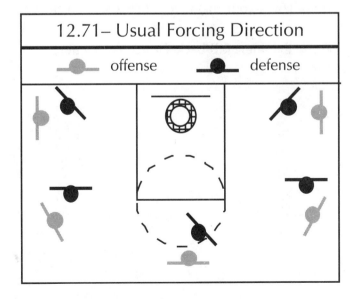

12.71– Usual Forcing Direction

offense   defense

12.71 D on Driver

There always is a direction in which the defense wants to force an offensive player with the ball.

Directions

The offense sets up, without the ball initially, in these positions–center, both sides, both baselines–and runs past the defense toward the basket. The offense can fake. The defense forces them in the most favorable direction as explained below. Groups alternate at each basket. Change positions every minute. Offense and defense switch roles after each run. Very experienced offensive players can use a ball. However, the defense gets better practice if the ball is not used for two reasons: one, the offense can move faster without the ball; two, the defense concentrates more on the player, rather than the ball. Players start 5-7 yards from the basket.

Center of court around key

1. Force a player in the center part of the court near the key or foul line toward either the player's weak hand or toward defensive help. Force left in the lesson.

Side and corner

2. Force a player positioned on either side, or corner, to the center where there usually is defensive help. Never give a player the baseline, since there is no help coming from out-of-bounds. Note, that sometimes you can trap on the baseline with more experienced players.

Dribbling down court (If this was done in Lesson 12.21, you can skip this now.)

3. The defense forces the player dribbling down court to either the sideline or toward the dribbler's weak hand.

12.72 2 on 1

1. Two offensive players set up just outside the lane between the foul line and key. The player on the right has the ball. He/she dribbles in for the layup. Pass only if the defense stops the dribbler.

2. The defense starts in the middle of the lane. Force the dribbler to the outside.

3. Make them pass. Most players have difficulty passing. Passing also slows down this break so that another defensive player can catch up. Have your inside hand ready to block the pass.

4. After you stop the dribbler, fall back for the pass, shot, or rebound.

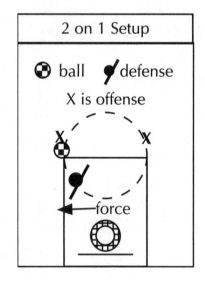

2 on 1 Setup

⊗ ball   defense

X is offense

force

Section 13
Picking or Screening

L E S S O N #	NAME	P L A Y E R S	C O U R T	B A L L	E F F O R T	LESSONS BEFORE	L E S S O N #	INTRO TIME	DAILY TIME
13.0	**Picking or Screening 1-2**	2+	x	x	1	10.6, 10.51	**13.0**	10-15	5
13.01	Defensing the Pick	4	x	x	2	13.0	13.01	10-30	5-15

13.0 Picking or Screening 1-2

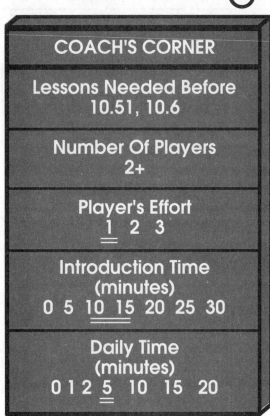

COACH'S CORNER

Lessons Needed Before
10.51, 10.6

Number Of Players
2+

Player's Effort
<u>1</u> 2 3

Introduction Time
(minutes)
0 5 <u>10</u> <u>15</u> 20 25 30

Daily Time
(minutes)
0 1 2 <u>5</u> 10 15 20

Brief:
A player sets a pick in the best position for a cutter.

Fundamental Notes

Picking is used to shake an offensive player loose from a tight defender. So, it is more important for older players than for novices. Pros pick the most. If you coach youngsters, skip this. Picks free up players to shoot, cut, dribble, and pass. Picking away from the ball is both more common and effective than picks on the ball, because off-ball defensive players are not as ready for picks as on-ball players.

Setup

The cutting line starts from the low post on the left side of the basket. The picking line starts at the high post on the right side of the basket.

Directions for Players

Part 1

1. The high post player runs straight across the lane to the left side to set a pick.

2. Your feet are slightly more than shoulder-width apart; legs bent, arms at the sides. Cross

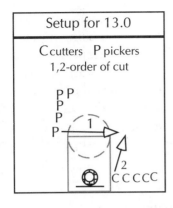

Setup for 13.0

C cutters   P pickers
1,2-order of cut

Elbows of a Pick

too much   too little   just right

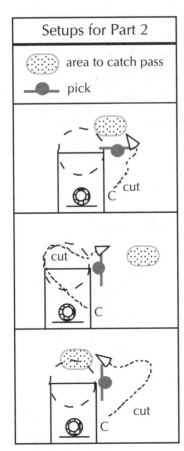

Setups for Part 2

area to catch pass

pick

cut

cut

cut

the forearms on the chest for protection. Move the elbows out slightly to take up more space.

3. Face the direction opposite the one that the cutter wants to go. This means that you face the cutter. In this case, the cutter is cutting out for the ball. Remain frozen in this position after setting up. It is a violation or foul to move right before the defense bumps into you. See the diagram.

4. The offensive player "wipes off" or "rubs off" the defense on the pick. Wait till the pick is set. Then maneuver the defense to run squarely into the pick. Cut by the pick so closely that you rub shoulders.

5. Switch lines.

Part 2

•Switch the direction or angle of the pick. The cutter must adjust the route as well. The diagrams show several situations. Some directions cutters can use: toward or away from the basket; toward the left or right sidelines; to the top of the key; to the low post, left or right side. Continue to execute the picking at the right side high post.

Troubleshooting

1. Remind the cutter to wait until the pick is set, or stationary, before cutting.

2. The cutter fakes before cutting.

Use of Assistants None

Weekly Practice 2-3 times per season

13.01 Defensing the Pick

This lesson adds defense on the cutter and the pick to Lesson 13.0. After the demonstration, players can work in groups of four at other baskets or anywhere in the gym. Make sure to assign starting spots to cutter and picker, as well as the approximate location of the pick. The pick needs to be stationary before the cutter uses it. The defense on the cutter should not be able to see the pick as they would in the previous lesson. See the diagram for a setup.

1. There are several options for defensing the user of a pick. In any case, the defender covering the pick needs to recognize that this is a picking situation. Then yell "pick left" (or right) as a warning.

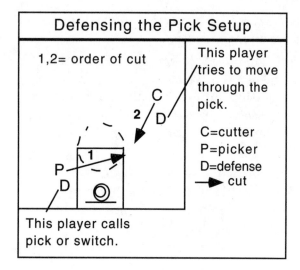

Defensing the Pick Setup

1,2= order of cut

This player tries to move through the pick.

C=cutter
P=picker
D=defense
→ cut

This player calls pick or switch.

2. Squeezing through a pick is easier to learn than the other methods for defensing a pick. The defensive player on the cutter steps or squeezes through the pick, so that he/she can not be rubbed off. To do this, the defense must be aware that a pick is set and then get to it ahead of the cutter. Repeat with offense and defense switching roles and then the cutters and pickers switching roles.

•Practice this.

3. A second way to defense the pick requires that the defensive player on the pick steps back, so that the defense on the cutter can slide between the defense and the pick. This method is used farther from the basket where there is not an immediate scoring threat.

4. A third way involves a switch. The defensive player on the cutter yells, "switch." The defense on the pick jumps to the far side of the pick to cover the cutter. The defensive player on the cutter steps back to cover the pick. Continue to play at half speed for 5-10 seconds after the pick. This may involve several switches back and forth. Change roles. Much coordination is needed for switches.

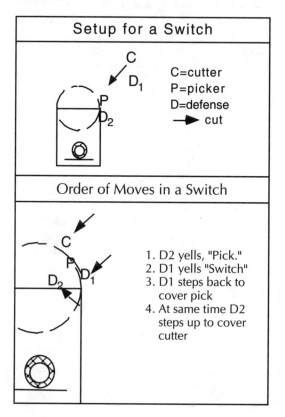

Setup for a Switch

C=cutter
P=picker
D=defense
→ cut

Order of Moves in a Switch

1. D2 yells, "Pick."
2. D1 yells "Switch"
3. D1 steps back to cover pick
4. At same time D2 steps up to cover cutter

Section 14
The Center Jump

L E S S O N #	NAME	P L A Y E R S	C O U R T	B A L L	E F F O R T	LESSONS BEFORE	L E S S O N #	INTRO TIME	DAILY TIME
14.0	**Center Jump**	T	x	x	1-3	12.1+	**14.0**	15-25	5-10
14.01	Practice Jumping	T	x	x	3	14.0+	14.01	5-10	2-5
14.02	D at Center Jump	T	x	x	3	all 12, 14.0+	14.02	5-10	5

14.0 Center Jump

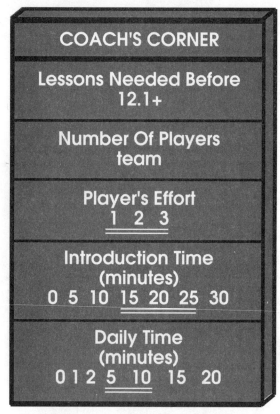
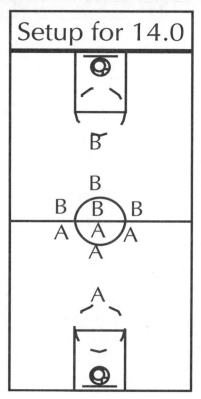

Setup for 14.0

Brief:

Players learn a simple defensive center jump.

Fundamental Notes

The only two sensible objectives for a center jump are to 1) get the ball and 2) prevent the other team from scoring. Designing tricky scoring plans from a jump ball is a waste of time and effort. Often these plans backfire and the opposite occurs; your opponent easily scores. The center jump described here is not only safe, but also has positive results–your team ends up with the ball.

Setup

See the diagram. Three players line up equidistant on the defensive side of the restraining circle. One player is about 10 yards back on defense. The other player is in the jump circle. Set up two teams. After each jump, players rotate counterclockwise so that each player plays each position.

Directions for Players

1. Jumpers, set up in the jump circle on the side facing your basket. Turn sideways for the jump. The knees are bent. The forearm of the hand used to tap the ball is bent upward, with the palm facing your body. See the diagram.

2. Before stepping into the circle, check several things. One, make sure your teammates are set up properly. If they are not, then direct them into place. Two, determine the best place to tap the ball. Look for two teammates next to each other, or an area where the offense is much closer than the defense. Communicate this information in a non-obvious, nonverbal way to your teammates.

3. Jump as the referee throws the ball up. If you wait for the ball to reach a peak, then the ball will be on the way down when you are up. Extend the arm fully as you jump. Again, you need

Position of Right Handed Jumper

right forearm and hand ready

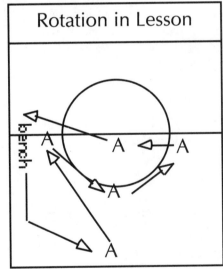

Rotation in Lesson

to be ready to tap the ball.

4. Lightly tap the ball with your fingertips, not your hand, to the previously picked spot. This spot is over your head in the direction that your team is positioned.

5. Players on the line take up as much space as possible. Set up quickly so you can freely choose your position. Nonverbally communicate with the jumper. Determine where the jumper wants to tap the ball. If you think the other jumper will control the jump, determine where they want to tap the ball. Look for obvious communication between players on the other team. Obviously, do not be obvious yourself.

6. After the ball is tossed, step in front of any opposing player for the tap. Get position, then go for the ball.

7. If you secure the ball, pass it to the guard back on defense.

8. The player back on defense does not go for the ball. You are strictly on defense. If our team wins the tap, the ball goes to you.

•In a game always put a guard in this position.

•Say "Ready," then toss the ball. Players rotate. Continue for the allotted time.

•See the diagram for the rotation. Rotate bench players as well into the center jump.

Troubleshooting

1. Most players jump too late.

2. They are also late extending their arm for the ball. See Lesson 14.01 for a simple jumping lesson.

3. The jumper must make sure everybody is in position before stepping into the jump circle.

4. The jumper must tip the ball back over the head rather than forward.

Use of Assistants   None

Weekly Practice   2-3 times at the start of the season

Extensions

14.01 Practice Jumping

Most novices need practice jumping at the center jump. This is a rapid fire jump lesson that takes 2-5 minutes. It needs to be practiced 2-4 times at the beginning of the season.

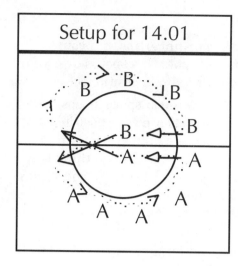

Setup for 14.01

Setup

Use two jumping lines that meet at the center jump. Curve the lines around the restraining circle so the players are in position to catch the taps. See the diagram.

Directions for Players

1. Players go from one line to the other.

2. I will say *ready* and then toss it.

3. The tapping arm and hand need to be extended almost before the jump. As you jump, the arm needs to be up, ready to tap the toss. Tap the ball backward over your head.

4. You need to expect errant tosses by the referees. Often the toss is too high, or too low, or too much to one side or the other. The toss counts, whichever way it goes.

•Without much effort you will teach players this. Toss some (additional) bad ones the way of a shorter player when they line up against a taller player. Players discover that the outcome of a jump is not foreordained.

14.02 D at Center Jump

If you play person-to-person defense, players pick up their defensive assignments at the center jump. The coach cannot do this ahead of time. Players pick their assignments and then communicate this to every other team member. Otherwise, three players may decide to cover the same person.

Setup

The setup is the same as Lesson 14.0: two teams ready to play at the center jump. The players start from the bench and walk out to the jump area.

Directions for Players

1. The jumper does not step into the circle until all players have their assignment.

2. Each player does two things to avoid mix-ups. One, walk toward and also point to the player that you will cover. Two, look at the selections of the other players. Work out any problems. When the team is ready, then the jumper steps into the circle.

•Shift both the lineups and the positions of the players after each jump. There is no need to actually toss the ball. When the players are ready, reposition them, and start over.

•As a check, instruct one team and then the other to cover the defense.

•After players learn how to pick up the defense, then work on making sure the match ups are sensible.

•In general you want tall players on tall players, athletic players on athletic ones and so on. Since the players on your team know each other well, the match-ups should be fairly accurate without your help. If they are not, explain any changes that you make.

The Basketball Coach's Bible

Section 15
Transition

L E S S O N #	NAME	P L A Y E R S	C O U R T	B A L L	E F F O R T	LESSONS BEFORE	L E S S O N #	INTRO TIME	DAILY TIME
15.0	**Foul Line Transition1-3**	T	x	x	1-3	all-11, 12+	**15.0**	15-30@	10-20@
15.1	Center Jump Transition	T	x	x	1-3	14.0, 15.0+	15.1	15-30	10-20
15.2	Play to Transition	T	x	x	2-3	9.6, 15.0, 16.0+	15.2	15-25	10-20

15.0 Foul Line Transition 1-3

COACH'S CORNER
Lessons Needed Before all 11-12+
Number Of Players team
Player's Effort <u>1</u> 2 3
Introduction Time (minutes per part) 0 5 10 <u>15</u> <u>20</u> <u>25</u> <u>30</u>
Daily Time (minutes per part) 0 1 2 5 <u>10</u>   <u>15</u>   <u>20</u>

Setup for 15.0 Part 1

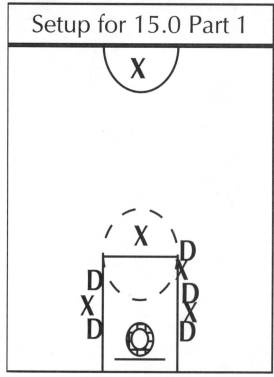

Brief:

This lesson teaches the free throw line and press setups as well as how to quickly make the transition between the two.

Fundamental Notes

Transitions, in general, are made from offense to defense and vice-versa; the exception is the transition from the neutral center jump to either offense or defense. In Part 1, the foul line setup is taught. The transition in Part 2 of this lesson is made to midcourt. Once learned, players quickly make transitions *to and from* any situation. In Part 3, the transition is made to a press. In addition, this lesson stresses boxing out, conditioning, and hustle.

Setup

Offense and defense wear different colors so you can easily differentiate them. Split all of your players into two teams (leave the 1/2s intact); nobody watches. With older players you may not want to put players in improper foul line positions. The defense sets up on the foul line in the first, third, and the position closest to the shooter. The offense sets up in the second and the forth positions; one player is at the foul line and another is past midcourt. Put as many players as possible on the lane. Put additional groups of players two steps away from the lane.

Directions for Players

Part 1 The Foul Line Setup

1. All players are in the half down position with your hands ready to catch the ball.

2. Defensive players line up as close to the offense as possible. Be careful; it is a violation to be on any line. Extend your arms outward; the elbows are slightly bent. Keep your arms above the arms of the offense.

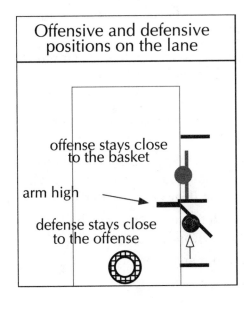

Offensive and defensive positions on the lane

offense stays close to the basket

arm high

defense stays close to the offense

3. When the ball is released, step in front of the offensive player. Expect a solid collision. Box them out before going for the ball.

4. The player closest to the shooter yells *shooter*. This informs your team that you will box out the shooter. After the ball is released, jump in front of the shooter.

5. Offensive players step inside as fast as possible when the ball hits the rim.

•More experienced players elude the defense by stepping outside as well.

6. Watch the shooter and ball with arms and hands in the ready position. Move when the ball touches the rim.

7. One offensive player is back at midcourt on defense. You sprint to the foul line on transition. Be careful; 10 players are sprinting in the other direction.

8. Play until the defense gets the ball. Play made shots like missed shots.

9. After each player on the offense shoots once, the offense and defense switch.

•Rotate positions after each shot. Make no transitions until Part 2 is completed.

•If novice players are not ready to shoot from the foul line, move them closer to the basket. If steps 1-5 take 20-30 minutes, do the following steps the next day.

Part 2 Transition to Midcourt

10. After each rebound, sprint to midcourt, setup in the defensive ready position and tap dance. The rebounder puts the ball on the endline before sprinting. The back player, on defense, sprints up to the foul line, not midcourt.

•Yell *go* as soon as the defense gets the ball.

Part 3 Transition to the Press

Setup

The shooting team becomes the defense. The guards set up on the right and left side high post; the forwards set up at midcourt behind the guards; the center is at the other foul line. This is a 2-2-1 zone press. See the diagram. Walk through this several times. Frequent switching familiarizes players with every position.

The offense sets up as follows: the player taking the ball out-of-bounds stands on either side of the backboard, not behind it, with the ball overhead. The other players set

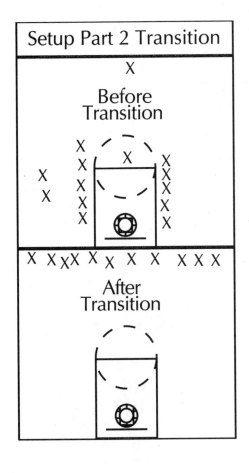

Setup Part 2 Transition

Before Transition

After Transition

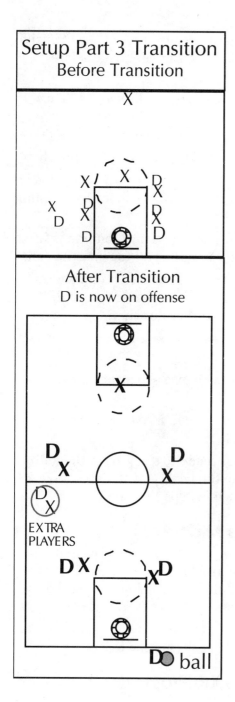

Setup Part 3 Transition
Before Transition

After Transition
D is now on offense

EXTRA
PLAYERS

D○ ball

up just behind and outside the defense near the foul line and at midcourt.

Set up additional players on offense and defense between midcourt and the foul line. *The court is big enough*.

11. Set up in the press positions.

• After the players set up properly, instruct them to run back to the foul line setup.

12. Set up on the foul line. As soon as the defense controls the ball, sprint to your positions and tap dance there. The rebounder puts the ball on the floor out-of-bounds.

• Initially, yell *go* when the defense controls the ball. Players should soon take off without urging.

• After each player takes a foul shot, the offense and defense switch. Repeat.

Use of Assistants None

Weekly Practice Everyday

Extensions None

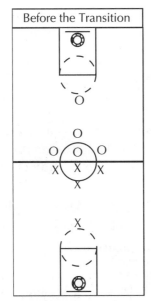
Before the Transition

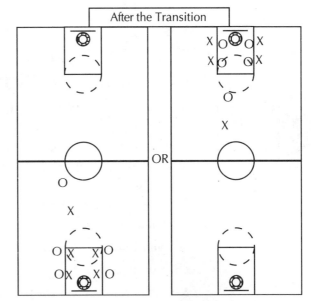
After the Transition

OR

15.1 Center Jump Transition

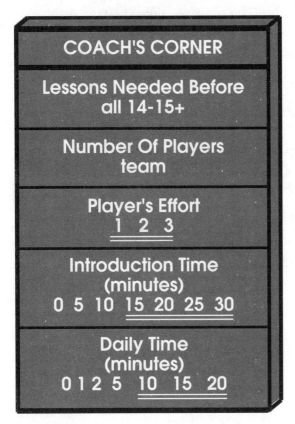

Brief:

Players make the transition from the center jump to half court offensive and defensive positions.

Fundamental Notes

The transition from the center jump is not a frequently made transition. However, practicing any transition lesson increases a player's ability to make any other transition because each transition lesson teaches players to react quickly after the ball changes hands. A half court offensive setup is introduced. Then, each player at the center jump chooses an offensive player to cover, makes the transition, and then picks up this player on offense. Finding this player after the transition, before they score, is a difficult task. Like all transition lessons this one involves conditioning and hustle as well.

Setup

Two teams start in the center jump setup. Extra players line up two yards away from the restraining circle. After the jump, one guard from the team that controls the tap brings the ball down to a simple offensive setup. The four other

players set up at the left and right, high and low post positions. The defense plays one-on-one. Extra players set up in the middle post area.

Directions for Players

•Starting at the center jump.

1. Point to the player that you cover. Check that nobody else points at the same player. In a game you must memorize the number of your opponent. The center should stay out of the jump circle until the team is ready.

2. After the jump, sprint to your position. Defense–play the person you are covering. Offense–go to the half court setup.

3. Each team go to your offensive positions now.

•Set up each team.

4. Okay, back to the center jump. Pick up a player. If you lose your assignment, sprint toward the basket. Don't stand around looking lost at midcourt. Set up in the middle of the lane and then look around.

•Toss the ball for the jump. The players make the transition. Stop play when the ball passes the top of the key.

5. Jog back to the center jump. Switch positions after each jump. Coordinate this switch with your teammates.

•This switching involves the important skill of communication. Help, if necessary. A rotation clockwise is okay. Repeat this lesson 4-10 times. Jump the ball at the end circles as well if they do this in your league. The team defending the basket close to the jump may want to put all 4 players on the restraining circle, instead of three on the circle and one back.

Troubleshooting

Watch for mismatches at the center jump. Help players recognize them and work them out.

Use of Assistants

Toss the jump ball

Weekly Practice   2-5 times at start of the season

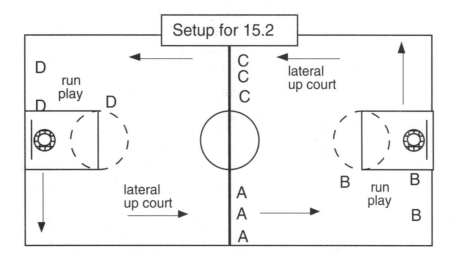

15.2 Play to Transition

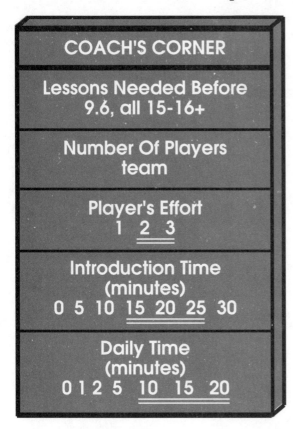
Brief:

The offense runs one play at each end of the court in a continuous motion lesson.

Fundamental Notes

This transition lesson is a dynamic way to work on plays while staying in continuous motion. Players pass as they make the transition. Use any play. Lesson 16.1 presents three basic plays.

Setup

One group of three sets up at each basket in position to run one play. The other groups wait at midcourt on the left and right sidelines. If there are more than four groups, either use more baskets or add more players to each group. Practice the play before you do this lesson.

Directions for Players

1. Run the play on the right side of each basket.

2. Rebound, pass the ball to the left corner. Lateral the ball down this side of the court.

3. Wait at midcourt for the previous group to finish. Jog in place while lateraling the ball back and forth.

4. Repeat the same play at the other end of the court.

5. Continue for a minute or two, until we switch directions. Then, run the play on the left side of each basket as you move around the court in the opposite direction.

•If desired, change the play every few minutes.

Troubleshooting

If there are more than two baskets, use them. If fewer are available, then increase the number of players in a group to 4 or 5. Keep the players moving.

Use of Assistants None

Weekly Practice As needed

Section 16
Team Offense

L E S S O N #	NAME	P L A Y E R S	C O U R T	B A L L	E F F O R T	LESSONS BEFORE	L E S S O N #	INTRO TIME	DAILY TIME
16.0	**Offense Setup 1-2**	T	x	x	1-2	all- 9, 10, 12+	**16.0**	10-20@	5-10@
16.1	Plays 1,2,3	3	x	x	2	16.0+	16.1	20-30	10-20
16.2	Figure 8	T	x	x	2	13.0, 16.0, 16.01+	16.2	10-25	5-15
16.21	8 with Defense	T	x	x	2-3	all 12, 16.2+	16.21	-	10-15

16.0 Offensive Setup 1-2

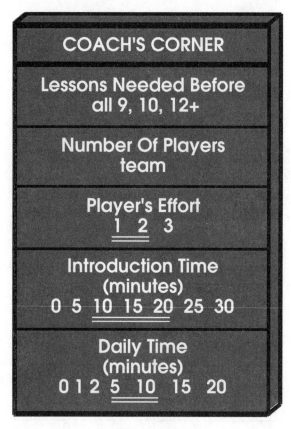

COACH'S CORNER

Lessons Needed Before
all 9, 10, 12+

Number Of Players
team

Player's Effort
1 2 3

Introduction Time
(minutes)
0 5 10 15 20 25 30

Daily Time
(minutes)
0 1 2 5 10 15 20

Brief:
Players learn the principles of half court offense.

Fundamental Notes

In a game, offensive players must react to each defense, rather than run rehearsed offensive routes. For this reason, simply spending a lot of time on these offenses will reap little benefit. Players, even novices, learn the plays quickly. However, the effectiveness of plays depends on each player's individual skills, so spend much time on these.

This offense involves all players. Not only are all five players on the court shadowed by one or two others, but also the play is designed so that every player on the court is involved. Timing is critical. Each play needs to look real, like there is a defense, to be beneficial. Otherwise this will be a waste of time.

Walk through the play with the players. You can use the offensive setup in Lesson 15.2, instead of the plays in Lesson 16.1. The team offensive principles below will work against any type of defense. All individual offensive principles still apply, even if they are not mentioned here.

Team Offensive Principles

•For all players:

1. Watch the ball.

2. Do not stop dribbling until you pass the ball.

3. Cut from the weak side to the strong side. Cut behind the defense, rather than in front.

4. Fake before cutting.

•For inside players:

5. Inside the foul line, cut to the open spot. Time the cut by communicating with teammates.

•For outside players:

6. Get the ball inside.

7. Look inside.

Setup for Part 1

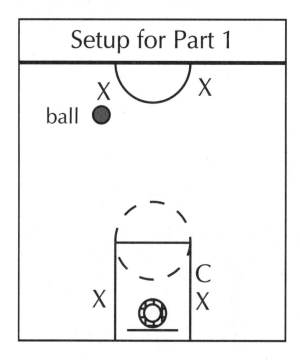

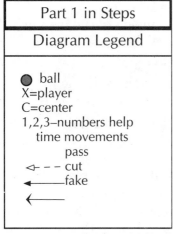

Step 1

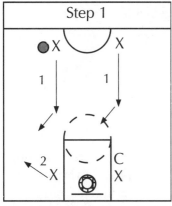

Step 2

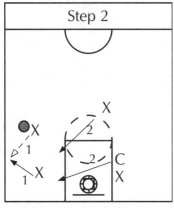

Step 3

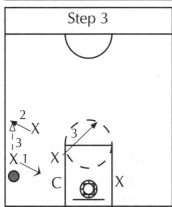

8. Hold the ball overhead, constantly faking, ready to pass.

9. Only dribble if necessary.

10. Cut to the ball from an angle that makes it difficult for the defense to intercept the pass.

11. Peripheral (outside) players move to provide the passer another outlet.

12. One player stays outside as a defensive safety.

Setup

1. Two guards start near midcourt, five yards apart three yards from the sidelines. The guard on the right has the ball.

2. The other three players line up in the low post; two on the opposite side of the ball, the left side; the other on the right side.

3. Set up a shadow team, or two, if necessary. The shadows perform the same lesson from two steps behind. Shadows do not interfere with passes or cuts. Regularly switch the shadows with the first team.

4. Walk through the directions with players.

5. When players are more expert, each group can run this lesson at a separate basket.

Directions for Players

Part 1

•The diagrams illustrate each step. Note that the small numbers in each diagram only refer to the timing of the moves shown, and not to the step or direction number. The center is designated by a C for clarity. Start with players in position.

Step 1

1. Left side players will eventually follow the same directions on the left side as the right side players on the right. So, listen carefully. (Say, "Joe, you will do the same thing as Pete. Gina the same as Nancy," and so on.) Jump and come to each pass like there is defense.

2. The right side guard dribbles the ball toward the right lane. The left side guard parallels his/her movements. At the top of the key, veer off to the right sideline. The right side forward cuts diagonally out for the ball.

Step 2

3. Pass the ball to the forward cutting out. The ball and the cutter meet at a spot.

4. The left side guard cuts to the high post right side. The center cuts to the low post.

Step 4

Step 5

Step 6

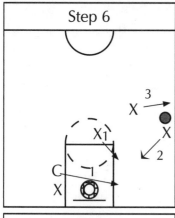

Step 7

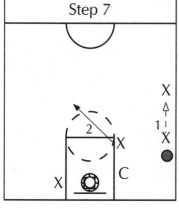

Step 3

5. The forward with the ball fakes a pass inside to the high or low post, just as these players reach these positions. The post players react like they are catching the pass.

6. The right guard cuts to a passing lane on the sideline to receive the pass back from the forward.

7. The left guard cuts back outside to the top of the key.

Step 4

8. The left guard passes to the right guard who dribbles left. This exchange is critical. The catcher may need to run to within steps or even run behind the passer to make this exchange safe. The right forward moves back to the low post, and the left forward starts a diagonal cut out toward the left sidelines for the ball. We now repeat the steps on the left side.

Step 5

9. The guard passes to the forward near the sideline. The right side guard starts for the left side high post.

Step 6

10. The left side guard cuts to the high post and the center cuts back to the low post on the left side. The forward fakes a pass inside just as the cutters reach their positions.

Step 8

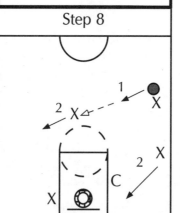

Step 9

11. The left side guard moves to the sideline for the pass back.

Step 7

12. The left side guard receives the pass on the sideline. The right side guard moves back to the key for a pass.

Step 8

13. The left guard passes to the right guard. The left forward moves back to the low post.

Step 9

14. When the guards move back toward the right side, we are back to the starting positions.

•After the first team works the ball left and right twice, the shadows repeat the lesson. After the

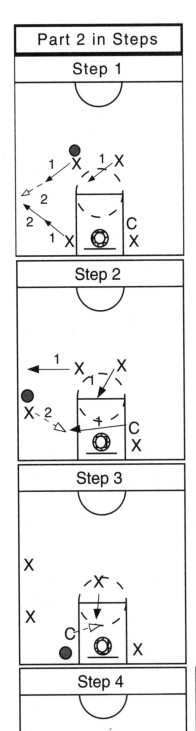

Part 2 in Steps

first presentation, run this lesson for 5-10 minutes on separate baskets.

Part 2

15. This is a continuation of Part 1; the ball goes inside this time. Walk through this.

• Start in the original starting positions.

Step 1

16. The guards move right and the right guard passes to the forward cutting out.

Step 2

17. This time the right forward passes to the center cutting across the lane. The left guard cuts down the center of the lane.

Step 3

18. The center passes (lateral or bounce pass) to the left guard cutting down the lane about five feet from the basket.

Step 4

19. This guard immediately passes to the left forward, who jumps into the lane and shoots a one-foot shot.

20. Everybody except the right guard follows up for the rebound. The right guard moves back to the top of the key.

Step 5

21. Move off the court quickly and set up out-of-bounds ready to repeat this play on the left side.

22. Shadows, let's do it.

• The shadow team repeats this lesson, then sets up out-of-bounds on the left side. The first team runs it on the left side and so on.

• The shadow teams, if more than one, alternate with the first team. A two- or three-player shadow team can alternate with players on another shadow team.

• Teams can practice on separate baskets when players are more expert.

Troubleshooting

1. Watch for realistic and coordinated faking, cutting, catching, and passing. Players need to play like there is a defense.

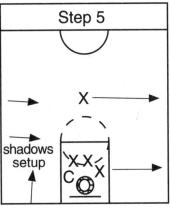

2. Watch for these things:

    a. the angle of the cut.

    b. the timing of the cuts.

    c. the faking before the cuts.

    d. catchers both coming to and jumping to the ball.

Use of Assistants
Dummy defense

Weekly Practice As needed

Extensions None

16.1 Plays 1-3

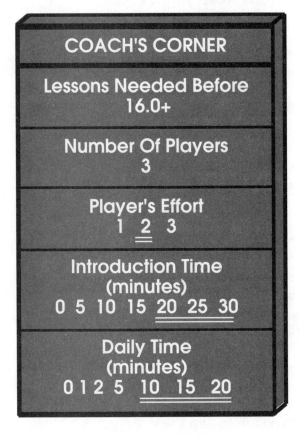

COACH'S CORNER

Lessons Needed Before
16.0+

Number Of Players
3

Player's Effort
1 <u>2</u> 3

Introduction Time (minutes)
0 5 10 15 <u>20</u> <u>25</u> <u>30</u>

Daily Time (minutes)
0 1 2 5 <u>10</u> <u>15</u> <u>20</u>

Brief:

Each play works the ball inside. Play 1 does it from the center; play 2 from the side; play 3 from the corner.

Fundamental Notes

Each defense presents particular problems and opportunities for the offense. It is difficult to predict what these will be. Practicing predetermined specific plays ignores this fact and thus defeats the purpose of the offense, which is to react to each defense. Sensible preparation involves understanding offensive objectives and how to achieve them. The objective, in general, of any offense is to pass the ball inside; to score from the inside. There are three different areas to pass the ball from–the center, the side, and the corner. Each one of the three plays covers one of these possibilities.

In games, plays are seldom run. If players have learned the tools, they recognize an opportunity and then go for it. Do not spend much time on these plays. Use them in Lesson 15.2 as well.

Setup

The starting setup for each play is the same. One guard with the ball at the top of the key. One player in the low post on each side. Other players are shadows. The plays were designed so that a different player ends up with the shot in each play. Walk through each play the first time. The directions start on the next page.

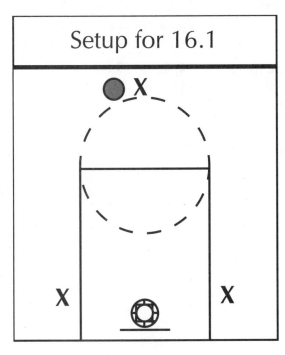

Setup for 16.1

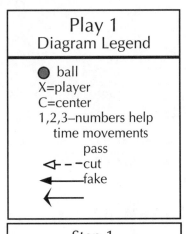

Play 1
Diagram Legend

● ball
X=player
C=center
1,2,3–numbers help
time movements
     pass
◁ – – cut
◀——— fake
◀———

Step 1

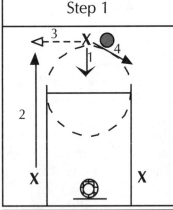

Step 2

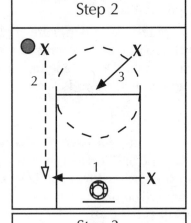

Step 3

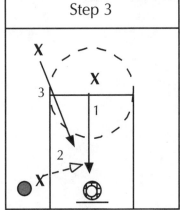

Directions for Players

Play 1–Pass from the center

Step 1

1. The play starts with the guard faking an overhead pass toward the basket. The right side player cuts to the high post for a pass.

2. The guard passes and moves 2-3 yards to the left. The high post player pivots around toward the right sideline, away from the guard.

Step 2

3. After the pivot, the left side player cuts across the lane and receives a pass at right side low post. The guard moves to the foul line.

Step 3

4. The guard cuts down the lane to the basket, receives a pass two feet from the basket, and shoots. The other players follow up the shot. Repeat this.

5. The shadows alternate with the first group.

•Each group does it 2-5 times. Then, run this play from the left side of the basket.

•Each group then practices at separate baskets for 2-5 minutes.

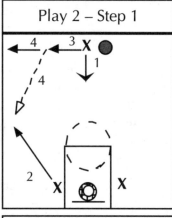

Play 2 – Step 1

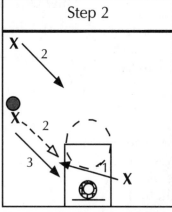

Step 2

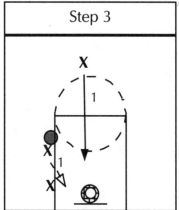

Step 3

Play 2–Pass from the side

Step 1

1. At the fake, the right side player cuts diagonally out toward the side.

2. The guard dribbles right, passes, and then moves further to the right as an outlet. As the ball moves back toward the center, so do you.

Step 2

3. After the right side player pivots around toward the basket, the left side player cuts across the lane to the middle post area. The pass and the cutter meet just outside the middle post area.

4. The passer cuts straight to the basket.

Step 3

5. The cutter receives a pass two feet from the basket, and then shoots. The passer pivots away from the cutter and then goes for the rebound. Again, all players go for the rebound. Each group runs it once, then switch sides.

•Use separate baskets if available.

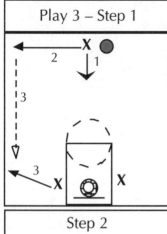

Play 3 – Step 1

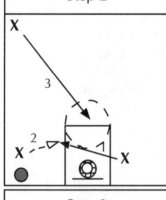

Step 2

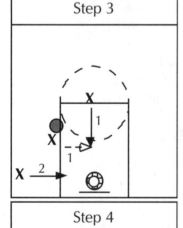

Step 3

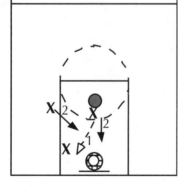

Step 4

Play 3-Pass from the corner.

Step 1

1. After the fake, the guard dribbles to the right sideline and passes to the right side forward cutting to the corner. It is better to cut a few yards from the endline.

Step 2

2. The left forward cuts across the lane after a fake pass to receive a pass at the mid-post area. The guard moves to the foul line.

Step 3

3. The guard cuts down the center of the lane to receive a pass six feet from the basket. The right forward cuts to the basket.

Step 4

4. The guard flips the ball right back to the right forward who shoots the ball. All players follow up the shot.

•The shadows alternate with the first team. Repeat on the left side of the basket, then practice at separate baskets.

•After several days, practice these plays with a token defense. The defense makes little effort and gets out of the way at the last second. Gradually instruct the defense to increase their effort.

Troubleshooting

1. A fake precedes every cut.

2. Players pass like there is defense. Use managers or shadows as dummy defensive players for the offense to pass the ball around.

3. Players jump to catch the ball like there is defense.

4. In games, these plays are seldom executed as in practice.

5. The timing of cuts and passes is critical.

Use of Assistants
As dummy defense.

Weekly Practice As needed

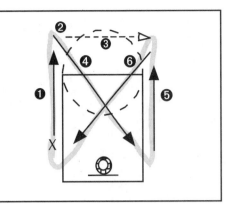

One player's path through the Figure 8

1-Cut out for ball
2-Fake inside pass
3-Pass to cutter
4-Cut across lane to low post
5-Cut out for ball
6-Fake, pass, and cut back to
   original position

16.2 Figure 8

COACH'S CORNER

Lessons Needed Before
all 13, 16.0, 16.1+

Number Of Players
team

Player's Effort
1 <u>2</u> 3

Introduction Time
(minutes)
0 5 10 15 <u>20 25 30</u>

Daily Time
(minutes)
0 1 2 5 <u>10 15 20</u>

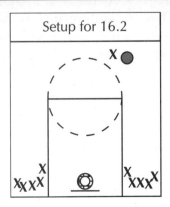

Setup for 16.2

Brief:

Players cut from the low post to the high post for the ball. They pass and then cut back to the basket.

Fundamental Notes

This is an offense for a person-to-person defense. The plays, 1-3, incorporate all the skills involved in the Figure 8. The Figure 8 is a way to practice these skills in a more continuous lesson, using the entire team at one basket. Defense against cutters is also taught. Note that the Figure 8 can be expanded into a four corners type of stalling offense.

Setup

The player with the ball stands on the left side of the lane extended to the key. The other players split into two lines, going away from the basket, starting at the right and left low post. See the diagrams.

Directions for Players

1. The passer fakes an overhead pass inside. This signals the right side low post player to cut up the lane past the high post. Do not stop running until you have the ball. The ball and the cutter should meet on the right side between the foul line and the top of the key. If the passer hesitates, continue running, even if you go to midcourt.

•Demonstrate this with a player. See if the player

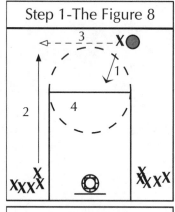

Step 1-The Figure 8

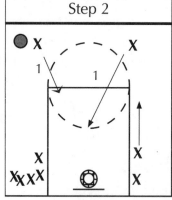

Step 2

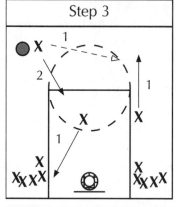

Step 3

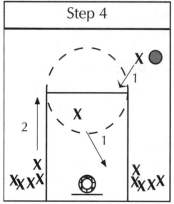

Step 4

**Diagram Legend
for the Figure 8**

● ball
X=player
C=center
1,2,3–numbers help
  time movements
◁ – – pass
◀—— cut
◀——— fake

slows down when you don't throw the pass at the expected point. Instruct players to move at full speed until they catch the ball.

2. After passing, cut to the basket. Slightly wave your arm to indicate that you are open, and expect the pass. You get the ball when I say "pass." Otherwise, the new passer just fakes to the cutter. The cutter goes into the line on the other side of the low post.

3. This fake to the cutter signals the left, or other, side low post player to cut up the side of the lane. The ball and the player meet again between the foul line and the top of the key.

•Continue ad infinitum.

Troubleshooting

1. Players fake before cutting.

2. Yell "pass" every third cut, or if a player is not ready to pass or catch.

3. Passer and cutter work on their timing.

4. Players sprint for the ball. They don't stop until they catch it. Sometimes, instruct the passer to *pause* to ascertain if the cutter slows down.

Use of Assistants

Managers can act as dummy defense.

Weekly Practice As needed

Extensions

16.21 8 with Defense

Run Lesson 16.2 with defense. Initially the defense plays at half speed. Never let them bat passes away. As the offense gets better, handle cutters like they are handled in the fronting and overplaying lessons, 12.4-12.6: stay one step ahead of the offense, stop in their path to cause collisions which impede the cut, step in front near the basket.

Section 17
Team Defense

L E S S O N #	NAME	P L A Y E R S	C O U R T	B A L L	E F F O R T	LESSONS BEFORE	L E S S O N #	INTRO TIME	DAILY TIME
17.0	**Defense-Helping Out 1-3**	T	x	x	1-3	all- 11, 12+	**17.0**	20-30	10-20
17.01	Help in Figure 8	T	x	x	1-3	17.0	17.01	-	10-20
17.1	2-1-2 Zone Shift	T	x	x	1-3	17.0+	17.1	10-15	5
17.11	Half Court Zone Trap	T	x	x	1-3	17.1+	17.11	10-20	5-10

17.0 Defense-Helping Out 1-3

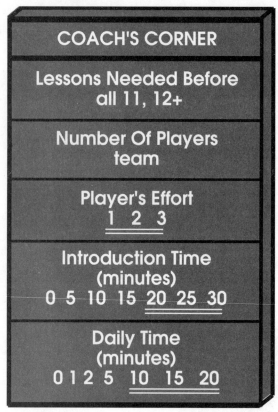

COACH'S CORNER

Lessons Needed Before
all 11, 12+

Number Of Players
team

Player's Effort
1 2 **3**

Introduction Time
(minutes)
0 5 10 15 **20 25 30**

Daily Time
(minutes)
0 1 2 5 **10 15 20**

Setup for 17.0

X=players
D=defense
M=managers
⬤ =ball

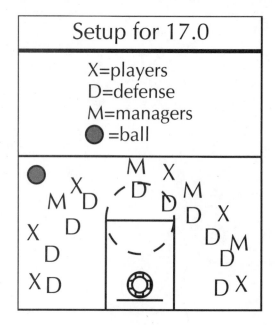

Brief:

Players learn strong -and weak-side play.

Fundamental Notes

A key to both person-to-person defense and any zone defense is helping out. Helping out means that other defensive players leave their positions to cover a particular player. One-on-one, the offense always has an advantage. When an offensive player gets close to the basket, other defensive players are in position to help. This lesson shows how to do this. Part 1 involves coverage of periphery players. Part 2 involves high and low post players. Part 3 combines Parts 1 and 2 in a game-like situation.

Setup

Split the number of players in half. Half, and all of the managers, are on offense. They set up around the periphery, initially. The other half of the team covers them one-on-one. Start the explanation with the defense overplaying the offense.

Directions for Players

Part 1 Periphery Players

1. The ball side of the court is the strong side. The other side is the weak side. The sides are separated by an imaginary line from the top of the key, through the middle of the lane, to the basket.

•See Lesson 12.6 for a further explanation of strong and weak side.

•Pass the ball to the right side, or walk it there.

2. The right side is the strong side. Overplay players on the strong side. Your body, shoulder-to-shoulder, points in the direction of the ball. Keep your eyes on the ball. Stay in touch with the offense by touch.

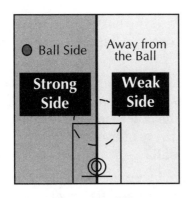

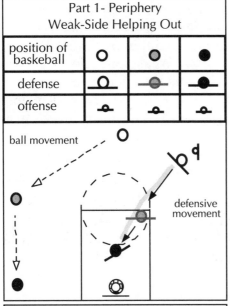

Part 1- Periphery Weak-Side Helping Out			
position of baskeball	○	◉	●
defense	⊖	⊖	⊖
offense	⊸	⊸	⊸

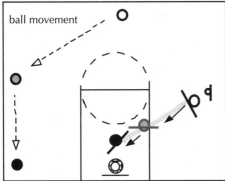

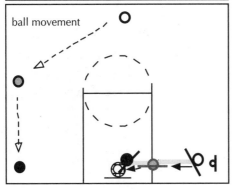

3. Offensive players on the weak side, far away from the basket and the ball, are not a scoring threat. This allows weak-side defense to cheat away from the offense toward the strong side. Move directly toward the basket until you are just inside the lane. Open up (rotate) your defensive stance halfway around toward the ball. This puts your body in a position facing the far end basket.

4. Watch both the ball and your offensive assignment. Protecting the basket is your primary job. If you lose your offensive assignment, step into the middle of the lane close to the basket. Pick up the offense from this position. Your eyes stay on the ball.

5. As the ball moves toward the right corner, weak-side players move toward the right side of the lane, one or two steps closer to the basket. Open up more to the ball. Your body faces the right side position.

6. Move toward your original position as the ball moves out to the side, and then back to the center. When the ball moves to the left side, right side players play weak side defense. Move toward the basket just into the lane. Open up halfway to the ball.

7. As the ball moves to the corner, weak side players move closer to the basket, more to the left side. Keep your eyes on the ball. If you lose the offense, move into the middle of the lane close to the basket. Protect the basket; pick up the offense later.

8. Offense, pass the ball at my signal. After each pass, stop, so I can check all positions.

•The offense passes the ball for 2-5 minutes. Switch offensive and defense. Repeat.

Part 2 High and Low Post Players

•Change the setup. Put offensive players in the high and low post on each side of the basket. Managers pass on the periphery.

•Defending the low post, strong and weak side, is covered in Lesson 12.6. In general, the closer a player is to the basket, the closer you play them.

9. High post defense sets up one or two steps away at most. Low post players set up right on the offense. (See 12.6 also.)

10. Move the ball from the center to the right side. Low post weak (left) side players open up halfway; right (strong) side players close down, shoulder-to-shoulder pointing to the ball. High post weak (left) side players

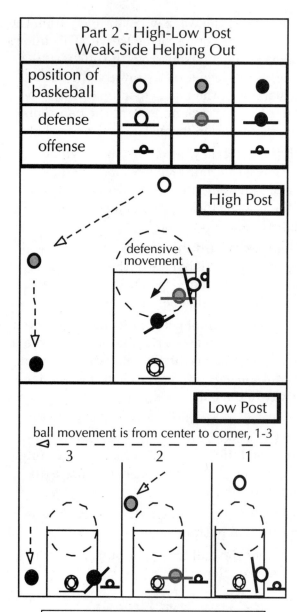

Part 2 - High-Low Post Weak-Side Helping Out			
position of baskeball	○	◐	●
defense	⊖	⊖	⊖
offense	↶	↶	↶

High Post

defensive movement

Low Post

ball movement is from center to corner, 1-3

3   2   1

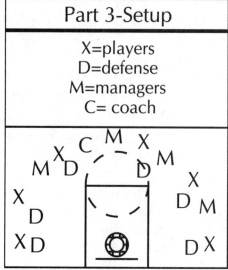

Part 3-Setup
X=players
D=defense
M=managers
C= coach

move one step toward the basket; strong (right) side players move to the other side of the offense from behind.

11. Move the ball to the corner. High post strong (right) side players stay behind the defense, overplaying from the other side; weak (left) side players move into the center of the lane and open up halfway to the ball.

•Repeat switching players left and right. Repeat again, switching offense and defense.

12. Low post strong (right) side players move in front to overplay on the other side (see Lesson 12.6); if necessary, remain in front with the offense on your back. Weak-side defense opens up to the ball, keeping the offense on your back. Boxing out this low post player prevents offensive weak-side rebounds which can devastate our team.

•Repeat these steps, moving the ball to the left side. Check defensive positions after each pass.

•Continue to move the ball, one pass at a time.

•When the defense is more expert, allow the offense to freely move the ball. Yell "freeze" when you want the ball and the players to stop.

Part 3 Stepping in Front

•The last and the most important part of this lesson involves stepping in front of an uncovered offensive player with the ball. All of the managers, as well as you, are extra, uncovered offensive players. Offense and defense set up around the periphery in a semicircle.

•Quickly move the ball around the periphery. An uncovered player, you or a manager, drives to the basket from the foul line every 3-6 passes. All defensive players should collapse in front quickly.

•Initially, players will not be ready for this. Every 5-15 seconds, send an uncovered player down the center of the lane. If the defense does not react, pass to this player. He/she should attempt to score.

Use of Assistants

As offensive players

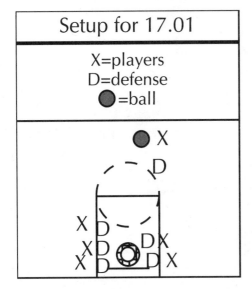

Setup for 17.01

X=players
D=defense
●=ball

Extensions

17.01 Help in Figure 8

See Lesson 16.2, The Figure 8. Use the same strong-weak-side instructions while the offense runs the figure 8. Freeze the action after each pass initially. Do not use managers. Here are the defensive situations to be concerned with:

1. Covering the cut out to the ball.

The defense stays one step ahead of the cutter until he/she reaches the foul line. Then slightly loosen up. Increase defensive effort as players become more expert on offense.

2. Covering the cutter to the basket.

The defense steps in front of the cutter as much as possible to prevent an easy cut. This results in minor collisions that slow down the cut and make it difficult to receive a pass. The defense should stay a step away, so that they can easily move around the offense. If too close, the offense can easily block out the defense, to one side or the other, to easily catch the pass.

Other defensive players on the lane need to be ready to step in front of an open cutter. Allow the offense to throw the pass. Weak side low post always stays tight on their assignment.

One player's path through the Figure 8

1-Cut out for ball
2-Fake inside pass
3-Pass to cutter
4-Cut across lane to low post
5-Cut out for ball
6-Fake, pass, and cut back to
     original position

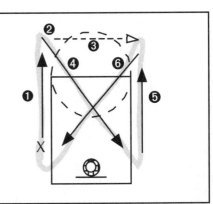

17.1 2-1-2 Zone

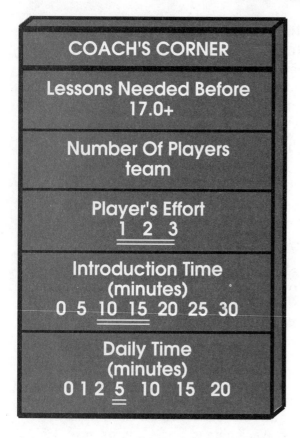
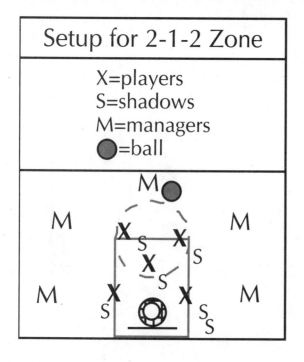

Setup for 2-1-2 Zone

X=players
S=shadows
M=managers
●=ball

Brief:

This lesson describes the shifting and communication in this type of zone.

Fundamental Notes

Players continuously shift position in a zone; they do not just graze in confined areas on the court. A 2-1-2 zone only looks this way when the ball is at the top of the key. As the ball is moved around, this zone has many looks. Once shifted to the proper position, players play one-on-one defense on any offense in the area; zones do not explain how to play defense–only how to shift as a unit. The defensive lessons in this book do. To play zone, you need to teach every player the individual defense for each position, just as you would if you played one-on-one.

One 2-1-2 zone may even set up differently than another. In one case, all the players may be packed into the lane to beef up rebounding and clog the lane. In another, the outside two may be past the top of the key to trap after the ball crosses midcourt. 2-1-2 zones also may shift differently, even though they initially set up the same. In one case, you might want to trap. In another, you may want to stop the outside shot. The 2-1-2 zone below is simple and effective. It can be learned in five minutes. That is, five minutes after you spend many hours practicing all of the defensive lessons.

Setup

The outside two players start one step outside the corner where the lane and foul line meet. The center plays in the middle of the lane. Put your best defensive player in this position. The back two are one step forward of the low post. Use shadows again. Use managers around the periphery as offensive players.

Directions for Players

1. Start in the half down defensive position with

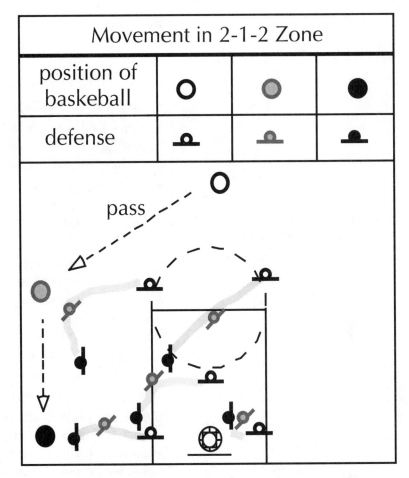

Movement in 2-1-2 Zone			
position of baskeball	O	◉	●
defense	⚊	⚊	⚊

pass

the arms both out and moving to cut down on the passing lanes. Cover any player in your area person-to-person. This zone, called a 2-1-2, is where we initially set up. This is how it looks when the ball is at the top of the key.

2. When the ball goes to the right side, the right side guard moves to the ball. The left side guard moves to the right and one step closer to the basket. The center moves to the edge of the lane. You are always in the lane right between the ball and the basket. The right side forward moves 1-2 steps right. The left side forward takes one step to the right. From the ball, this setup looks like a 1-3-1.

3. When the ball goes into the corner, the right side forward moves out to the ball–not more than 12 feet. The center quickly moves into the position vacated by the right side forward. Step in front of any player in the area. The guards move directly toward the baseline. The right guard moves 2-3 yards. The left side guard moves into the center of the lane. The left side forward turns toward the ball but does not move. You need to cover the weak side rebound. Step in only to cover the ball in the middle. This setup looks like a 2-2-1 from the corner.

4. When the ball is shot, box out any player in the area. Outside players collapse to the boards as well.

•Run this to the left side.

•Some coaches teach that the three players closest to the basket form a boxing out triangle. Actually, the players just move together to box out as a group.

•Move the ball around the periphery to the right and left sides. Switch players on the right and left sides as well as the shadows into the game.

•Offensive teams usually go right. This puts the left side guard near the boards and the right side guard on the ball. Put your better rebounder on the left side and your better defensive player on the right. Do the same with the forwards since the right side forward goes out to the ball and the left side forward stays under.

•Teach each player how to play every position. Sometime you will either want or need to switch. For a guard trap a taller player is used outside.

•Offensive players should set up behind defensive players in the zone. This is a good place to cut from, to catch a pass, or to set a pick. Inside defensive players need to inform outer defensive players when this occurs. Yell a player's name, the one you are communicating with, and then "behind" or "left" or "right."

Decisions to Make in a Zone

•You need to vary how far forwards and guards move to cover the ball. Keep novices as close as possible to the lane.

•You need to decide the positions of the guards when the ball is at the top of the key: do you trap, play tight, or loose.

•Do you pick up the ball outside the top of the key, at the top of the key, or do you stay back near the foul line.

•These choices depend on the idiosyncrasies of the offense and your personnel.

Troubleshooting

1. Person-to-person defense is needed before practicing the zone. A player does not learn individual defense in a zone. Teach individual defense in the appropriate setup.

2. Each player needs to learn every defensive position.

Use of Assistants

Assistants act as offense around the periphery.

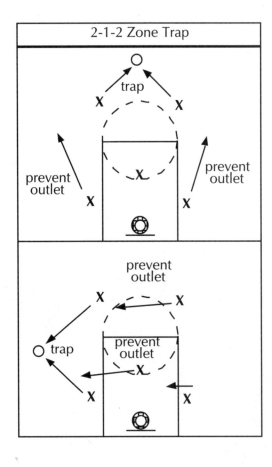

2-1-2 Zone Trap

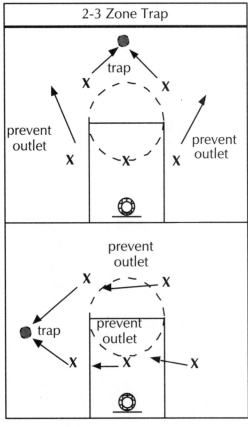

2-3 Zone Trap

Weekly Practice As needed

Extensions

There are several zone formations that coaches use besides a 2-1-2. These include the 2-3, 3-2, 1-2-2, and several others. In any case, the switching or movement in the zone is more important than the initial setup. In each zone used, three switching situations must be addressed:

1. who covers the ball

2. who covers the lane, middle and low post areas

3. who covers weak-side rebounding

17.11 Half Court Zone Trap

In a 2-1-2 zone, the two players closest to the ball trap. This action involves either the two guards or a guard and a forward. Trapping changes the look to a 2-2-1 from any position except dead center. The other three players shift closer to the ball, away from the basket, to prevent or intercept the outlet pass. Because of this shift, trapping leaves you more vulnerable for easy baskets underneath.

The 2-3 is a better initial setup for trapping, because the forwards, the ends of the 3, are more outside to begin with. To switch to the 2-3 from the 2-1-2, move the forwards 2 steps diagonally away from the basket. The shifts in the 2-3 are the same as those in the 2-1-2. So, just instruct the players to move out; you don't necessarily need to mention that this is the 2-3.

The disadvantage of a trap is that your players are farther from the basket. This makes your team more vulnerable in the low post areas and under the boards. If the trap is effective, this is not a problem. With experienced players, traps are more effective when used on an irregular basis, like every third time the offense comes down court. If used regularly, the offense quickly adjusts and find ways to beat it. Then you have lost a potent weapon. Novices will not adjust as quickly as experienced teams.

(Notes)

The Basketball Coach's Bible

Section 18
Out-of-Bounds Plays

L E S S O N #	NAME	P L A Y E R S	C O U R T	B A L L	E F F O R T	LESSONS BEFORE	L E S S O N #	INTRO TIME	DAILY TIME
18.0	**Out-of-Bounds Plays**	T	x	x	1-3	16.0+	**18.0**	10-15	5-10
18.01	4 in Line	T	x	x	1-3	18.0+	18.01	10-15	5-10

18.0 Out-of-Bounds Plays

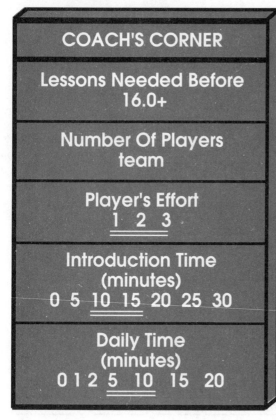

COACH'S CORNER

Lessons Needed Before
16.0+

Number Of Players
team

Player's Effort
1 2 3

Introduction Time
(minutes)
0 5 10 15 20 25 30

Daily Time
(minutes)
0 1 2 5 10 15 20

Brief:

This lesson gives both the offensive and defensive setup for an in-bounds play used underneath your own basket.

Fundamental Notes

One special out-of-bounds play is needed for both inbounding the ball under your own basket and defending the inbound under the other team's basket. In other situations use either the full court pressure setup or regular half court setup.

In this setup players always fake before moving to the open spot. They continue to sprint toward the ball and then fake away, until the pass is thrown.

Setup

1. Offense–four players form a box around the lane; two in the high post and low post on both sides of the lane.

2. The player taking the ball out is just to the right side (facing the basket) of the backboard.

3. The defense fronts all players. Line up extra players on the weak side, outside the low post.

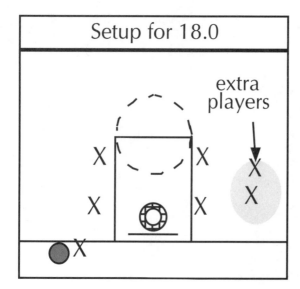

Setup for 18.0

extra
players

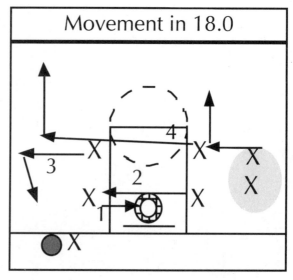

Movement in 18.0

Defending the Passer

Directions for Players

•Designate one or two players to take the ball out-of-bounds in the game.

1. The player out-of-bounds does not pick up the ball until the team is ready. Look down court immediately. When ready, grab the ball, step out-of-bounds to the right of the backboard, not under the backboard.

2. Start counting loudly to five; say, "timeout" in the place of five. Do not count out loud in a game. It is okay to walk behind the endline, not so on the sidelines. Do not step back onto the court before you pass.

3a. The player closest to the ball slides to the basket.

3b. The player at the low post on the weak side cuts behind the other player across the lane and stops at the low post.

3c. The high post strong-side player cuts to the sideline and then toward the ball.

3d. The weak-side high post player cuts to the sideline and then back toward midcourt.

4. The low post players cut first, as soon as the ball is overhead; next, the high post players cut. Continue faking away and then cutting to the ball or the open spot until the pass is thrown.

5. Usually, it is easiest to pass to the high post strong-side player. Look for the players near the basket first. Then look for the high post players, first the strong side, then the weak side.

6. The defense on the passer stands one foot toward the basket side to block passes into the lane. The hand on the side of the basket is waist high or below; the other hand is high.

7. The other defensive players front the offense. Be aware of, and communicate, picks. The closer the player comes to the basket, the tighter the defense. Step in front of any player attempting to cross the lane.

•Run this at half speed initially with a dummy defense. Increase the intensity as players gain expertise.

•Offense and defense switch roles.

•Additional groups set up one yard away from the high post on the weak side. Nobody watches. The offensive player in these groups take two steps toward the basket and then cut back to the foul line.

Troubleshooting

The player taking the ball out-of-bounds needs to wait till the team is set up and then look near, then far, to pass.

Use of Assistants None

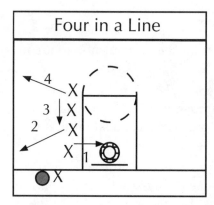

Four in a Line

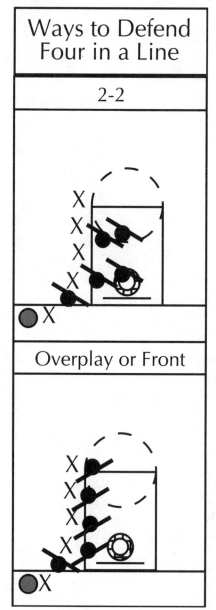

Ways to Defend Four in a Line

2-2

Overplay or Front

Extensions

18.01 Four in Line

This is another out-of-bounds play and defense that is used under your own basket. Follow the general directions in Lesson 18.0.

Setup

1. Offensive players set up packed in one line on the lane, strong side.

2. The closest player slides to the basket.

3. The second in line cuts to the near corner.

4. The third moves straight forward after the other two cut.

5. The last player moves diagonally back toward the near sidelines as an outlet. The directions for any two players can be swapped.

6. The defense sets up as a 2-2 pushed into the lane with the fifth player covering the pass.

> • Face the ball and block any cuts.

> • One player can play on the other side of the four in line setup.

> • Be concerned with inside passes.

> • The defensive player on the passer stands one step toward the inside (basket); inside arm low; outside arm mid or high. Do not allow any pass inside.

7. Fronting or overplaying person-to-person can work as well on defense. In either case, the defense forces the offense away from the basket.

Section 19

Full Court Pressure

L E S S O N #	NAME	P L A Y E R S	C O U R T	B A L L	E F F O R T	LESSONS BEFORE	L E S S O N #	INTRO TIME	DAILY TIME
19.0	**Full Pressure Offense**	T	x	x	1-3	16.0, 17.0+	**19.0**	20-30	15-30
19.1	Trapping Zone Press	T	x	x	1-3	19.0+	19.1	15-30	15-20
19.11	Switch Zone to 1-on-1	T	x	x	1-3	17.1, 19.1+	19.11	-	5-15

19.0 Full Pressure Offense

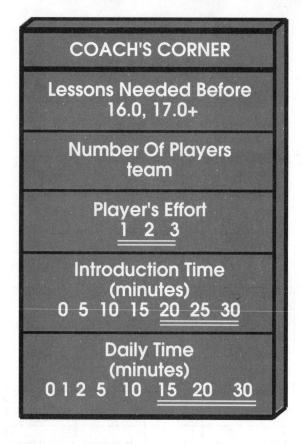

Brief:

This lesson presents a full court pressure defense and an offense to combat it.

Fundamental Notes

This is the ultimate lesson or test for the offense– playing against a press. If your team can do this well, you can play and win against any team. Without this ability you are sunk. You can have a 20-point lead going into the fourth quarter and be destroyed by a press. Even a novice coach will press, if you get a big lead in the first half. The key to defeating a full court press is cutting and catching, lessons 10.0 to 10.9. For this lesson, put seven or eight players on defense against the offense. Compared to practice, the presses in games will seem easy. This is a lesson that you need to reach as soon as possible. However, skipping steps to reach it will not work.

Setup

One player with the ball sets up out-of-bounds to the right or left of the backboard. One player is on the foul line. Two players set up at midcourt–

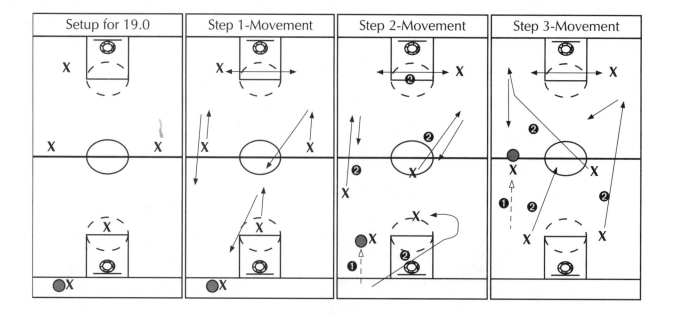

| Setup for 19.0 | Step 1-Movement | Step 2-Movement | Step 3-Movement |

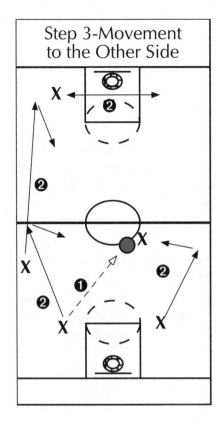

Step 3-Movement to the Other Side

one on the far right, the other on the far left. One player sets up near your own basket. Use shadows as token defense. Station extra players at mid or downcourt. All defensive players overplay the offense except the one close to the ball who fronts.

Directions for Players

1. There is no dribbling in this lesson.

2. The player out-of-bounds stands to the right or left of the backboard. Do not stand under the backboard. Doing so can interfere with a long pass. You are allowed to move. Start looking down court before you pick up the ball. Always look long first. When the team is ready, pick it up and step out-of-bounds. Count to 5. Call timeout after 4, if you still have the ball.

3. The player at the foul line fakes away until the passer is ready. Then cut to the ball. A fake away involves jogging 5-10 yards away.

4. Strong-side players always fake away and then cut to the ball; weak-side players fake away and then cut to the center of the court. If the ball is in the center of the court, you can't cut to the strong or weak side. So, do what is easiest and/or most effective. If you do not receive the pass, fake away again and repeat your movements. If you do receive a pass, pivot around and immediately look to pass downcourt.

5. The player down court stays on the weak side. When ready to catch a pass, cut to the strong side. Stay out of the lane. Three seconds will be called.

6. If the ball is passed to the player who starts at the foul line, the passer cuts to the weak side so that the setup looks like a 2-2-1. Move to maintain this approximate setup.

•Players repeat the faking movements to move the ball up court.

7. When the ball moves up court, all players quickly shift their positions in that direction. If a pass is made to a forward, the strong-side guard cuts toward the center, the weak-side guard cuts straight up court. The weak-side forward cuts diagonally to the strong side.

8. From these new positions, players fake away and then move toward the ball.

9. If the ball goes to the weak-side forward in the center of the court, the movements of the offense are similar. The other forward cuts diagonally across the court. The guard, who passed the ball, cuts straight downcourt past the ball and then comes back directly to it. The other guard either cuts straight down court, or diagonally to the other side, since the ball is in the center.

10. Repeat these movements up court. Time your cuts. Wait till a player is ready to pass.

•Move the players up court, one pass at a time. Repeat this 2-4 times.

•Initially, the defense is token. One team brings the ball down court to their half court setup. Then, let the other team run the offense in the other direction. No half court playing unless a team scores before the half court setup.

Troubleshooting

1. Designate several players as the initial passers. Switch positions frequently, so players are able to play all of them.

2. Players have a tendency not to look long. Signal the defense on the player down court to walk off the court to see if the passer reacts. The offensive player is now wide open and should receive the inbounds pass.

Use of Assistants

Use managers as additional defense.

Weekly Practice   Everyday

Extensions   None

19.1 Trapping Zone Press

COACH'S CORNER

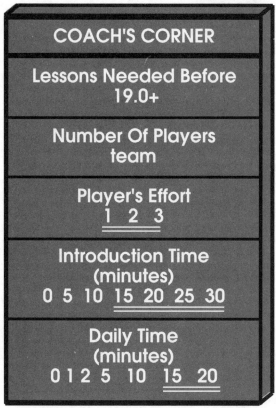

Lessons Needed Before
19.0+

Number Of Players
team

Player's Effort
<u>1</u> <u>2</u> 3

Introduction Time
(minutes)
0 5 10 <u>15 20 25</u> 30

Daily Time
(minutes)
0 1 2 5 10 <u>15 20</u>

Setup for 19.1

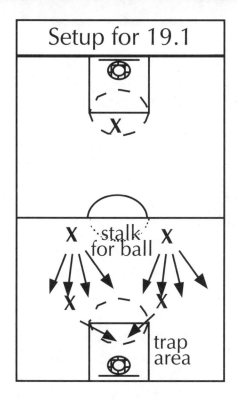

stalk
for ball

trap
area

Brief:
A full court 2-2-1 trapping zone press is presented.

Fundamental Notes

Often younger teams have one good dribbler, but have not learned cutting and catching techniques. A trapping defense prevents dribbling and forces a team to pass. Applying the 2-2-1 trapping press in this situation can be very advantageous.

There is a problem with the offensive setup in this lesson. For the defense to be effective, the offense needs to play the wrong way. You don't want your offense to play the wrong way. So, let a manager do the initial dribbling and get trapped or start off with one of the regular players trapped. Once the defense learns how to trap well, use the offense in Lesson 19.0 against it. Make sure the offense being trapped follows the guidelines below:

1. Stay in the middle of the court, so there are more passing lanes.

2. Don't dribble.

3. Make many quick passes.

These things defeat a trap.

Setup

The first 2 of the 2-2-1 are two steps both behind and to the side of the foul line. The second 2 are at midcourt on the left or right sides directly behind the first 2. The 1 is down court on the foul line. Initially, set up the offense however you like.

Directions for Players

1. The first two on defense allow the offense a short pass to one side. Wait for the dribbler to start dribbling. Then, trap this player as soon as possible; the closer to the sideline the better. The objective is to tie this player up after he or she stops dribbling.

2. The next two defensive players look for players who can be outlets for a pass. Overplay these players. Be ready to intercept a pass as the dribbler is being trapped. Stay low, coil up and then spring forward to steal the pass. Maintain a stalking distance.

3. The defensive player furthest back only moves up when a clear interception can be made.

4. After the trap, the zone looks like a trap-2-1.

5. If the ball is played backward to the other side of the court, trap again on this side.

•The more the midcourt weak-side player moves down-court to trap or cover the ball, the riskier the situation.

6. If the ball gets by the trap, immediately sprint back to half court defensive positions. Set up in a 2-1-2 zone.

•Practice this last step 5-10 times in a row. This is the most difficult part of the lesson.

7. Continue trapping until the ball goes forward past midcourt.

•Switch offense and defense. Change the positions of players frequently.

•Run the offense from Lesson 19.0 against this defense. Only allow managers to dribble.

Troubleshooting

1. This type of defense is not as effective on a team that passes well (like your team).

2. Use managers to dribble the ball into the trap, not your players, or start the lesson from the trap with your players.

3. Have players practice sprinting downcourt when the ball gets past the trap.

4. Players should tie up the trapped passer. Players should not try to steal the ball. Let the defense give it to them.

Use of Assistants

Assistants can be offensive dribblers and players as well as additional defense.

Weekly Practice At least 3-5 times per season

Extensions

19.11 Switch Zone to One-on-One

To switch back from a zone defense to one-on-one, the farthest back player yells *switch*. The ball must be outside the top of the key. Do not attempt to switch while the ball is being passed into the lane. Players point to the player that they will pick up. If the forward farthest back or center yells *okay*, the offense is covered. The team switches to one-on-one. Do this only after completing Lesson 19.1.

(Notes)

List of Appendices

A. **Strategies with Players Plus**

B. **Warm Down**

C. **How to Keep Game Statistics and User Forms**

D. **Inside Shot Statistics and User Form**

E. **Sample Practices**

F. **User Forms**

   1. Practice Planning Guide

   2. Weekly Practice Planner

G. **Tables**

   1. Table of Lessons-This Table lists all of the lessons in this book in the exact order presented.

   2. Table of Individual Skills-This Table lists the lessons by skill category in the order that you would teach them to one player.

Appendix A

STRATEGIES WITH PLAYERS PLUS

A. Walking into a New Gym

One disadvantage of playing away games is that the gym and surroundings are different. At Overbrook High School in 1963, the gym was more than minuscule. I still remember the stunned look on the face of a tall opponent *snuffed* by gymnastic rings hanging down from the ceiling. Swollen palms and elbows resulted from banging off small portions of wall that intruded onto the court near the baskets.

At more modern gyms, there are still problems. Often, I found holes in the floor and warped floors because of ceiling leaks. Often there were dead spots on the floor. Usually, schools use gyms for so many sports that the overlapping court lines make it difficult to tell the badminton border from the basketball endline. Court sizes vary as well. Regulation-size courts can be 50% larger than the puny one you practice on. Background lighting, as well as solid or glass backboards, affect shooting. Unexpectedly having to look into a sunny window (or bright TV lights) while shooting is another obstacle to overcome. These anomalies cause violations, lost balls, missed shots, and more, often critical situations.

There is an easy way to avoid many of these problems. Walk around the court with your team before the game, before the players even change. Walk single file on the sidelines and endlines. Point out any problem and/or difficulties detected as a group. Players feel more comfortable on the court after this stroll. They also recognize boundaries, bad spots, and many other court idiosyncrasies.

B. Game Warm-Ups

Use warm-ups for more than just loosening up the bones. In a game most players rarely handle the ball, so players need to warm up ball handling skills as well. Since warm-up time is limited, use efficient drills. The regular layup drill is not one of them, because players stand around most of the time. All players need a ball, just like practice. Practice shooting technique, one-foot shots, layups, and passing. With novices, practice pivoting and other beginning skills just as you do in practice. Use this time wisely. Here are some suggestions (use any extension as well):

#	Game Warmups	
	Skill	Lesson
1.	Shooting technique	5.0, 5.1
2.	Shooting practice	5.3
3.	Layups	5.4, 5.5, 5.8
4.	Passing	9.7, 9.1

C. Substituting

Games are for players; daily practice is for the coach. Gametime is the only time for players to apply practice teachings. Play as many players as possible for at least a quarter. Mix better players with the others in the lineup. Inform players in practice that they will report in for so-and-so. This is a time of learning and development for players, not a time to let your ego run wild. Benching players because you have to win creates lifelong scars.

D. Timeouts

Take timeouts to relay information to your players. Take one just after the start of the game if players are confused. In tight situations, decide if the timeout will help the other team more than your own. A well-coached team may be better off not calling a timeout if the other team will benefit more.

Talk slowly in timeouts. Base instructions on the players' skills; players must possess the ability to successfully execute them. Often I knew exactly what my players needed to do. Unfortunately, they did not have the skills (yet) to do so. In one case, after one week of practice, players (11th and 12th graders) did not know how to cut to the ball. The opponent's press squashed us. I once taught players (10th grade) a 2-1-2 shifting zone defense during a timeout, only because these players possessed all the needed skills.

Remain overtly calm and light, especially in tight situations; players mimic you. If you are uptight, players will play this way. Calm coaching reaps great reward. My uptight record for close (one or two point) games is 0-7 (my first full season); my calm record is about 20-1.

What if you need to relay much information to your players? Inform the refs ahead of time that you will take another timeout after the first one. Assign a manager to time it, using a stop watch, to insure that anxious refs do not cut 15 seconds or so off the second one. Young players often do not understand clipboard explanations. It is okay to bring them out on the court to describe a new setup. Even if the other team pays attention, which is not very probable, they still need to figure out what you are talking about and then plan a counter strategy. I'd worry more about being hit by lightning.

E. Psychology

Pregame

Players always seem to be up for games. Never tell players how important a game is to you; it's your problem. Players must concentrate on their specific job. Plant ideas the day before the game. Direct players to focus on two things at most. Better, just one. Never discuss standings unless asked. This is the job of sportscasters. Players intuitively know if a game is important. Emphasizing the point psyches them out. For example, bet 50 cents on a shot. Take it, and then bet one million dollars on the same shot. It won't be the same. Fifty-cent shots are easier.

Game

Stay cool. All games are for the players. Success or failure has already occurred at practice. Here you can only score more or fewer points than the other team. This is hardly significant, especially since your players can play well and lose and play poorly and win. Expert planning yields predictable results; players do exactly the same in games as they do at practice. Surprises and anger suggest poor planning.

F. Dealing with Referees

Referees possess a variety of abilities. A coach can only hope for consistent calling. Sometimes consistent calls work against your team. For example, referees decide they are not going to call all the fouls because they have experienced so much fouling with players at this level. You have taught your team not to foul or hack. The result is that the other team is hacking the heck out of your team; the refs only call one of every five fouls. This gives the other team a great advantage.

What do you do? The refs are probably not aware that one team is hacking and the other isn't. Point it out to them. Tell them that your players do not flail their arms or hack. The hacking is one way and this is putting your team at an unfair disadvantage. Most refs notice this immediately and then call more fouls on the hackers.

If you do not understand a call or you think the refs have made a mistake, attempt to get an explanation. If you can't get the refs' attention on an important matter call a timeout. Before discussing the problem, state that you want an official timeout because there is a mistake. If the ref agrees after the parley, you get the official timeout. If not, you get to explain yourself and find out what the refs are thinking. Usually, they are decent people who want what is best for everybody. You can also ask a ref about a less important call at halftime or after the game.

Never argue. Understand their rationale. Inform them of yours. Usually the bad calls will balance out by the end of the game. If they don't, be persistant during the game and, especially, after it. Refs with chips on their shoulders will penalize your team more unless the other ref works to even things out. Continued explantions of unfair or improper calls will affect one ref.

G. Locker Room Talks

Let's set the scene. The locker room; halftime; your team is down by 10; players sit on benches with sweaty, dispirited faces. Ronald Reagan comes in and gives an inspiring talk that ends with, "Let's do it for the Gipper." Faces radiate energy, the sweating stops, veins explode from muscles raring to go; the team rejuvenates. Your team beats the crap out of the opponent in the second half. ...only in the movies. Even Geritol can't help your team (or you). Winning and losing are not even the problem; quality of play is. There are no surprises in games unless you have problems every day in practice. Take care of problems in practice.

Never did I experience players who needed a pep talk. The bigger problem is keeping players calm and focused. You can only do this if you are calm and focused. Planning ahead helps.

H. Keeping Statistics

If possible, have an assistant keep game statistics. See the Appendix on statistics for more specific information. The most important statistic is the offensive rebounds by the opposing team. These lead to easy scores. The next is turnovers and violations by your team. Other important statistics are shooting and foul shooting percentage, and offensive and defensive rebounds.

Use these numbers for planning your practices, not to beat your players with. It is foolish to tell your players that they need to practice shooting, for example. You plan the practices. Shooting poorly is a result of your poor teaching and planning. So, beat yourself, not your players. Give players any statistics they want. They are not secret information.

I. The Beginning of the Season

A. Choosing a Team

Teach as many players as you can handle. The methods in this book allow you to handle twice as many players as you might have initially thought you could. Give players ample opportunity to cut themselves before you do it. Wait 2-4 weeks before cutting a team down to a minimum level. Twelve may be a nice number, an even dozen, for a team, but if you carry 15 players you can field three complete teams. This is easier than figuring out what to do with those two extras. The only thing special about the number 12 is that they sell donuts cheaper by the dozen.

If 12 is such an optimal number for teaching, why do school districts assign 30-60 students to normal classes?

B. Choosing Assistants

Assistants are of great help. Given specific directions, just as you give to players, assistants enhance your efforts. A talented assistant may be able to handle players as well as you. Five or six assistants are not too many. If necessary, use them as a dummy team. Choose assistants as you do players. High schoolers can be a great help with players at any level. Usually they have an interest in basketball, so they listen closely and often work with the team. Adults, on the other hand, can be a problem. Most sports aficionados and even coaches think they know it all without any study or preparation. Make it clear that you are going to follow these methods (this book plus whatever) and that you want them to do so as well. If they think *winning is the only thing* direct them to the closest professional team that needs assistants.

Appendix B-Warm Down

This is a warm down with a few strengthening exercises. It is similar to the one I used. As soon as possible, assign one player to lead it. The coach watches and talks during a long stretch. Emphasize that players should perform the exercises gently, using steady pressure—no jerky or forced movements that can cause injury. The goal is to gradually extend the range of muscle movement. Instruct players to inhale during the first part of an exercise, like a sit up, and exhale when lowering to the original position. Make sure your players know the goal for the exercise. Joe Fareira, a veteran track coach from the Philadelphia area, assisted me in developing this warm down.

Two sets of muscle groups are mentioned often in the exercises. The **hamstrings** are located at the back of the thigh. The **quadriceps** are located at the front outside of each thigh.

# NAME	DIRECTIONS	DIAGRAM
1 Hurdler's Stretch	Start this common runners' stretch sitting on the floor with both feet straight out in front of you, knees straight. Bend the right thigh back so that it makes an L with the other foot. This may be very difficult, so instruct players to go only as far as possible. Bend the calf towards the body. See the Diagram. Bend forward at the waist as far as possible. Hold the ankle or the furthest part on the leg that can be reached for 10 seconds. This stretches the hamstrings. Lay backward as far as possible from this same position for 10 seconds to stretch the quadriceps. Repeat this with the right leg forward.	
2 Feet over head	Lie down with the back on the floor. Bring the legs straight up together and back over the head. Try to touch the floor with your toes. Hold this position for 10 seconds. See diagram. Lower the legs slowly to the floor. This exercise strengthens the lower back.	
3 Sit-ups	Do 10 sit-ups slowly with the legs bent. Inhale as you count to 4 on the roll up and exhale counting to 4 as you roll down. Have a partner hold the feet down if there is nothing to put their feet under. This strengthens the mid-section and lower back.	 hold feet

Appendix B continued

# NAME	DIRECTIONS	DIAGRAM
4 Back ups	Lie on the stomach, arms behind the back. Bring the chest and head upwards. Inhale, counting to 4 on the way up, and then exhale, counting again to 4 on the way down. Do 5 slowly. This strengthens the stomach area.	initial motion
5 Back stretch	Lie on stomach. Bend calves up and extend arms behind back to grab feet. Pull for 10 seconds. Repeat. This stretches back, arms and other parts of body.	back stomach
6 Twister	Standing up with hands behind head, slowly rotate downward to the left. At the halfway point the head is between the legs as close to the ground as possible. Continue rotating upward to the right to the original position. Keep the legs in one position while rotating; if your legs are straight, keep them straight, if bent, keep them bent. Count to 6 or 8 on each rotation. Repeat, rotating in the opposite direction. Do 3 times.	rotate from the waist
7 Toe touches(3)	(1) With the feet together, bend from the waist and touch your toes. Hold for 10 seconds. (2) Repeat this with the feet far apart. This time hold the left foot with both hands for 10 seconds. Repeat, holding the right foot. (3) For a third stretch, crisscross the feet first one way, then the other. The back foot is stretched in this exercise. These stretch all muscles up to the hip.	together straddled crossed
8 Push up	Start on the knees and walk with the hands to a push up position. Do a push up and walk back. Repeat 3 times.	
9 Windmills	From a standing position rotate both arms forward (Clockwise) making a circle with the hands. Repeat 10 times. Rotate the arms 10 times in the opposite direction.	

Appendix B continued

# NAME	DIRECTIONS	DIAGRAM
10 Head rotations	Rotate the head from left to down to right to back. Count to 6 on each rotation. Repeat 3 times. This exercise relieves tension.	top view
11 Hamstring exercise	Place the heel of one foot forward on a raised object 3 feet off the ground. Lean forward, keeping the leg straight. Grab ankle and hold for 5-10 seconds. Repeat, raising the other foot. Use a partner to hold the foot if no objects are around. Repeat again.	
12 Quadriceps exercise	Stand near a wall or object you can touch for balance. Raise one foot behind and grab it with the same side arm. Lift gently. Hold for 5-10 seconds and then repeat, using the other foot and arm. Repeat again.	
13 Wall leans (3)	(1) With feet one yard from the wall, lean towards the wall keeping the heels on the floor and the legs straight. Hold for 5-10 seconds. This stretches the Achilles tendon and the calf. (2) Repeat this with your toes on a 3 inch high piece of wood or other object. You want the heels to be lower than the toes. Hold for 10 seconds. (3) Now step forward with one foot and raise the other off the ground. Hold for 10 seconds and repeat with the other foot. This also stretches the Achilles tendon and the calf.	(1) (2) (3)

Appendix C–Game Statistics

This is a simple way for a coach or manager to keep a detailed record of what occurred in a game. You can also use these statistics in case the official scorers make a mistake with fouls, points, or timeouts. Usually I also assign a manager to keep unofficial score on a copy of the official score sheet as an additional precaution.

Many helpful statistics can be calculated using this information. Here is an explanation of how to use the form and analyze the statistics. Blank sheets for your use follow.

Use the following abbreviations to detail game action. Put the letter in the Us or Opponent box in the chart. Continue in order, left to right, top to bottom as you fill out the chart. When a quarter or half ends draw a dark line and use the next open line to write the new letter.

J–won jump   R–rebound. Offensive if after a shot.

X–missed shot, X^F–fouled on shot   2–made shot

0–missed foul shot   1–made foul shot

T–turnover, bad pass, lost ball   V–violation, 3 seconds, walking

F–non-shooting foul

?–missed or do not understand what happened. Write what happened if there is time.

Line	Opponent	Us
1	J X R 2	2
2	X	R 2
3	X R V	T
4	X^F 0 1	X R X R X R 2
5		

Sample Data with Interpretation

Interpretation

LINE 1 The opponent won the jump(J), missed a shot(X), got the offensive rebound(R), then made the shot(2). In our next possession we took a shot and made it(2). If we had gotten possession after the jump, then the opponent's box on **line 1** would be empty.

LINE 2 In their next possession, the opponent missed the shot(X). We got the rebound(R). This is a defensive rebound. At the other end of the court, we made the shot(2).

LINE 3 On their next possession our opponents missed a shot(X), got another offensive rebound(R), then walked or committed a violation(V). We then turned the ball over(T) as our team came down the court.

LINE 4 We fouled an opponent on a missed shot(X^F). Do not count missed shots as shots when

Appendix C continued

a player is fouled. The first foul shot was missed(0). The second one was made(1). On our possession we shot three times(X's), pulled down 3 offensive rebounds(R's), and then scored(2).

Analysis

At the end of the game or quarter, you can analyze this information. The darker an area is shaded the more important this statistic category. All rebounding is important. Because the opponent's offensive rebounds usually lead to easy scores I consider this the most important statistic. Our turnovers, violations, shooting percentages, and fouls committed are other important numbers. Note that the analysis of these statistics will help you more in planning practice than in a game.

SUMMARY OF GAME STATISTICS		
Type	**Opponent**	**Us**
OFFENSIVE REBOUNDS	2	3
DEFENSIVE REBOUNDS	1	1
TURNOVERS	0	1
VIOLATIONS	1	0
JUMPS WON	1	0
SHOTS MADE	1	3
SHOTS MISSED	3	3
SHOOTING %	1/4, 25%	3/6, 50%
FOULS MADE	1	0
FOULS MISSED	1	0
FOUL SHOT %	1/2, 50%	0
FOULS BY	0	1

Appendix C continued-User Form

Game Statistics

Use the below abbreviations to detail the game action.

J - won jump   R - rebound.   X - missed shot
2 - made shot   0 - missed foul shot   1- made foul shot
F - non-shooting foul   T - turnover, lost ball   V - violation, 3 seconds, walking
? - missed or do not understand. Write what happened if there is time.
Circle multiple foul shots. Write the quarter or half number on the next open line.

Date_____Us_____Opponents_____Played at_____

Line	Us	Them	Us	Them
1				
2				
3				
4				
5				
6				
7				
8				
9				
10				
11				
12				
13				
14				
15				
16				
17				
18				
19				
20				
21				
22				
23				
24				
25				
26				
27				
28				
29				
30				
31				
32				
33				
34				
35				
36				

The Basketball Coach's Bible

Appendix C continued-User Form

Summary of Game Statistics

At the end of the game or quarter you can analyze this information. The shaded areas indicate what I think most important. Compare the shooting and foul information with the official score sheet.

SUMMARY OF GAME STATISTICS		
Type	**Opponent**	**Us**
OFFENSIVE REBOUNDS		
DEFENSIVE REBOUNDS		
TURNOVERS		
VIOLATIONS		
JUMPS WON		
SHOTS MADE		
SHOTS MISSED		
SHOOTING %		
FOULS MADE		
FOULS MISSED		
FOUL SHOT %		
FOULS BY		

Appendix D—Inside Shot Statistics

The ideal percentage of shots taken inside varies from game to game, team to team, and from young to old. Work for over 50%; 100% is great; 0% stinks. In any case you want to shoot more inside shots than your opponents.

How to Use the Statistic

Instruct a manager to put a small x for a missed shot or a small two (2) for a shot made on the diagram at the corresponding spot on the court where the shot was taken. Don't worry about being slightly off. It is more important to record every shot. Switch to the next diagram when the current one is full, or at the next half or quarter. Make sure to show your manager the **inside area** on the actual court.

How to Calculate the Statistic

Count the total number of shots both made and missed in each quarter, half, or game. Calculate the percentage of inside shots made using this formula:

$$\frac{\text{inside shots}}{\text{total shots}} \times 100$$

What the Statistic Means

There are no absolutes with this statistic because of the many variables such as the age and ability of the players. So, use it on a relative scale to compare your team to the opponent, though the inside percentage of your team should be over 50%.

If your inside percentage is low or lower than the other team, it could mean several things:

1. Your team is not looking to work the ball inside.

2. Your players have not mastered the basic offensive skills in sections 9 (Passing) and 10 (Catch-cut technique).

3. Your team is not rebounding well, especially offensively.

If the opponent's inside percentage is high or higher than yours, then it could mean that your team is not playing defense well. Work on overplaying, boxing out, and helping out.

Appendix D continued-User form

INSIDE SHOT STATISTICS

Use a small X for a missed shot or a small two (2) for a shot made. Be accurate.
You do not need to be exact. Record all shots.

Date_____

Us _____
First Quarter, Half, or_____

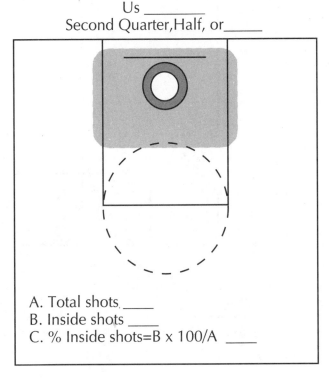

A. Total shots ____
B. Inside shots ____
C. % Inside shots=B x 100/A ____

Them _____
First Quarter, Half, or_____

A. Total shots ____
B. Inside shots ____
C. % Inside shots=B x 100/A ____

Us _____
Second Quarter, Half, or_____

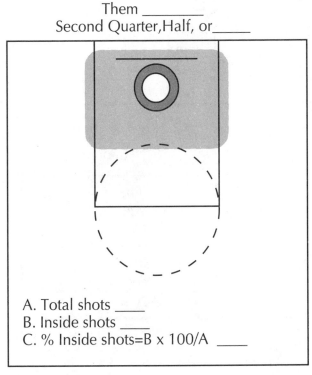

A. Total shots ____
B. Inside shots ____
C. % Inside shots=B x 100/A ____

Them _____
Second Quarter, Half, or_____

A. Total shots ____
B. Inside shots ____
C. % Inside shots=B x 100/A ____

Appendix E—Sample Practices

Sample Practices

Order Number	Reccomended Lesson	First Day 6-8 grade	First Day 9-11 grade	First Day 12+ grade	1-2 months later 9-11	Mid season 9-11
1	individual warm-ups any 1-13 5-15 minutes	watch 5 minutes		work with players 10-30 minutes		
2	continuous movement 1.2+,1.3, 9.32, 9.4+ 15-30 minutes	skip		1.2+ext	1.2+ext 1.3	9.3,9.4
3	individual skills new lessons,1-13 15-30 minutes	1.0,2.0	1.0,2.0 2.1	1.0, 2.0+ext	15.2	19.0
4	shooting technique 3,5-8 10-30 minutes	3.0,5.0 5.1	3.0,5.0 5.1+ext	3.0,5.0 5.1+,5.3	5.1+,5.32 5.6	5.0-5.3, 5.6,5.7
5	defense 12, 11.3 10-15 minutes	12.0	12.0, 12.1	12.0, 12.1	12.2-3 12.6	12.21, 12.5-6
6	individual skills, 1-13 transition, team 14-19 10-15 minutes	9.0,9.1	9.0,9.1	9.0,9.1 9.11-12	9.6,10.6 15.2	10.8, 15.2
7	layups 5.4-5.5,5.8 5-10 minutes	5.41-2	5.41-2	5.41,5.44 5.5,5.51	5.51,5.8	5.51,5.8
8	warm down see Appendix B 5-10 minutes	can skip	do	do	do	do
9	individual practice any 1-13 0-20 minutes	work with players individually				

Adjust lesson times during the practice based on player need. Use a stopwatch. The maximum recommended practice is 2 hours.

Appendix F—User Forms

	Practice Planning Guide		
Order Number	**Reccomended Lesson**	**Lesson**	**Time Needed (minutes)**
1	individual warm-ups any 1-13 5-15 minutes		
2	continuous movement 1.2+,1.3, 9.32, 9.4+ 15-30 minutes		
3	individual skills new lessons,1-13 15-30 minutes		
4	shooting technique 3,5-8 10-30 minutes		
5	defense 12, 11.3 10-15 minutes		
6	individual skills, 1-13 transition, team 14-19 10-15 minutes		
7	layups 5.4-5.5,5.8 5-10 minutes		
8	warm down see Appendix B 5-10 minutes		
9	individual practice any 1-13 0-20 minutes		
TOTALS- 2 Hour Maximum			

Appendix F–User Forms continued

Order Number	Reccomended Lesson	MON	TUES	WED	THUR	FRI
1	individual warm-ups any 1-13 5-15 minutes					
2	continuous movement 1.2+,1.3, 9.32, 9.4+ 15-30 minutes					
3	individual skills new lessons,1-13 15-30 minutes					
4	shooting technique 3,5-8 10-30 minutes					
5	defense 12, 11.3 10-15 minutes					
6	individual skills, 1-13 transition, team 14-19 10-15 minutes					
7	layups 5.4-5.5,5.8 5-10 minutes					
8	warm down see Appendix B 5-10 minutes					
9	individual practice any 1-13 0-20 minutes					
TOTALS- 2 Hour Maximum						

Weekly Practice Planner

If the total is more than 2 hours, then adjust the time for each lesson based on player need during practice. Use a stopwatch.

The Basketball Coach's Bible

Appendix G-Tables

Table Explanation

All of the table features are discussed in more detail in other sections and are also part of each lesson.

Lesson # and Name
The lessons are listed in order with the first lesson in each section in bold. The name of the first lesson in each section denotes the type of skill involved.

Players
The players needed in each group involved in the lesson. Note that the directions are given for many groups.

Court and Ball
X means you need a court or a ball for this lesson. A dash (-) means you do not.

Effort Level
1=little physical activity, technique level lesson

2=moderate activity, practice level

3=maximum physical effort involved, game level

Lessons Before
These lessons are needed before you do the current one. Usually only the lesson before is needed. However, sometimes many other lessons are needed, and it would be difficult to complete the current lesson without them.

Intro Time and Daily Time
The Intro Time is the time needed to teach a lesson for the first time. Usually it is double the Daily Time, the time needed after players understand the lesson.

Appendix G-Table of Lessons

L E S S O N #	NAME	P L A Y E R S	C O U R T	B A L L	E F F O R T	LESSONS BEFORE	L E S S O N #	INTRO TIME	DAILY TIME
1.0	**Holding the Ball**	1	-	x	1	none	**1.0**	5-10	1-2
1.1	Take Away	2	-	x	1	1.0	1.1	5-10	1-5
1.11	Hold High	2	-	x	1	1.1	1.11	-	1-5
1.12	Hold Low	2	-	x	1	1.1	1.12	-	1-5
1.2	Grab Full Court	2	x	x	2	1.1, 5.4	1.2	10-20	10-20
1.21	Short Pass Full Court	2	x	x	2	1.2	1.21	-	10-20
1.22	Tricky Pass Full Court	2	x	x	2	1.2	1.22	-	10-20
1.3	Line Lesson	T	x	x	2-3	1.1, 1.2	1.3	15-55	5-15
1.4	Move Ball	2	-	x	3	1.1	1.4	5-10	2-5
2.0	**Start Pivoting**	1	-	-	1	none	**2.0**	10-15	5-10
2.1	Pivoting with Ball	1	-	x	2	1.0, 2.0	2.1	15-20	2-20
2.2	Pivot with Defense	2	-	x	3	1.4, 2.1, 7.1	2.2	15-20	5-10
2.21	Pivot with D Pass	2+	x	x	3	2.2	2.21	10	5-10
2.22	Pivot 2 on D	3	x	x	3	2.21	2.22	10	5-10
2.23	Pivot 2 on D Pass	3+	x	x	3	2.22	2.23	10	5-10
3.0	**Flick of the Wrist - Shoot,Pass,Dribble**	1	-	-	1	none	**3.0**	10-15	2
4.0	**Dribbling D Position**	1	-	x	1	3.0	**4.0**	5-10	1-2
4.1	Look at the Leader 1-2	1+	x	x	2	4.0	4.1	20-30	5-15
4.11	Look and Count	1+	-	x	2	4.1	4.11	"	"
4.12	Watch the Game	1+	-	x	2	4.1	4.12	-	-
4.13	Twist Around	1	-	x	2	4.1	4.13	-	5-15
4.2	Follow the Leader	1+	-	x	2	4.1, 4.13	4.2	15-20	5-15
4.21	Follow Step Ahead	1+	-	x	2	4.2	4.21	-	5-15
4.22	Follow Back & Sideways	1+	-	x	2	4.2	4.22	-	1-5
4.23	Twister	1	-	-	2	4.22	4.23	5-10	1-5
4.24	Twister with Ball	1	-	x	2	4.23	4.24	-	5-10
4.3	Protect Ball	2	-	x	2-3	4.2	4.3	10-25	5-10
4.31	Protect with 2 on D	3	-	x	3	4.3	4.31	-	5-10
4.32	Dribbler Vs Dribbler	2	-	x	2	4.3	4.32	-	10-20
4.4	Dribble with D Layup	1+	x	x	2-3	4.3, 5.41	4.4	15-25	10-20
4.5	Dribble Pass with D	3	-	x	3	4.4, 9.3, 9.6, 10.5	4.5	20-30	10-20
4.51	Dribbler Shoots Ball	3	x	x	3	4.5	4.51	-	10-20
4.52	With D on Cutter	4	x	x	3	4.5	4.52	-	10-20
5.0	**Shot Technique Wrists**	1	-	-	1	none	**5.0**	10-15	2
5.1	Flick Up	1	-	x	1	5.0	5.1	10-20	2-5
5.11	Opposite Hand Flick Up	1	-	x	1	5.1	5.11	-	2-5
5.12	Flick Up High	1	-	x	1	5.1	5.12	-	2-4
5.13	Shoot Up	1	-	x	2	5.12	5.13	-	1-2
5.2	One-Inch Shot	1	x	x	1	5.13	5.2	10-30	5-10
5.3	One-Foot Shot	1	x	x	2	5.2	5.3	10-20	5-15
5.31	Regular One-Foot Shot	1	x	x	2	5.3	5.31	-	5-10
5.32	One-Foot Shot +Dribble	1+	x	x	2	4.3	5.32	-	5-15
5.33	One-Foot Jump Shot	1+	x	x	2	5.31	5.33	-	5-10

Appendix G-Table of Lessons continued

LESSON #	NAME	PLAYERS	COURT	BALL	EFFORT	LESSONS BEFORE	LESSON #	INTRO TIME	DAILY TIME
5.4	The No-Step Layup	1	x	x	1	1.0	5.4	15-30	5-20
5.41	One-Step Layup	1	x	x	1	5.4	5.41	-	5-20
5.42	Layup Lesson	T	x	x	2	5.41	5.42	10-20	10-15
5.43	Layup with Dribble	1	x	x	2	4.2, 5.42	5.43	15-20	5-15
5.44	Layup with Passing	T	x	x	2	5.42, 9.1	5.44	15-25	5-15
5.5	One Dribble Layup	1	x	x	2	4.2, 5.42	5.5	15-25	5-15
5.51	Two Dribble Layup	1	x	x	2	5.5	5.51	-	5-15
5.6	Foul Shot Technique	1	-	x	1	5.3	5.6	10-15	2-5
5.61	Technique Short Shot	1	-	x	1	5.6	5.61	10-15	5-15
5.62	Technique Longer Shots	1	-	x	1	5.61	5.62	-	5-15
5.7	Foul Shot Practice	1	x	x	3	5.6	5.7	5-15	5-15
5.8	Lateral Layup Lesson	T	x	x	2	2.1, 5.43, 9.5, 10.61	5.8	15-25	5-15
5.81	Bounce Pass Layup	T	x	x	2	5.8	5.81	-	5-15
6.0	**Moves**	x	x	x	-	2.1, 5.3	**6.0**	5-15	0-20
6.1	Pivot Around Shoot	1	x	x	2	6.0	6.1	5-15	0-20
6.2	Pivot Backward Shoot	1	x	x	2	6.1	6.2	5-15	0-20
6.3	Step Fake Shoot	1	x	x	2	6.0	6.3	5-15	0-20
6.31	Fake Pivot Shoot	1	x	x	2	6.3	6.31	5-15	0-20
6.32	Fake Pivot Back Shoot	1	x	x	2	6.31	6.32	5-15	0-20
6.4	Pivot Fake Shoot	1	x	x	2	6.0	6.4	5-15	0-20
6.41	Pivot Fake Back Shoot	1	x	x	2	6.4	6.41	5-15	0-20
6.5	Hook Shot 1-2	1	x	x	2	6.0	6.5	5-15	0-20
6.51	Jump Hook	1	x	x	2	6.5	6.51	5-15	0-20
6.52	Hook with Fake	1	x	x	2	6.51	6.52	5-15	0-20
6.53	Step Hook	1	x	x	2	6.51	6.53	5-15	0-20
6.54	Fake Step Hook	1	x	x	2	6.52-3	6.54	5-15	0-20
6.55	Underneath Hooks	1	x	x	2	6.54	6.55	5-15	0-20
6.6	Jump Shot	1	x	x	2	6.0	6.6	5-15	0-20
6.61	Fake Jump	1	x	x	2	6.6	6.61	5-15	0-20
6.62	Fake Pivot Around Jump	1	x	x	2	6.61	6.62	5-15	0-20
6.63	Pump Fake	1	x	x	2	6.6	6.63	5-10	5-10
7.0	**Pressure Shot**	1	x	x	2-3	6.1 or 6.6	**7.0**	5-15	5-15
7.01	Pressure Shot with D	2	x	x	3	7.0	7.01	-	5-15
7.02	Pressure Shot Two	2	x	x	3	7.01, 10.3, 11.0	7.02	-	5-15
7.1	Run Stop Shoot	1	x	x	2-3	6.6	7.1	5-10	2-5
7.11	With D	2	x	x	3	7.1	7.11	-	2-5
7.12	Run Catch Shoot	2	x	x	3	7.1, 9.1 10.6	7.12	10-20	5-15
7.2	Catch Up	2	x	x	3	5.51, 7.0	7.2	5-10	5
7.3	Defense in Face Shoot	2	x	x	3	5.3	7.3	5-10	2-5
7.31	Defense in Face Rebound	2	x	x	3	7.3, 11.3	7.31	-	2-5
7.32	Fouled Shooting	1	x	x	3	7.3	7.32	-	2-5
8.0	**Practice Shooting**	-	x	x	-	-	**8.0**	-	-
8.1	Driving to the Basket	1	x	x	2	2.1, 5.51	8.1	10-15	5
8.11	Fake Then Drive	1	x	x	2	6.4, 8.1	8.11	5-10	5

LESSON #	NAME	PLAYERS	COURT	BALL	EFFORT	LESSONS BEFORE	LESSON #	INTRO TIME	DAILY TIME
8.12	Drive Opposite Foot	1	x	x	2	8.1	8.12	5-10	5
8.2	Full Court Shoot	1	x	x	2	4.24, 6.6, 8.1	8.2	5-10	5-15
8.3	Near to Far	1	x	x	2	5.62	8.3	-	5-15
9.0	**Passing Technique**	1	-	-	1	2.0, 3.0	**9.0**	5	1-2
9.1	Overhead Short Pass	2	-	x	1-2	9.0, 10.0	9.1	5-10	5
9.11	Side Short Pass	2	-	x	1-2	9.1	9.11	-	5
9.12	Bounce Pass	2	-	x	1-2	9.1	9.12	-	5
9.13	Pivot Away Back Pass	2	-	x	1-2	2.1, 9.1	9.13	-	5
9.2	Baseball Pass	2	x	x	2	none	9.2	5-10	5
9.3	Baseball Pass Cut	2	x	x	2	7.1, 9.2	9.3	10-15	5-10
9.31	Midcourt Cut	2	x	x	2	9.3	9.31	-	5-10
9.32	Continuous Half Court	T	x	x	2	9.31	9.32	-	5-10
9.4	Continuous Full Court	T	x	x	2	7.2, 9.3	9.4	20-30	10-20
9.41	Full Court Pass	T	x	x	2	9.4	9.41	20-30	10-30
9.5	Pivot Pass & Communication	2	-	x	2	2.1, 9.1, 10.0	9.5	10-15	5-10
9.51	Pass Communication	2	-	x	2	9.5	9.51	10-15	5
9.52	Communication 2	2	-	x	2	9.51	9.52	-	5
9.6	D Overhead Side Pass	3	-	x	2-3	2.2, 9.51, 12.0	9.6	12-25	5-10
9.61	Defense Bounce Pass	3	-	x	2-3	9.6	9.61	-	5-10
9.7	Front Weave	3	x	x	2	5.8	9.7	15-20	10
9.8	Back Weave	T	-	x	2	1.1	9.8	10-15	5
10.0	**Catch Cut Technique**	1+	-	x	1	1.0, 9.0	**10.0**	10-20	5-10
10.01	Catching Technique 2	2	-	x	1	10.0	10.01	-	5-10
10.1	"Go Fetch It"	1+	-	x	1-2	10.0	10.1	5-20	2-10
10.11	Coming to the Ball	1+	-	x	1-2	10.1	10.11	5-10	5-10
10.2	Jump to Ball	2	-	x	1-2	10.0	10.2	10-15	5-10
10.3	Loose Ball Lesson	2	-	x	3	1.1, 11.2	10.3	5-10	3-5
10.31	Go for It	2+	-	x	3	10.3	10.31	-	3-5
10.4	Catching Bad Passes	1+	-	x	2	10.2	10.4	3-8	2-5
10.5	Cut Fake Technique	1	-	-	1	none	10.5	10-20	5-15
10.51	Cutting Off A Pick	3	-	-	1	10.5	10.51	10-20	5-15
10.6	Cut to the Ball	2	-	x	2	10.2, 10.5	10.6	10-20	5-15
10.61	Cut Communication	2	x	x	2	10.6	10.61	10-20	5-15
10.7	Three Second Lesson	1	x	-	1	10.2, 10.5	10.7	3-6	3-4
10.71	Cut into Lane	2	x	x	2	10.2	10.71	10-15	5-10
10.8	Overplay the Catcher	2	x	x	3	9.5, 10.6, 12.5	10.8	10-20	5-20
10.81	Front the Catcher	3	x	x	3	9.5, 10.6, 12.4	10.81	10-20	5-20
10.82	D on Catcher, Cut	3	x	x	3	10.8	10.82	-	5-15
10.9	D Pass, Overplay Catch	4	x	x	3	9.6, 10.82	10.9	5-20	5-15
10.91	D Passer, Front Catch	4	x	x	3	9.6, 10.81	10.91	5-10	5-15
10.92	D on Catcher,Passer Cut	4	x	x	3	10.82-10.91	10.92	5-20	5-15
11.0	**Rebound Grab Ball**	2	x	-	1	1.1, 2.1	**11.0**	5-10	2-5
11.1	Watching the Ball	1	-	-	1	none	11.1	5-10	5
11.11	The Ready Position	1	-	-	1	11.1	11.11	3	1

Appendix G-Table of Lessons continued

L E S S O N #	NAME	P L A Y E R S	C O U R T	B A L L	E F F O R T	LESSONS BEFORE	L E S S O N #	INTRO TIME	DAILY TIME
11.12	Move to Rebound	1	-	-	1	11.1	11.12	5	5
11.2	Step in Front Box Out 1-2	2	x	x	3	10.3, 11.12	11.2	10-15	5-10
11.3	Blocking Boxing Out 1-2	2	x	x	3	11.2, 12.5	11.3	15-30	10-20
12.0	**Defensive Position**	1	-	-	1	4.0	**12.0**	10-20	2-4
12.1	Move in D Position	1	-	-	1	12.0	12.1	10-30	5-25
12.2	Force Left & Right1-5	2	-	-	1-2	12.1	12.2	5-10@	2-5@
12.21	Three Yard Lesson	2	-	-	2-3	12.2	12.21	15-30	5-15
12.22	Mirror Lesson	2	x	x	3	12.21	12.22	-	5-10
12.3	Trapping 1-3	3	-	-	2-3	12.21	12.3	15-25	10-15
12.31	Trapping Game	3	-	-	2-3	12.3	12.31	-	10-20
12.4	Front Keep Out of Lane	2	x	-	3	12.1	12.4	10-20	10-15
12.41	Front and Box Out	2	x	-	3	11.3, 12.4	12.41	10-15	10-15
12.5	Overplaying 1-6	2	x	-	1-3	10.7, 12.2	12.5	~5-30	~5-15
12.6	Defense the Low Post	2+	x	-	1-2	12.5	12.6	20-30	10-15
12.61	Low Post with Passing	2+	x	-	2-3	12.6	12.61	-	10-20
12.7	D on Shooter	2	x	x	2	5.3, 11.3	12.7	10-15	3-8
12.71	D on Driver	2	x	x	2-3	12.7, 12.21	12.71	10-20	5-10
12.72	2 on 1	3	x	x	3	12.7,9.52+	12.72	10-20	5-10
13.0	**Picking or Screening 1-2**	2+	x	x	1	10.6,10.51	**13.0**	10-15	5
13.01	Defensing the Pick	4	x	x	2	13.0	13.01	10-30	5-15
14.0	**Center Jump**	T	x	x	1-3	12.1,+	**14.0**	15-25	5-10
14.01	Practice Jumping	T	x	x	3	14.0,+	14.01	5-10	2-5
14.02	D at Center Jump	T	x	x	3	all 12,14.0,+	14.02	5-10	5
15.0	**Foul Line Transition1-3**	T	x	x	1-3	all-11,12,+	**15.0**	15-30@	10-20@
15.1	Center Jump Transition	T	x	x	1-3	14.0,15.0+	15.1	15-30	10-20
15.2	Play to Transition	T	x	x	2-3	9.6,15.0,16.0+	15.2	15-25	10-20
16.0	**Offense Setup 1-2**	T	x	x	1-2	all- 9,10,12,+	**16.0**	10-20@	5-10@
16.1	Plays 1,2,3	3	x	x	2	16.0,+	16.1	20-30	10-20
16.2	Figure 8	T	x	x	2	13.0,16.0-1,+	16.2	10-25	5-15
16.21	8 with Defense	T	x	x	2-3	all 12,16.2,+	16.21	-	10-15
17.0	**Defense-Helping Out 1-3**	T	x	x	1-3	all- 11,12,+	**17.0**	20-30	10-20
17.01	Help in Figure 8	T	x	x	1-3	17.0	17.01	-	10-20
17.1	2-1-2 Zone Shift	T	x	x	1-3	17.0,+	17.1	10-15	5
17.11	Half Court Trap Zone	T	x	x	1-3	17.1,+	17.11	10-20	5-10
18.0	**Out-of-Bounds Plays**	T	x	x	1-3	16.0,+	**18.0**	10-15	5-10
18.01	4 in Line	T	x	x	1-3	18.0,+	18.01	10-15	5-10
19.0	**Full Pressure Offense**	T	x	x	1-3	16,0,17.0,+	**19.0**	20-30	15-30
19.1	Trapping Zone Press	T	x	x	1-3	19.0,+	19.1	15-30	15-20
19.11	Switch Zone to 1-on-1	T	x	x	1-3	17.1,19.1,+	19.11	-	5-15

Appendix G-Table of Individual Skills

Shooting		Moves (after Shooting)		Practice & Pressure shot (after Shooting)		Pass (also see Cut-Catch)	
LESSON NAME	#	LESSON NAME	#	LESSON NAME	#	LESSON NAME	#
Holding the Ball	1.0	Moves	6.0	Practice Shooting	8.0	Holding the Ball	1.0
Flick of the Wrist	3.0	Pivot Around Shoot	6.1	Driving to the Basket	8.1	Take Away	1.1
Flick Up	5.1	Pivot Back-ward Shoot	6.2	Fake Then Drive	8.11	Move Ball	1.4
One-Inch Shot	5.2	Step Fake Shoot	6.3	Drive Opp-osite Foot	8.12	Flick of the Wrist	3.0
One-Foot Shot	5.3	Fake Pivot Shoot	6.31	Near to Far	8.3	Start Pivoting	2.0
The No-Step Layup	5.4	Fake Pivot Back Shoot	6.32	Full Court Shoot	8.2	Pivoting with Ball	2.1
1 Step Dribble Layup	5.5	Pivot Fake Shoot	6.4	Pressure Shot	7.0	Pivot with Defense	2.2
Foul Shot Technique	5.6	Pivot Fake Back Shoot	6.41	Pressure Shot Two	7.02	Passing Technique	9.0
Foul Shot Practice	5.7	Hook Shot 1-2	6.5	Run Stop Shoot	7.1	Overhead Short Pass	9.1
Start Pivoting	2.0	Jump Hook	6.51	Run Catch Shoot	7.12	Side Short Pass	9.11
Pivoting with Ball	2.1	Hook with Fake	6.52	Catch Up	7.2	Bounce Pass	9.12
Pivot with Defense	2.2	Step Hook	6.53	Defense in Face Shoot	7.3	Crossover Step Pass	9.13
		Fake Step Hook	6.54			Baseball Pass	9.2
		Underneath Hooks	6.55			Baseball Pass Cut	9.3
		Jump Shot	6.6			Pivot Pass	9.5
		Pump Fake	6.63			Pass Commu-nication	9.51
						D Overhead Side Pass	9.6
						Front Weave	9.7
						Back Weave	9.8

Appendix G-Table of Individual Skills continued

Cut-Catch (see Passing)		Dribbling		Defense		Rebounding	
LESSON NAME	#	LESSON NAME	#	LESSON NAME	#	LESSON NAME	#
Catch Cut Technique	10.0	Holding the Ball	1.0	Defensive Position	12.0	Start Pivoting	2.0
Go Fetch It	10.1	Flick of the Wrist	3.0	Move in D Position	12.1	Pivoting with Ball	2.1
Coming to the Ball	10.11	Dribbling D Position	4.0	Force Left & Right1-5	12.2	Pivot with Defense	2.2
Jump to Ball	10.2	Look at the Leader 1-2	4.1	Three Yard Lesson	12.21	Rebound Grab Ball	11.0
Loose Ball Lesson	10.3	Twist Around	4.13	Trapping 1-2	12.3	Watching the Ball	11.1
Catching Bad Passes	10.4	Follow the Leader	4.2	Front Keep Out of Lane	12.4	The Ready Position	11.11
Cut Fake Technique	10.5	Follow Step Ahead	4.21	Overplaying 1-6	12.5	Stepping In Front	11.2
Cut to the Ball	10.6	Follow Back & Sideways	4.22	Defense the Low Post	12.6	Boxing Out	11.3
3 Second Lesson	10.7	Twister	4.23	D on Shooter	12.7		
Overplay the Catcher	10.8	Protect Ball	4.3	D on Driver	12.71		
D Pass, Over-play Catcher	10.9	Dribble with D Layup	4.4	Defensing the Pick	13.01		
Picking or Screening 1-2	13.0	Dribble Pass with D	4.5				
Cutting Off a Pick	10.51	Dribble Full Shoot	8.2				
Defensing the Pick	13.01						

Index

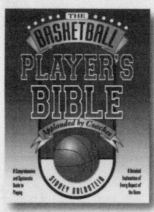

About The Author...

Question:

Why is Sidney Goldstein "Mr. Basketball Basics"?

Answer:

Because he wrote the books!

*A biophysicist, a science and mathematics teacher, and a lover of all things basketball. Sidney Goldstein has played high school, college-level, and independent team basketball for well over 20 years. He's coached men's and women's basketball, enjoying several championship seasons, over a period of 17 years. He developed **The Nitty-Gritty Basketball Series** because, after years of searching for information and attending coaching clinics, he realized there was little usable material to help coaches teach players the fundamentals of the game. So he quit his day job to literally write the books himself.*

The Series is winning rave reviews from coaches at every level of the game and is already a practice-partner for some of the biggest names in collegiate and professional basketball.

about The Basketball Coach's Bible

The Basketball Coach's Bible is aptly described by knowledgeable coaches as "long overdue" and "more detailed" than any other book on the fundamentals. The author who has successfully coached both men's and women's teams spent three years writing this practical action book so that anyone can coach.

• Part I discusses and graphically defines the fundamentals.

• Part II explains how to plan–the key to coaching– and teach at practice.

• Part III, the largest part, systematically presents over 200 lessons in 19 sections.

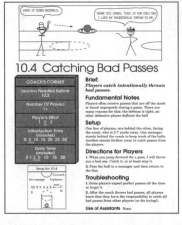

• Twenty-three pages of Appendices supply other useful coaching information such as: strategies; a practice warm down; game statistics and more. The large Index, Table of Contents, and over 400 illustrations help separate this book from lesser efforts.

• This book supplies the know how to teach successfully all players, women and men, of all abilities from Biddy League to professional. With these methods players improved conspicuously during each and every practice. Others can now benefit as well.

To the left is a sample page from Section 10, Catching and Cutting.

The Nitty-Gritty Basketball Series	Applauded by coaches as providing the most detailed and understandable explanation of the fundamentals.	Cost $93.55	#	Total
The Basketball Coach's Bible ISBN 1-884357-07-5 350 pages 8.5 x 11	Everything you need to know about the fundamentals of both coaching and basketball. over 400 illustrations	$24.95		
The Basketball Player's Bible ISBN 1-884357-13-X 270 pages 8.5 x 11	Everything you need to know about fundamentals and teaching the skills to one or two players. 300 illustrations	$19.95		
The Basketball Guide Set ISBN 1-884357-21-0 7 Mini-Guides	Covers the most critical aspects of basketball play. one topic at a time. From The Basketball Bibles	$48.65		
•**The Basketball Shooting Guide** ISBN 1-884357-14-8 45 pages 8.5 x 11	Techniques that yield rapid and permanent improvement. From **The Basketball Player's Bible.**	$6.95		
•**The Basketball Scoring Guide** ISBN 1-884357-15-6 47 pages 8.5 x 11	Teaches the moves used by the pros step-by-step. From **The Basketball Player's Bible.**	$6.95		
•**The Basketball Dribbling Guide** ISBN 1-884357-16-4 46 pages 8.5 x 11	Anyone can be a good dribbler. These methods show how. From **The Basketball Player's Bible.**	$6.95		
•**The Basketball Defense Guide** ISBN 1-884357-17-2 46 pages 8.5 x 11	Teaches how to play defense in every situation. From **The Basketball Player's Bible.**	$6.95		
•**The Basketball Pass Cut Catch Guide** ISBN 1-884357-18-0 47 pages 8.5 x 11	Be an effective team and all-around player with these skills. From **The Basketball Player's Bible.**	$6.95		
•**Basketball Fundamentals** ISBN 1-884357-08-3 46 pages 8.5 x 11	All about the fundamental skills of basketball. From **The Basketball Coach's Bible.**	$6.95		
•**Planning Basketball Practice** ISBN 1-884357-09-1 46 pages 8.5 x 11	Plan practice, use time efficiently, keep statistics, and more. From **The Basketball Coach's Bible.**	$6.95		

Up to 50% Off

CALL FOR DETAILS
SATISFACTION GUARANTEED
SPECIAL DISCOUNTS FOR YOUR TEAM OR ORGANIZATION
ALSO AVAILABLE THROUGH LOCAL BOOKSTORES AND MAJOR BOOK WHOLESALERS

PA Residents: add 6% tax

Philadelphia: add 7% tax   _____

Shipping Charges   _____

TOTAL ORDER   [_____]

3 WAYS TO ORDER

Order by mail:
Golden Aura Publishing
P.O. Box 41012
Phila., PA 19127-1012

Order by phone:
1-800-979-8642

Order by fax:
1-215-438-4459

Date: _____ Bill To/SendTo:

Name_____

Address_____

City_____State_____Zip_____

Phone (area code 1st)_____ fax_____

Shipping Charges:
Purchases
up to:
$25 . . . . . .$5
$50 . . . . . .$5.75
$75 . . . . . .$6.50
$100 . . . . .$7.50
each add'l $25. 50¢